THE DEVELOPMENT DANCE

THE DEVELOPMENT DANCE

How Donors and Recipients Negotiate
the Delivery of Foreign Aid

Haley J. Swedlund

CORNELL UNIVERSITY PRESS   **ITHACA AND LONDON**

First published 2017 by Cornell University Press

Printed in the United States of America

Library of Congress Cataloging-in-Publication Data

Names: Swedlund, Haley J., author.
Title: The development dance : how donors and recipients negotiate the delivery of
    foreign aid / Haley J. Swedlund.
Description: Ithaca : Cornell University Press, 2017. | Includes bibliographical
    references and index.
Identifiers: LCCN 2017012409 (print) | LCCN 2017013994 (ebook) |
    ISBN 9781501712425 (epub/mobi) | ISBN 9781501709784 (pdf) | ISBN
    9781501712876 | ISBN 9781501712876 (cloth : alk. paper) | ISBN
    9781501709401 (pbk. : alk. paper)
Subjects: LCSH: Economic assistance—Political aspects—Africa, Sub-Saharan. |
    International agencies—Political aspects—Africa, Sub-Saharan. |
    Non-governmental organizations—Political aspects—Africa, Sub-Saharan. |
    Economic development—Political aspects—Africa, Sub-Saharan. | Africa,
    Sub-Saharan—Foreign economic relations.
Classification: LCC HC800 (ebook) | LCC HC800 .S955 2017 (print) |
    DDC 338.910967—dc23
LC record available at https://lccn.loc.gov/2017012409

Cornell University Press strives to use environmentally responsible suppliers and materials to the fullest extent possible in the publishing of its books. Such materials include vegetable-based, low-VOC inks and acid-free papers that are recycled, totally chlorine-free, or partly composed of nonwood fibers. For further information, visit our website at cornellpress.cornell.edu.

Contents

Figures and Tables

Acknowledgments

This book is the product of over seven years of research on donor–government relations across many different countries. I did not start out intending to write a book on bargaining between donor agencies and recipient governments. I arrived in Kigali, Rwanda, in 2009 in order to do research on the post-genocide period. I very quickly became fascinated by the dense network of policy dialogues and the amount of effort that donor and government officials put into keeping these dialogues alive. I therefore set in motion a research project designed to understand how donors and recipients negotiate the delivery of aid in Rwanda.

After completing an initial wave of research in Rwanda, I was curious if the theories I had started to develop were applicable elsewhere. With the help of a grant from the Research Executive Agency of the European Commission (CIG Project no. 322228), I embarked on a multiyear project that took me to Accra, Ghana; Kampala, Uganda; Dar es Salaam, Tanzania; and back to Rwanda. The project also allowed me to carry out a survey of development practitioners working in twenty countries across Africa. Throughout this period, the research subject matter has continued to captivate me. Development practitioners invest so much time in maintaining their relationships with one another, yet we know so little about how this affects the delivery of aid.

Like all scholarship, this book has benefited from the assistance of many people. First and foremost, I am indebted to the literally hundreds of people who shared their professional experiences in development aid, taking time out of their often very hectic and busy schedules to speak with me, to answer my survey, or to attend one of my workshops. I am also particularly grateful to those who, in addition to taking an hour or more out of their day to answer my questions, opened up their Rolodex so that I could also talk with their colleagues and friends. My experience talking to practitioners served as a constant reminder that the vast majority of aid workers truly want to help. They work, however, within a system that is often failing. Only by learning from the people who work within that system day in and day out will we be able to make any headway in improving it.

I am also indebted to the student assistants who helped me carry out background research and the survey: Samuel Andreas Admasie, Rik van Hulst, Marije Oude Hengel, Elisabeth Krämer, and Maya Turolla. Each of them contributed to the success of the project by, for example, laboring to acquire names and contacts and carrying out the painstaking work of cleaning the data for analysis.

Many scholars provided me with feedback on the project at different stages. I am first grateful to Hans Peter Schmitz, who let me explore these topics way back in 2009. On the book manuscript, I particularly appreciate the comments I received at a workshop held at Radboud University in June 2015. Two external reviewers—Stephan Klingebiel and Stephen Brown—traveled all the way to Nijmegen and provided truly excellent advice and feedback at a critical moment. Comments from my colleagues at Radboud, including Romain Malejacq, Lotje de Vries, and Mathijs van Leeuwen, also helped me to shape the final book. I am also very grateful to Jan Pronk for being willing to chair the workshop. Not only did he do an excellent job of keeping us on track; his vast experience in international development helped ground the book in the everyday practices of development cooperation.

I am very grateful to Naomi Levy and Matt Winters for their willingness to read a draft of the manuscript in its entirely. Two anonymous reviewers also provided truly excellent feedback and advice. Heather Pincock, Ryan Jablonski, Malte Lierl, Reyko Huang, Michael Tierney, and Nicolas van de Walle all gave excellent advice and comments on various parts of the manuscript. I am also appreciative of my editor at Cornell, Roger Haydon, for providing his own comments at several points and for identifying such thoughtful external reviewers.

During the final stages of writing, I benefited enormously from the opportunity to be a visiting fellow at Yale University's MacMillan Center. My time there allowed me to sharpen both my argumentation and my prose. During this period of revision, Seth Fischer helped bring the manuscript, in particular the first three chapters, to life.

On a more personal note, I am incredibly thankful to my family. My parents have always encouraged me to pursue my dreams, allowing me from an early age to not put boundaries on ideas. They also instilled in me a strong midwestern work ethic that helped me stubbornly finish this project. I am also grateful to my paternal grandfather. I cannot remember a time when he didn't have a pen in hand. He, more than anyone else, instilled in me the desire to write a book. Finally, I am thankful for the loving support of my husband. From the moment I called him on a choppy phone line from Kigali to share my excitement about "finding" my research topic, he has steadfastly believed in me and in this research. His support has time and time again been instrumental in my belief that I should write this book.

Abbreviations

AfDB	African Development Bank
BRN	Big Results Now (Tanzania)
BSHG	Budget Support Harmonization Group (Rwanda)
CCM	Chama Cha Mapinduzi [Kiswahili] (Revolutionary Party, Tanzania)
CG	Consultative Group (Ghana)
CIDA	Canadian International Development Agency
DAC	Development Assistance Committee
Danida	Development Cooperation Agency of the Danish Ministry of Foreign Affairs
DFID	Department for International Development (United Kingdom)
DG DEVCO	Directorate-General for International Cooperation and Development (European Commission)
DPAF	Donor Performance Assessment Framework (Rwanda)
DPCG	Development Partners Coordination Group (Rwanda)
DPG	Development Partners Group (Tanzania)
DRC	Democratic Republic of the Congo
EC	European Commission
EDPRS	Economic Development and Poverty Reduction Strategy (Rwanda)
FDI	foreign direct investment
FY	fiscal year
GBS	general budget support
GNI	gross national income
GNP	gross national product
HIPC	Heavily Indebted Poor Countries
HoC	head of (development) cooperation
IBRD	International Bank for Reconstruction and Development
IDA	International Development Association
IMF	International Monetary Fund
JAST	Joint Assistance Strategy for Tanzania
JBSF	Joint Budget Support Framework (Uganda)
LRA	Lord's Resistance Army
MDBS	Multi-donor Budget Support (Ghana)
MDGs	Millennium Development Goals

MKUKUTA	Mkakati wa Kukuza Uchumi na Kupunguza Umaskini [Kiswahili] (National Strategy for Growth and Reduction of Poverty, Tanzania)
MoFEP	Ministry of Finance and Economic Planning (Ghana)
NDC	National Democratic Congress (Ghana)
NDPC	National Development Planning Council (Ghana)
NPP	New Patriotic Party (Ghana)
NRA	National Resistance Army (Uganda)
ODA	official development assistance
OECD	Organisation for Economic Co-operation and Development
PAF	performance assessment framework
PIU	project implementation unit
PRSP	poverty reduction strategy paper
RBA	results-based aid
RPF	Rwandan Patriotic Front
SAP	structural adjustment program
SBS	sector budget support
SIDA	Swedish International Development Cooperation Agency
SWPs	sector-wide approaches
UNDP	United Nations Development Programme
USAID	United States Agency for International Development

THE DEVELOPMENT DANCE

THE DEVELOPMENT DANCE

The besetting sin of development policy throughout its life has been vulnerability to fashion.

—Mosley, Harrigan, and Toye (1995, 308)

As country director for the United States Agency for International Development (USAID) in Uganda, it is your job to oversee the disbursement of roughly $300 million in foreign aid every year.[1] This money is given on behalf of the American people with the expectation that it will help raise thousands of people out of poverty, increase life expectancies and levels of education, and limit the spread of HIV/AIDS in Uganda. How do you make sure foreign aid dollars are well spent? How do you make sure that the aid you have been tasked with allocating is not wasted?

To deliver the foreign aid, you will have to navigate a minefield of competing demands. You will need to manage expectations from USAID headquarters, taxpayers, Congress, the State Department, and the White House. You will also need to make sure that there is sufficient buy-in from the Ugandan government. How can you be sure that your counterparts in government are equally committed to putting the aid dollars to good use? If you want to build ten new schools in Uganda, you will want to make sure children can afford to attend those schools and that when they get there they have something to learn. Therefore, in exchange for your aid dollars, you might ask the Ugandan government to commit to staffing the schools and limiting school fees. For government officials to be willing to make these commitments in exchange for American aid dollars, you will need to convince them that your commitment to fund ten new primary schools is credible. The success of the aid project depends on the credibility of both parties' commitments.

How likely is it, however, that the Ugandan government will keep its commitment to staffing the schools and lowering enrollment fees? Maybe, as in 2011, campaign promises made by the Ugandan president, Yoweri Museveni, will draw money away from the education sector and toward the military. At the same time, how likely is it that you will be able to keep your commitment to the Ugandan government? Perhaps in the midst of the initiative, which is scheduled to last five years, there is a U.S. presidential election, and the new president decides that he wants to invest more money in HIV/AIDS in Africa, decreasing the amount of money available for educational investments in Uganda. As a result, you have only enough funds to build six schools.

This book wrestles with a basic problem: both agencies and governments have trouble making credible commitments. The book is about how donor agencies like USAID and recipient governments like Uganda negotiate the delivery of foreign aid. It is about how the two parties engage in aid policy bargaining, or what I refer to in this book as the "development dance." More specifically, it is about how donor agencies and recipient governments attempt to demonstrate the credibility of their promises, and how their difficulty doing so affects the sustainability of aid policy compromises over time.

In *The Development Dance*, I explain that, because aid agencies and recipient governments have a hard time making credible commitments to one another, the policy compromises reached by the two parties frequently break down. This not only causes a great deal of frustration among donor and government officials; it also means that the two parties are continuously searching for new ways of delivering aid that help to limit this problem.

In developing countries, there is a virtual "aid bazaar" with lots of good ideas, lots of projects, and lots of wasted money (Pomerantz 2004). Needs are vast, and donor agencies have many different options for how they can deliver foreign aid. Imagine that as part of your new position at USAID you have $2 million specifically earmarked to invest in increasing school enrollment for girls ages ten to fourteen. You could disburse the aid to the Ugandan Ministry of Education to help offset school fees for girls, or you could set up a stand-alone project implementation unit to administer programs that educate parents on the value of a formal education for girls and distribute sanitary pads to help keep girls from missing school. To increase the total amount of aid available for the initiative, you could also form a joint "basket fund" with other donor agencies,[2] or you could partner with a local or international NGO already doing this kind of work. You could even simply transfer the money into the treasury of the Ugandan government, allowing them to use it as they see fit but making clear that, in exchange for the money, you would like to see them place more emphasis on girls' education.

Each of these different approaches to delivering foreign aid—what I refer to in this book as aid delivery mechanisms—has been in vogue at some point or other. From microfinance to results-based aid, from basket funding to general budget support, development aid is continuously reinventing itself, claiming to have finally found the next big idea that is going to make aid more effective. This relentless innovation—what some call aid fads or fashions—leads to rapid paradigm shifts in development cooperation that are difficult, if not impossible, for development practitioners to keep up with.

In this book, I offer an explanation for why foreign aid jumps from one fad to the next and a plan for how we can go about building more sustainable, or longer lasting, ways of delivering foreign aid. I argue that choices in how to deliver aid are influenced by the difficulty each side has ensuring that the other party will uphold its promises. Because donor agencies like USAID or the World Bank desire reform in exchange for aid dollars, they engage in negotiations with recipient governments like Uganda or Mozambique. These negotiations result in an aid policy compromise, in which the donor agency agrees to provide a certain amount of aid in exchange for specific actions by the recipient government. However, changing circumstances are continuously undermining these negotiated compromises. Following the global economic recession in the late 2000s, for example, many donor countries slashed aid budgets, forcing donor agencies to back out of promises already made to recipient governments.

The breakdown of negotiated compromises between donor agencies and recipient governments is so commonplace that most development practitioners consider it an inherent feature of development aid. My argument is that this common feature in the aid system has profound implications on how aid is actually delivered to beneficiaries. Because donor agencies and recipient governments anticipate that the other party might be unable or unwilling to uphold its promises over the long term, there is a relentless search for new ways of delivering foreign aid that are more effective at ensuring credible commitments from both parties. Unless, however, the negotiated compromises reached by donor agencies and recipient governments are measurable and enforceable by both parties, they will not be sustainable past an initial period of enthusiasm, perpetuating a continual search for new and more effective ways of delivering foreign aid.

Accompanying aid fads are what former World Bank country director Phyllis Pomerantz calls "aid mood swings," or highs and lows in the aid relationship. Likening these mood swings to what happens when a person has manic depression, she notes that "beyond the objective facts are very real feelings of disappointment, failed expectations, and even betrayal among the donor representatives. Perspectives can and do become warped. . . . The 'highs' are high, but the 'lows' are really low" (2004, 3). As enthusiasm about a new aid delivery mechanism dies, frustration grows. But because donor agencies and recipient governments are deeply dependent on one another, the two parties have little choice but to pick up the pieces and try again. The result is a never-ending cycle of excitement over new aid delivery mechanisms, followed by deep frustration over failure to produce credible commitments yet again.

In this way, the concept of commitment problems—or the difficulty donor agencies and recipient governments have upholding their promises—assists us in two ways: not only does it help us to understand why there are so many fads in development aid, but we also gain a tool for assessing the sustainability of a proposed aid delivery mechanism. If we want to know whether an aid delivery mechanism, such as budget support or results-based aid, is likely to be sustained, we need to look at whether it induces credible commitments from *both* donor agencies and recipient governments over the long term. In other words, we need to make sure that the Ugandan government follows through with its commitment to staff the schools built by USAID, and that USAID follows through with its commitment to build ten primary schools in Uganda.

Aid Delivery and Aid Effectiveness

The principal question driving debates on foreign aid is whether or not aid is effective. This is of course an extremely important question. Billions of people around the world depend on foreign aid to receive basic services, such as clean drinking water and safe housing. It therefore makes sense that we would want to know in what cases and circumstances foreign aid is actually working. However, the relentless focus on measuring the effectiveness of aid often causes us to overlook how policies of foreign aid actually come to exist in the first place and how likely it is that such practices will remain in place over the long term. It also means that foreign-aid scholars often assume—either implicitly or explicitly—that aid programs are actually designed to be effective, and evaluate them accordingly.

In my research, I ask a fundamentally different set of questions: Why is foreign aid given in the way it is, and why is it that aid delivery mechanisms seem to change and evolve so rapidly? I do not ask whether the money Uganda receives from USAID to support girls' education is actually improving access to primary education for Ugandan schoolgirls. Rather, I look at how foreign aid is distributed and how fads in distribution mechanisms have changed over time. I take as a given that a certain amount of foreign aid has been allocated to a recipient country, focusing instead on how donor agencies make decisions about how to disburse that aid. Donor politicians and high-level bureaucrats back in the donor country are largely responsible for decisions regarding how much aid a recipient government receives. Once that aid has been allocated, however, how do donor officials working at the recipient-country level negotiate the delivery of foreign aid with representatives of the recipient government? By starting with aid delivery, I avoid assuming that aid delivery mechanisms are inherently designed to be effective, but am still able to address three important empirical questions related to the effectiveness of foreign aid:

First, what determines the sustainability of an aid delivery mechanism over the long term? A common complaint among development practitioners is that new aid practices and policies are not given enough time to become effective. Why is this? Best practices regarding aid delivery are notoriously fickle. In the eighties, structural adjustment was the norm. In the nineties, project aid and support to NGOs became fashionable. At the turn of the twenty-first century, budget support was all the rage. Now donor agencies are crazy for results-based aid. Yet we know very little about why policies and practices often fall by the wayside (sometimes only to be picked up again twenty, thirty years down the road). Scholars of foreign aid often implicitly assume that changes in aid delivery over time are driven by changing beliefs about how best to deliver aid. I argue that there is a more fundamental logic driving the sustainability of aid delivery mechanisms: fads and fashions in development aid are attempts to overcome particular types of commitment problems that undermine the credibility of policy compromises reached by international donors and recipient governments.

Second, how will exogenous shocks impact donor–government relations at the recipient-country level? It is widely assumed that shocks to the aid system, such as a financial crisis or a global conflict like the War on Terror, affect the distribution of aid. However, we know very little about how such events affect *the relations* between donor agencies and recipient governments. Understanding the logic of aid delivery can help to illuminate how exogenous shocks affect the bargaining processes between donor agencies and recipient governments, and thus the types of aid policy bargaining compromises that emerge between the two parties. For example, how did the Netherlands negotiate its aid to Tanzania after a financial crisis in the late 2000s resulted in a shrinking of the Dutch aid budget by more than 25 percent?

Third, and most important, how can we go about inventing better ways of delivering foreign aid? Without understanding the logic of aid policy bargaining and how it affects choices in aid delivery, we are stuck evaluating aid programs and initiatives based on the problematic assumption that they exist in order to be effective. This is, of course, unlikely to be true. In the midst of a brutal civil war, the World Bank, for example, spent more than $45 million in Sierra Leone on building and maintaining roads. Thirty-three percent of the funds went toward compensating contractors for lost time and the destruction of their efforts (Easterly 2003a, 36). There is disagreement about why the World Bank continued to fund road projects in the midst of a civil war, but it is clear that it was not about effectiveness. Once we understand the reasons behind the adoption of certain aid delivery practices and their potential staying power, we can begin the arduous task of designing institutions of foreign aid that are more resilient to external shocks and fluctuation.

The Evolution of Aid Delivery Mechanisms

Foreign aid, which is sometimes called development aid or development assistance, is commonly defined as financial flows, technical assistance, and commodities that are provided as either grants or subsidized loans in order to promote economic development and welfare (Radelet 2006a). While many different actors provide foreign aid, in this book I concentrate on official development assistance (ODA) provided by publicly funded development agencies like the Swedish International Development Cooperation Agency (SIDA) or the European Commission's Directorate-General for International Cooperation and Development (DG DEVCO).[3] I exclude from my analysis foreign aid provided by private foundations like the Bill and Melinda Gates Foundation, as well as aid provided exclusively for short-term humanitarian purposes (for example, after a natural disaster).[4]

Within development agencies, there has long been a tension between two types of aid: program aid and project aid. Project aid is the financing of specific development projects or initiatives.[5] In Burkina Faso, for example, SIDA funds the construction and rehabilitation of rainwater basins, so that Burkinabe farmers can store water during the dry season for cattle and agriculture. Program aid, on the other hand, is not linked to a specific project or initiative. Rather, it is financial contributions that are extended to the recipient country for more general developmental purposes (Arakawa 2006, 432). For example, also in Burkina Faso, between 2013 and 2016, SIDA gave the Ministry of Environment $5.6 million. Instead of funding a particular aid project, the money went toward supporting the ministry and its capacity to implement the country's forestry-sector plan. While at any given time, donors use both project and program aid, preferences for each have changed over time. As far back as the 1960s, Alan Carlin of the RAND Corporation wrote about the tension between project and program aid as one of the "longest-standing controversies in the administration of foreign aid" (Carlin 1966, 1).

In the post–World War II period, development cooperation as we now know it began to take shape with the passage of the Marshall Plan by the United States in 1948.[6] Widely considered a huge success, the Marshall Plan provided support to finance general categories of imports and strengthen the balance of payments in order to rebuild Europe's crumbling infrastructure after the devastating war period (Arndt, Jones, and Tarp 2014, 20). That is, the initiative offered program aid to European governments, which then used these funds to carry out infrastructure projects and to purchase goods from the United States. While grateful to receive the aid, European partners did not simply open their arms to U.S. aid. Instead, the negotiations that led to the Marshall Plan were long and complex, with each country bringing its own concerns and interests. Need also did not guarantee participation. Finland opted not to participate in order to avoid antagonizing the Soviets, who flat out forbid Poland and Czechoslovakia from joining the negotiations (Schain 2001).

In the 1950s, attempting to replicate the success of the Marshall Plan, developed countries began to focus their attention on developing countries, laying the groundwork for what would eventually become bilateral cooperation programs. During this period, aid was very much driven by Cold War politics. Between 1953 and 1961, the United States gave more aid per capita to Bolivia than to any other country. While the original objective was to prevent the new revolutionary government from turning toward the Soviet Union, once a diplomatic foothold had been achieved, aid was also used as a lever for policy reforms like the adoption of the 1956 Bolivian Oil Code, which proved to be highly beneficial to U.S. oil companies (Fraser 2009, 49; Rabe 1988, 79–80).

It was also during this period that international institutions originally designed to help with postwar recovery in Europe, such as the International Bank for Reconstruction and Development (IBRD)—now a part of the World Bank Group—and the International Monetary Fund (IMF), starting turning their attention toward developing countries. During this period, the IMF, for example, issued "standby agreements" to countries like Peru and Bolivia, allowing them to withdraw funds over a specific period. Originally, the recipient was given just six months to make requests, but the time period was eventually extended to one year under the condition that the IMF could rescind the aid if it disagreed with actions taken by the recipient during the agreement period (Jeanne, Ostry, and Zettelmeyer 2008).

In the 1960s (designated the United Nations Development Decade by the UN General Assembly), development cooperation was professionalized. Developed countries like the United States, Canada, and France formally established bilateral development agencies,[7] and the World Bank, with strong support from the United States, established the International Development Association (IDA) to provide very soft loans to countries like Honduras (which received the first IDA credit for highway maintenance), Chile, Sudan, and India.[8] As donor agencies proliferated, there was also a growing emphasis on international coordination. In 1960, the Development Assistance Group,[9] which would later become the Development Assistance Committee (DAC), was established to provide a forum for consultations among different aid donors. And after a series of meetings in Washington, London, and Tokyo, the World Bank established the first consultative group for Nigeria in 1962, attempting to harmonize Nigeria's growing number of international donors (Führer 1996).

In contrast to the Marshall Plan era, throughout the fifties and sixties, foreign assistance was largely disbursed via project aid, which was given to support the implementation of specific capital investment projects like the building of dams, roads, and irrigation systems (Arndt, Jones, and Tarp 2014). Aid agencies favored discrete projects over program aid, because this gave them more control over how aid was allocated and how the funds were used (Fraser 2009). To help ensure the success of their aid, many donor countries complemented project aid with technical assistance, or financing designed to build local capacity and support the implementation of development projects (Arndt 2000).

Project aid was not the preferred mode of delivery for recipient governments. Recipients, however, were able to work around the constraints of project aid, because aid is fungible (Collier 1997; Fraser 2009). If a recipient country like Rwanda can attract aid for a project it is already planning to support, aid funds allow the government to redirect funds toward another initiative that donors are less likely to fund. At the same time, Cold War politics allowed for some strategic maneuvering on the part of recipients, who were able to use superpower support to balance external and internal power threats (Fraser 2009).

In the 1970s, the political climate changed. Economic crises in countries like the United Kingdom negatively affected the economies of developing countries, particularly in Africa. The crisis made clear that, despite most being independent for over twenty years, many developing countries were still very dependent on their former colonizers. Following the rise of popular movements that challenged the effectiveness of trickle-down economics and the Washington Consensus, a focus on poverty alleviation came to dominate the agenda of organizations such as the World Bank and the IMF (Arndt, Jones, and Tarp 2014; Mosley et al. 2012). Developing-country governments tried as much as possible to use popular sentiments to their advantage. In 1974, the group of seventy-seven developing countries (the G77) drafted the UN General Assembly Declaration on the Establishment of the New International Economic Order, which demanded, among other things, "more aid with less political conditions" (Fraser 2009, 53).

Although there were important changes in development ideology in the 1970s, the dominant aid delivery mechanism—project aid—remained the same (Arndt, Jones, and Tarp 2014; Hjertholm and White 2000). This changed in the 1980s. Following a second oil shock in 1979, the international debt crisis erupted, and huge macroeconomic imbalances became widespread in developing countries. The crisis was particularly hard on African economies, where countries like Senegal found themselves with a fiscal deficit exceeding 12.5 percent of their gross national product (GDP) and no way to pay off their debt. In response to the need to disburse high volumes of aid quickly, program aid, and in particular balance-of-payment support, began to flourish, with financial program aid and structural adjustment lending becoming fashionable toward the end of the decade (Mosley and Eeckhout 2000). The adjustment model dates to 1956, when Argentina convened all its creditors at a meeting in Paris, persuading them to forgive some of its debt in order to prevent the complete collapse of its economy and ensure at least minimal repayment. It was not, however, until the 1980s that the World Bank and the IMF took a central role in managing creditors and developed a system of conditionality that came to be known as "structural adjustment" (Fraser 2009).

The Berg Report, published in 1981 by the World Bank, laid out the intellectual origins of structural adjustment. The report argued that, as investment projects would inevitably fail in "poor policy environments," the World Bank should increase policy-based lending and also tie project-specific loans to macroeconomic conditions (Fraser 2009, 58). Between 1976 and 1980, adjustment lending constituted just 0.5 percent of all lending from the World Bank. In the period between 1986 and 1990, it rose to 26 percent of total spending (Williams 1997, 155). Most developing countries were hamstrung by structural adjustment. The policies were deeply unpopular with populations. In Africa, for example, they often resulted in a rise in prices of staple commodities like bread and milk. But recipient governments needed the financing. As a result, governments often engaged in non-negotiation and non-implementation (Whitfield 2009a): recipient governments formally accepted the conditionalities required by lenders in order to receive the funds, but in practice failed to implement many of the reforms (Killick 1998; Mosley, Harrigan, and Toye 1995; N. van de Walle 2001).

The end of the Cold War in the early nineties marked an important shift in donor–government relations, as recipients could no longer play the Soviet Union and Western countries off one another. Among many development professionals there was initially hope that the end of the Cold War meant that aid would be less politicized. This initial wave of optimism, however, was quickly damped, as fiscal conservatives in Western countries used the end of the East-West conflict as an excuse to cut aid funds. Via the OECD-DAC, donor agencies pushed back at such declines by arguing that aid was needed to advance "human development" and recasting development as a "partnership" between donor agencies and recipient governments (Fraser and Whitfield 2009).

In the context of these debates, a stronger focus on the social sectors like health and education emerged, exemplified by the approval of the Millennium Development Goals (MDGs) in 2000. The MDGs set a number of global targets, such as reducing global child mortality by two-thirds, attempting to the use the momentum behind such targets to mobilize aid dollars. At the same time, global funds like the Global Fund to Fight AIDS, Tuberculosis and Malaria emerged as a popular alternative to traditional bilateral and multilateral aid, and there was a noticeable increase in the number of private foundations and development NGOs.[10] Bilateral and multilateral aid donors funded these programs largely via project aid. To help coordinate the growing number of funds from multiple sources, in the nineties, recipient governments and donor agencies starting using sector-wide approaches (SWPs), drafting operating principles for individual sectors like agriculture or health in order to harmonize the activities of the government bodies, donors, and other stakeholders, such as civil society, working in that sector (WHO 2000, 123).

Also during this period, the World Bank and the IMF launched an ambitious new program in 1996 called the Heavily Indebted Poor Countries (HIPC) Initiative. The goal of HIPC was to provide debt relief and low-interest loans (program aid) to developing countries that, once again, possessed unsustainable levels of debt. Thirty-eight countries—thirty of them in Africa—opted into the program. Despite strong criticism of the lending practices of the World Bank and IMF and a growing rhetorical emphasis on partnership, conditionality was far from abandoned during the early days of HIPC. The World Bank, for example, introduced "short leash" lending, in which funds were closely tied to recipients' prior actions (Collier 1997, 61). In some cases, the funds were not released until after the recipient demonstrated that it had actually implemented the reforms. Longer-term loans also began to be released in tranches, which were tied to certain targets referred to by the World Bank as "benchmark criteria" (Fraser 2009, 69).

Toward the end of the decade, there was a stark and surprising change in the rhetoric around conditionality. Drawing on Uganda's experience drafting a poverty reduction strategy—the Poverty Eradication Action Plan (PEAP)—the HIPC process was reformed in 1999 to include the official requirement that participants draft a poverty reduction strategy paper (PRSP) that met the approval of the boards of the IMF and World Bank (Mosley et al. 2012). The PRSP process tried to ensure that recipient countries had in place the proper policies for aid to be effective without the heavy hand of conditionality. By 2005, poverty reduction strategy credits, the funding mechanism for PRSP-based lending at the World Bank, accounted for almost 60 percent of IDA policy-based lending and a quarter of the World Bank's total policy-based lending (World Bank 2010, xi).

It was not just the World Bank, however, that embraced what is now commonly called "budget support" in the 2000s. Budget support is a type of program aid in which aid is transferred directly into the recipient country's treasury, allowing the recipient country to use its own allocation, procurement, and accounting structures to manage the aid (Koeberle, Stavreski, and Walliser 2006). While sector budget support is targeted toward specific sectors, such as health or education, general budget support gives the recipient country the freedom to use the aid however it would like. Either in conjunction with the PRSP process or on their own, several bilateral donor agencies, as well as the European Commission, began providing budget support. In 1990, donors disbursed approximately $11.5 billion in general budget support worldwide. By 2002, this figure had increased to $98.6 billion.[11]

The tide, however, is once again shifting. By 2013, budget support totals were back down to just over $10 billion.[12] In the place of budget support, an emphasis on new, so-called "innovative approaches" has emerged (Sumner and Mallett 2013). In particular, results-based aid (RBA), or what is sometimes called cash on delivery, is currently fashionable. Compared to budget support, RBA takes a very different approach, disbursing foreign aid only *after* the recipient's performance has been rigorously assessed using prespecified indicators (Klingebiel 2012; Pearson, Johnson, and Ellison 2010; de Renzio and Woods 2010; Rogerson 2011). For example, the UK's Department for International Development (DFID) has a pilot program in Ethiopia where it makes a payment of between £50 to £100 for each additional schoolchild who partakes in a set of national-level exams, paying more if the child actually passes the exam. To provide an incentive to the government to pay more attention to "lagging groups," the payout is higher for girls and for students from certain regions (Birdsall and Perakis 2012). While we lack concrete numbers on the amount of aid being channeled through RBA, the aid delivery mechanism is clearly rapidly growing in popularity.

This brief look at the history of the global aid industry reveals two important points. First, development aid is always trying to reinvent itself. Since the 1950s, donors have continually tried out a number of different aid delivery mechanisms. At different time periods, different approaches have risen in popularity, only to eventually be replaced by something new. These different approaches are not directly attributable to particular historical events or milestones in development thinking. The history of foreign aid is instead a history of fads and fashions. Second, throughout this period, donor agencies have tried to use foreign aid to leverage reforms, while recipient governments have pushed backed against such pressures. Recipients have not always had much negotiating capital (Whitfield 2009a). Nonetheless, they use whatever strategies are available to them to resist donor demands and intrusions, trying to carve out as much space for their own preferences as possible.

Commitment Problems in Foreign Aid

What is shaping choices in aid delivery mechanisms? Under what conditions are aid delivery mechanisms politically sustainable? And on what grounds do donor agencies and recipient governments negotiate the delivery of foreign aid at the recipient country level? The difficulty of delegating aid delivery and enforcing aid conditionalities is well documented (Gibson et al. 2005; Killick 1998; Mosley, Harrigan, and Toye 1995; Ostrom et al. 2002; N. van de Walle 2001). We know relatively little, however, about how donor agencies and recipient countries make choices regarding how to deliver aid, and under what conditions their policy compromises are sustainable.

To unmask bargaining between donor agencies and recipient governments, I draw on institutional economics—especially the work of the Nobel prize–winning economist Douglass North. Economic institutionalism argues that institutions, which North (1990) defines as the "rules of the game" governing social interactions, change and evolve as the parties involved attempt to decrease transaction costs—or the costs associated with measurement and accountability. By this, North means that the parties engaged in a given bargaining relationship seek out agreements that help to ensure that the other side actually lives up to its promises. Importantly, for North, there is no guarantee that the two parties will actually reach a sustainable compromise. Competing interests, the complexity of the environment, and the lack of a third party to enforce commitments can all prevent sustainable compromises from emerging (North 1990, 33).

Applied to the study of foreign aid, institutional economics provides us with the analytical tools to break open the black box of aid policy bargaining. It tells us that if USAID is negotiating the delivery of ten public health clinics with the Ugandan government, it will do what it can to make sure Uganda lives up to its promises to make specific investments like limiting school fees or staffing the schools. At the same time, the Ugandan government will do what it can to make sure USAID actually delivers on its promise to build the ten primary schools. Both sides will innovate in order to try to get the other side to live up to its commitments. There is, however, no guarantee that institutions will emerge that can effectively measure and enforce the commitments made by USAID and the government of Uganda.

In the following chapters, I demonstrate that aid policy compromises are reached through a dynamic bargaining process between donor agencies and recipient governments. In this "dance," the two parties each try to secure preferential agreements based on their own interests and negotiating capital (Mosley et al. 2012; Whitfield 2009a). Crucially, however, aid policy compromises are constrained by the difficulty each side has guaranteeing that the other side will uphold its commitments. This affects both choices in aid delivery and the sustainability of aid delivery mechanisms.

Consider, for example, the negotiations surrounding structural adjustment in Ghana in the 1990s.[13] In this process, World Bank staff perceived Ghanaian officials to be "tough negotiators" (Armstrong 1996). Via continuous bargaining, the Provisional National Defense Council government that led Ghana at the time was able to moderate conditionality, resulting in a more gradual reform process than either the World Bank or the IMF would have preferred (Tsikata 2001). Ghanaian officials were able to push back on conditionalities, because donor officials wanted to make sure that the reforms would actually be implemented. On both sides, however, there was always a great deal of uncertainty. Would the Ghanaian government actually follow through with the reforms? And, if not, would donors actually pull funding? In practice, there often was a great deal of flexibility in implementation. What mattered, according to Tsikata (2001), was that donor officials *believed* that the government was actually committed to the reform.

It is not just the World Bank or the IMF that tries to leverage aid for reforms. Every day, in developing-country capitals throughout the world, multilateral and bilateral donor agencies try to leverage their financial contributions for specific policy actions. In the case of the World Bank, these might be large macroeconomic reforms, like the liberalization of the Ghanaian cocoa market. But in the case of bilateral donors, these reforms and policy changes might be much smaller. For example, donor officials may want the government to extend the electricity grid (perhaps to include a school or hospital it is building) or to enact a new public procurement law to make sure that their aid dollars are properly accounted for in the national budget. As Pomerantz (2004) explains, just as aid money gives donor agencies leverage, the knowledge that donors need recipient governments for reforms gives recipient governments leverage. In the words of one European ambassador, "Mozambique needs us and we need a successful Mozambique—and they know it."[14]

The problem is that even if the agreement between the donor agency and the recipient government is relatively straightforward (and often it is not), it is frequently difficult for either party to uphold its promises. In the case of the electricity grid, for example, election promises made by the recipient government may take money away from the expansion by diverting the money elsewhere. Similarly, reforming the public financial management systems of a country may face an uphill battle in some government circles if the reforms tighten loopholes used by politicians to extract rents. As a result, despite a commitment by the government to push through both reforms, the electrical grid remains unexpanded and the proposed public procurement law languishes in parliament. It might also be the case that the government simply does not want to make a particular reform. Throughout the nineties, the World Bank tried to get Ghana to liberalize its cocoa market. As a part of negotiations in 1991, Ghana did allow private buyers into the market. Additionally, in 2003, it conceded to liberalizing the internal marketing system. However, the government has flat-out refused to liberalize the export of cocoa (see Whitfield and Jones 2009, 198).

It is not just recipient countries that have a hard time keeping promises, however. As a donor official in Uganda told me, "We promise we'll do this and then midway we cancel or leave."[15] Statistics on aid predictability tell us that the fact that promised aid dollars are not actually delivered is a consistent problem for developing-country governments. In sub-Saharan Africa between 1990 and 2005, aid disbursements deviated from aid commitments by 3.4 percent of GDP on average, with some countries reporting deviations of up to 10 percent of GDP (Celasun and Walliser 2008, 558–59). To put that into perspective, the economy of Tanzania was valued at just over $14 billion in 2005 (current USD). Even a modest 2 percent gap in commitments versus disbursements means a loss of $280 million in aid for the Tanzanian government.[16]

This has real impacts for recipient governments. Take the case of Malawi in the 1990s, where aid inflows bounced up and down between 8 to 20 percent of GDP (Bulíř and Hamann 2001). As Nancy Birdsall of the Center for Global Development explains, "This would be the equivalent in the U.S. of quintupling the deficit in one year, and then a year later absorbing a huge recession-like effect on jobs and incomes" (2005, 18). Aid unpredictability means that recipient governments cannot plan for foreign aid in advance, resulting in lower rates of investment, vulnerability to economic shocks, and lower levels of growth (Lensink and Morrissey 2000). It would be poor fiscal planning for you to invest in a home, if you are not sure that you can make the payments for the foreseeable future. Similarly, for low-income countries, it would not be prudent to scale up a teacher-training program or create a new program for the treatment of HIV/AIDS without predictable and reliable donor financing (Birdsall 2005).

Yet donors frequently renege on their promises, sometimes because aid budgets dry up, sometimes because priorities shift elsewhere. After the implementation of the HIPC program, for example, countries *not* participating in the initiative saw a reduction in their financing of between 24 and 56 percent over a two-year period between 1998 and 2000 (Killick 2004). Because the program shifted donors' attention elsewhere, nonparticipants lost out on aid dollars.

Despite widespread recognition of the existence of both donor and recipient commitment problems, we don't yet fully understand the political implications of unpredictability on the aid system. My argument is that the popularity of aid delivery mechanisms waxes and wanes because recipient governments and donor agencies are trying to find bargaining compromises that are more easily measured and enforced. This is, however, an extremely difficult task, so despite attempts to make commitments easier to measure and enforce, promises go unfulfilled and partners get frustrated. Consequently, the aid policy compromises reached between donor agencies and recipient governments falter and require renegotiation.

The Shift toward Budget Support

To test the saliency of my argument, I empirically examine the evolution of aid policy bargaining and donor–government relations in four sub-Saharan Africa countries—Ghana, Rwanda, Tanzania, and Uganda—from the early 2000s until the mid-2010s. This time period allows me to trace both the adoption and the subsequent decline of a specific aid delivery mechanism—budget support—in each of the four countries. Budget support's rise and decline—both in rhetoric and in actual aid dollars distributed—represents a unique opportunity to study the implementation and repudiation of a particular aid delivery mechanism that was both innovative and puzzling. Given poor governance and public financial accountability in many recipient countries, why would donor agencies suddenly decide to trust recipient governments with large sums of aid funds, delivered with limited conditions directly into the recipient country's treasury?

In the late nineties, donors began promising more control over foreign aid to recipient countries. In 1999, the president of the World Bank, James Wolfensohn, famously argued that what was needed was to put recipient countries in the driver's seat. In 2005, these ideals were institutionalized in the Paris Declaration on Aid Effectiveness, which was signed by over 130 donor and recipient countries. At the heart of the Paris Agenda is an emphasis on moving from "donor-driven" development aid toward recipient-country "ownership," and the aid delivery mechanism most commonly associated with ownership is budget support (Armon 2007). After all, what would give a recipient country more ownership—or control over implemented policy outcomes (Whitfield and Fraser 2009a, 4)—than the ability to directly control where aid dollars are spent.[17]

While rhetorically appealing, the embrace of budget support in the 2000s is puzzling analytically. The idea of ownership in development cooperation is not new (see, for example, L. B. Pearson 1969), and there is little empirical evidence supporting the claim that budget support is actually more effective than other aid delivery mechanisms (Easterly 2007; IDD and Associates 2006; Koeberle, Stavreski, and Walliser 2006; de Renzio and Mulley 2006). Budget support requires donor agencies to trust governments who often have a relatively poor record of governance, including the management of aid funds. Why would donor officials, who are responsible for distributing taxpayers' funds, be willing to relinquish control over aid funds to recipient governments?

If my theoretical framework is correct, budget support was appealing to both donor agencies and recipient governments because it promised to increase the credibility of commitments, opening up the possibility for new bargaining compromises that were more favorable for both parties. Recipient governments received more technical control over aid dollars, which were now transferred directly to the recipient government in large sums at the beginning of the year, with limited conditions. In exchange, donor agencies were granted higher levels of access to recipient-government officials and more influence over development policy. Over time, however, the two parties were unable to live up to their commitments. The financial crisis in Europe strained donor budgets, and recipient governments made less headway with reforms than promised.

As a result, budget support has gradually fallen out of favor, and in its place new aid delivery mechanisms that promise to more effectively solve commitment problems have become fashionable.

As I explain in more detail in chapter 3, I focus my empirical analysis on Ghana, Rwanda, Tanzania, and Uganda, because these countries received some of the highest rates of budget support in the world. In each country, I examine the shift toward and away from budget support, as well as changes in the country's aid architecture—or the sets of rules and guiding frameworks that govern donor–government relations in a given recipient country. In conjunction with budget support, the aid architecture in all four countries went through major changes in the late 1990s and early 2000s. These changes provide valuable insights into how donor agencies and recipient governments seek to manage their relations with one another and provide an essential context for understanding donor–government relations at the recipient-country level.

To gain insight into the evolution of aid policy bargaining and donor–government relations during the budget support era, I collected data at multiple levels of analysis in each of the four countries of the study. I followed the evolution of aid policy bargaining over multiple years, interviewing key decision makers involved in aid policy bargaining on both the government and donor sides. In total, I formally interviewed over 150 high-level policy makers involved in aid policy bargaining (see appendix 1). Additionally, I combed through hundreds of policy documents on budget support and donor–government relations in each of the four countries, looking for evidence of how aid policy bargaining works at the recipient-country level. Policy documentation from each country allowed me to understand how changes in aid policy are framed at the recipient-country level. It also provided me with another way of comparing and contrasting the four country contexts.

Finally, I supplement data from the case studies with data from a large-N survey of high-level donor officials in twenty countries throughout sub-Saharan Africa. The survey is, to my knowledge, the first multicountry survey of high-ranking donor officials working at the mission level, and it targeted those individuals who are responsible for a donor agency's development program in a particular country. These individuals are often referred to as the head of cooperation or the head of development cooperation and serve as the key interlocutor for the donor agency at the recipient-country level. In total, 114 individuals from twenty-three different donor agencies participated in the survey. I use data from the survey to gauge the generalizability of my theory beyond the four country case studies.

This book is about two things: first, how donor agencies and recipient governments negotiate the delivery of foreign aid, and second, how such negotiations affect the sustainability of aid delivery mechanisms over time. It is not a book about the genesis of innovation regarding aid delivery mechanisms. Explaining where innovation in foreign aid comes from would require a fundamentally different approach, as potential sources of innovations are manifold (e.g., changing norms, leadership, organization incentives, and policy entrepreneurship). Instead, the goal of this book is to provide a theoretical framework for understanding under what conditions aid delivery mechanisms will last.

The argument I make—which is borne out in empirical evidence from detailed country case studies in four countries and a cross-national survey of donor officials in twenty countries—is that donor agencies and recipient governments continuously engage in an intense back-and-forth about the content of aid packages. A key concern for both parties in these negotiations is whether the promises made by the other side are credible. Concerns about the credibility of the other party's commitments influence choices regarding what to fund and how to fund it, and these concerns also determine whether an aid delivery mechanism is politically sustainable over the long term.

My findings make clear that choices in aid delivery are neither random nor driven exclusively by aid effectiveness concerns or the strategic interests of donor countries. Rather, choices in aid delivery are the product of a negotiated compromise between donor agencies and recipient governments. If the Norwegian Agency for Development Cooperation (Norad) wants to deliver foreign aid to the people of Burundi, it has to negotiate with the Burundian government. The problem is that aid policy compromises between donor agencies like Norad and governments like Burundi are constrained by the credibility of each side's commitments. This introduces a great deal of uncertainty, not to mention frustration, into development cooperation.

As I will explore in greater detail in the concluding chapter, my results ultimately suggest that designing more effective ways of delivering foreign aid is not just about finding better ways of meeting recipient needs. It is also about incentivizing *both* donor agencies and recipient governments to keep their promises over the long term. It is about making sure that a country like Uganda agrees to and carries out promised electoral reforms; but it is also about making sure that an agency like the UK's DFID delivers on its promise to fund the electoral commission for the foreseeable future. Incentivizing recipient governments and donor agencies to live up to their commitments is not likely to be an easy task. There are always good reasons for both donor agencies and recipient governments to withdraw from their commitments to one another. Ensuring the credibility of commitments is, however, essential to ensuring the sustainability of aid delivery mechanisms. Without a concentrated effort to limit commitment problems in the negotiated compromises between donor agencies and recipient government, fads and fashions in foreign aid will continue to rule the day, undermining the overall effectiveness of foreign aid.

IT TAKES TWO TO TANGO

Aid Policy Bargaining

Neither donors nor recipients can be forced into a policy straitjacket without a cost to the other party.

—Bertin Martens (2005, 662)

Let's say you work at the UK's Department for International Development (DFID) and you've been told that £3 million has been approved to help combat the high rate of infant mortality in Zambia over the next three years. You know that to implement an effective program you will have to work with lots of other stakeholders within a health care system that is lacking in capacity and personnel. But having been involved in Zambia for several years, you have also seen the human cost of the country's high rate of infant deaths. You want to get the money there quickly, and you want it to be effective. How do you use the power you have to decide how to spend the foreign aid?

Like at most donor agencies, actual funding amounts are out of your control, decided by politicians back home. But you have the opportunity to influence spending and allocation patterns by drafting and proposing both individual aid programs and national-level aid strategies that determine the direction of your agency's portfolio in a given recipient country for the next several years (typically three to five years). This is true even when politicians place strong oversight on your agency, such as restricting the spending of aid on family planning.

When drafting proposals for aid projects, a first point of call for donor officials like you is the recipient government. You have been working in Zambia for a few years, but you don't know it as well as the people who have lived there their whole lives, and local people will need to be on board for the program to be successful. You would like to be able to quickly earn the cooperation of the recipient government. Rarely, however, are their wishes immediately granted. Instead, what occurs is a back-and-forth between your agency and the government about the terms and the conditions of the aid. The Zambian government may prefer that the £3 million be used to shore up its health budget, allowing the government to limit user fees for citizens. Your agency, however, prefers to have something more tangible to show for its aid dollars. What about using the funds to build a clinic in the slums of Lusaka to provide pre- and post-natal care, you ask? The government agrees with the idea of a new clinic, but requests that it be built outside Lusaka in an area that it argues has more urgent needs (and might also be politically salient for the ruling party). You agree to build the clinic, but in return ask the government to commit to staffing the clinic with a doctor and several nurses and to run electricity to the site. You also ask that the government commit to prioritizing pre- and post-natal care in its new health-sector strategy plan, which is scheduled to be approved next month.

These types of negotiations go on every day in recipient countries. Far from simply deciding to build a new health clinic, donor agencies engage in lengthy discussions with recipient-country policy makers in order to come up with aid initiatives that are seen as useful and sustainable (although neither is of course guaranteed). In these discussions, recipient governments are not powerless but have a say in how the aid is disbursed. They have a say because donor agencies want their initiatives to work and want something in return for their aid money, like co-financing or reform promises. An essential part of these negotiations is how the aid money will actually be delivered—that is, the aid delivery mechanism—and the conditions attached to the delivery of such aid.

In this chapter, I provide a theoretical framework for understanding aid policy bargaining between donor agencies and recipient governments. The chapter is intended to provide the reader with insight into how aid is actually delivered at the recipient-country level. I want to convince you that aid is always negotiated and that in these negotiations both donor agencies and recipient governments have a commitment problem. My goal is not to provide an exhaustive account of the aid system. Rather, my focus is on the bargaining and negotiation that take place between recipient governments and publicly funded donor agencies, and how the commitment problems faced by both parties in these negotiations affect the political sustainability of aid policy compromises. In other words, it is about how DIFD officials work with Zambian government officials to determine how aid will be delivered and how the commitment problems plaguing these negotiations affect aid policy bargaining and the sustainability of aid initiatives.

Understanding Aid Delivery in Recipient Countries

Scholarship on foreign aid has predominantly focused on either aid allocation (i.e., "who gives foreign aid to whom and why")[1] or aid effectiveness (i.e., does foreign aid actually promote development in recipient countries).[2] In doing so, it has frequently overlooked decision making regarding *how* aid is actually delivered in recipient countries.[3] Once the decision to allocate aid to a given recipient country has been made, who is responsible for actually delivering the aid, and how are choices around aid delivery determined?

An aid delivery mechanism is the way in which a given amount of foreign aid is actually disbursed to the recipient. It's how DFID gives its money to Zambia. Components of an aid delivery mechanism include not only how the aid is distributed but also how the aid is managed. For example, in the case of the clinic, will the £3 million be managed through a stand-alone project implementation unit (PIU), or be transferred to the Ministry of Health or an NGO? When (and how) does the Zambian government need to report back to DFID, and is any co-financing required? Related to choices about aid delivery are the policy conditions attached to the aid—that is, what types of reforms or promises are required from the Zambian government to secure the aid. For example, does the government need to promise to approve a new health-sector plan, or does it need to promise to roll out a national-level education campaign on prenatal care?

As I noted in chapter 1, over time, different types of aid delivery mechanisms have fallen in and out of fashion. But even within these core fads—such as structural adjustment, project aid, budget support—there are hundreds of different ways of designing aid delivery. For example, a donor agency may decide to give budget support through a joint basket fund established in conjunction with other donors, or it may decide to go it alone, establishing its own mechanism for disbursing the funds. One donor might decide to set up a self-standing project to help treat Ebola victims in Makeni, Sierra Leone, while another donor may opt to transfer aid funds directly to the Ministry of Health and Sanitation in order to support programs already in place. Different funders may even attach radically different (and at times contradictory) conditions to their aid. One donor might require that funds go through the country's national procurement system, while another might forbid it.

Who Is Responsible for Aid Delivery?

At the recipient-country level, donor agencies like DFID or the African Development Bank are responsible for delivering aid. In discussions about foreign aid, donor countries and donor agencies are often lumped together under the generic label "donors." However, when analyzing aid policy bargaining, it is important to distinguish between the *countries* that provide foreign aid and the *agencies* that distribute it. USAID is not synonymous with the United States government. While it is frequently hamstrung by the policies of the State Department,

Congress, and the White House (Radelet 2006b), USAID is a distinct organization with its own preferences and objectives.

As Martens explains, donor agencies are the "the chief mediator between the preferences and interests of all persons involved in the aid delivery chain" (2005, 656). If there were zero transaction costs and fully shared preferences between donors and recipients, donor countries could simply directly transfer the funds without employing donor agencies as a middleman. If a country like the Democratic Republic of the Congo and a country like Germany had precisely the same goals, there would be no need for an intermediary in the form of Germany's development bank, KfW. However, because of the high transaction costs involved in the drafting and monitoring of aid agreements, it became necessary for donor countries to establish aid agencies: "As long as donors and recipients live in different political constituencies with no overarching political institution to work out a policy compromise between them, aid agencies will fill that gap and act as mediators between donors and recipients, proposing aid delivery instruments that reduce transaction costs and ex-post uncertainties in delivery" (Martens 2005, 662).

As an agent of the donor country, donor agencies are responsible to the donor country or donor countries (in the case of multilateral aid). However, this does not mean they always act in ways that perfectly align with the interests and preferences of the donor country (Martens 2002, 2005; Seabright 2002; Hawkins et al. 2006). For example, while parliaments in donor countries prefer to minimize spending on foreign aid in order to free up funds for other constituent demands, donor agencies seek to maximize aid budgets (Pomerantz 2004; Schneider and Tobin 2013; Svensson 2003). From the donor official's perspective, more aid extends the reach and the potential impact of the donor agency. From the donor politician's perspective, increasing foreign aid draws money away from other domestic priorities.

But how much leeway do donor agencies actually have to act in ways that are different from the preferences of donor countries? The answer is much more than one might first assume. The degree of oversight donor politicians can exercise over aid policy varies from donor country to donor country. Foreign aid is subject to much more political influence in the United States, France, and Japan than it is in the Scandinavian countries. Political oversight can also change over time, as new donor governments come in and out of power, and agencies are reorganized according to the government's preferences. After the Labour Party came to power in 1997 in the UK, Prime Minister Tony Blair created a new ministry (DFID) to oversee aid and development policy, appointing the new head, Clare Short, a full member of his cabinet (Barder 2005). Even, however, when donor politicians heavily constrain the actions of donor agencies, it is donor agencies that are responsible for designing and implementing programming at the recipient-country level.

Mutually Cooperative Bargaining

To deliver foreign aid, donor agencies must work with recipient governments. This is true even when donor agencies "bypass" recipient governments and channel aid money through entities like NGOs (Dietrich 2013; Knack 2013). To deliver aid, donor agencies not only negotiate the terms under which aid is disbursed with the recipient government but also engage in policy dialogue with the recipient government (Gibson et al. 2005; Mosley, Harrigan, and Toye 1995; Mosley et al. 2012; Whitfield 2009a). In other words, donor agencies like the World Bank not only talk to wealthy countries like the United States and Germany; they also have to negotiate with recipient countries like Zambia and El Salvador.

In aid policy bargaining, donor agencies exercise a great deal of power and influence. After all, donor agencies have the power of the purse. It would be incorrect, however, to characterize the relationship as being purely donor driven (Fisher 2013; Hyden 2008; Whitfield 2009a; Whitfield and Fraser 2010). Instead, the relationship is best characterized as one where there is mutual gain to be had by working together (Axelrod 2004; Tsekpo 2008). The end result of the bargaining process between donor agencies and recipient governments is what I call an aid policy compromise (see figure 2.1). The precise nature of a given aid policy compromise depends not only on the context, but also on the donor agency and the recipient government in question.

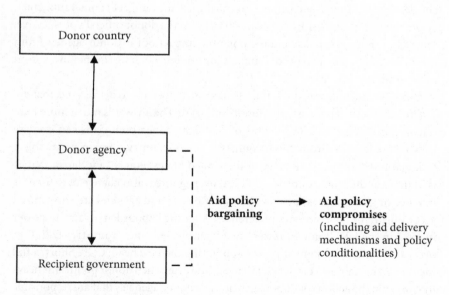

FIGURE 2.1 Aid policy bargaining

In Ghana, for example, the World Bank wanted the government to use HIPC funds only in the social sectors. However, the minister of finance wanted some of the funds to be used in sectors that that would generate more growth and employment. After a period of negotiation, the government and the World Bank came to an agreement that 20 percent of the HIPC savings would be used to pay off interest on domestic debt, with the rest going to projects for both poverty reduction and economic growth, as well as to fund specific projects submitted by government bodies (Whitfield and Jones 2009, 200). Such a negotiated agreement is what I refer to as an aid policy compromise.

As this example shows, at a basic level the donor agency promises to disburse foreign aid in exchange for certain promised actions on the part of the recipient country. This means that the aid policy compromise includes more than just the amount of aid. It also includes commitments by the donor agency to deliver the aid in a particular way and commitments by the recipient to undertake specific policy actions, reforms, or both. In some cases these commitments are explicitly spelled out to both parties; however, in many cases, aid policy compromises are based on verbal or nonbinding agreements between donor and recipient-government officials.

Donor agencies must negotiate aid with recipient governments for at least three reasons. First, recipient governments must (at least) tacitly consent to the donor agency being active in the country (Ostrom et al. 2002; W. Brown 2013). While rare, there are examples of recipient governments throwing out donors either individually or entirely. In 2006, Rwanda severed diplomatic ties with France for several years, after a French judge accused the Rwandan president Paul Kagame and several other senior Rwandan officials of being behind the 1994 murder of Rwanda's Hutu president Juvénal Habyarimana (BBC 2009).[4] In 1979, Tanzanian president Julius Nyerere expelled the IMF after it conditioned future support on the government implementing a macroeconomic adjustment program, including a large devaluation of the Tanzanian shilling, fiscal restraint, and parastatal reform. The situation was not resolved until 1986, when Nyerere decided not to seek another term and the new government reopened negotiations with the IMF (Edwards 2014a, 9).[5]

Second, donor agencies rely on recipient governments to effectively implement aid programs and projects. Take, as an example, a very simple aid project: the distribution of textbooks to a primary school in Tanzania. At a minimum, the donor agency needs to know how many students attend that particular school, as well as their current education level. To find out this information, the donor agency could send someone to the village to do a head count and to assess current education levels. This is, however, expensive and time consuming, particularly if the donor wants to distribute textbooks in more than one village. A better solution is for the donor agency to work with Tanzania's Ministry of Education and local governments to identify the number and needs of the students. This is what the Swedish International Development Cooperation Agency (SIDA) did throughout the eighties and nineties, financing a book-management unit in the ministry that helped increase the number of textbooks in circulation from just over six hundred thousand to more than four million (World Bank 1999, 100). Even if the donor agency decides to bypass the government and use an NGO to deliver the textbooks, it will still need input from the Ministry of Education, including a commitment to actually use the textbooks once they have been distributed. More complex governance reform projects will necessitate even more input, because by definition they require the government to undertake specific actions.

Third, donor agencies rely on recipient governments to carry out policies and reforms that they desire in exchange for aid. Take the example of the health clinic mentioned at the outset of this chapter. In this hypothetical scenario, DFID promises to build a clinic to help lower rates of infant mortality, but in return asks for the government to staff the clinic and to provide electricity. They also ask the government to include a section on pre- and post-natal care in its new health-sector plans. Donor agencies ask for these commitments, because the project will be less successful without them. A clinic is of limited use if there is no one to staff it and if there is no electricity (although neither scenario is uncommon in developing countries). The clinic is also more likely to accomplish the donor's objective of decreasing infant mortality if it is part of a larger set of policies being implemented by the government to improve pre- and post-natal care. Of course, donor agencies also might want something more self-interested in return for aid money. For example, they might require that the Zambian government use contractors or building materials from the donor country to build the clinic, or require that the recipient government pass an economic policy that is advantageous to domestic companies. However, whether it is for strategic, commercial, or altruistic reasons (or most likely a combination of all three), the donor agency depends on the recipient government to implement policies and reforms.

The model of aid policy bargaining illustrated in figure 2.1 is admittedly simplified. There are a host of other development actors like NGOs and development contractors that factor into aid policy bargaining at the recipient-country level. At the same time, neither the donor agency nor the recipient government is a unitary actor. Differences between donor agencies—both in how they are organized and in the political preferences of the countries they represent—can clearly affect the outcomes of aid policy bargaining. It matters, for example, that USAID is often hamstrung by Congress and the White House, while the development minister in the UK has more license to act independently (Swedlund 2017a).

In the empirical analysis, I am attentive to the role of NGOs and other development contractors, as well as to differences across donors and recipients in terms of preferences and organization. My research is not, however, designed to test the impact of these potential sources of variations on policy outcomes. This is not because I underestimate the complexity of the aid system or the actors that work within it. I explicitly choose to develop a theoretical model of donor–government relations that is broadly generalizable, because this relationship is fundamental to all types of aid distribution. Even when bilateral and multilateral aid donors use NGOs to distribute aid, there must be at least tacit consent from the recipient government for the donor agency to be active in the recipient country. And even when differences across donors and recipients alter specific policy outcomes, there are commonalities in the preferences and objectives of donors and recipients that transcend national boundaries. I draw on these common preferences and objectives to build a theoretical framework that can be expanded and adapted to account for potential sources of variation as need.

What Do Donor Agencies and Recipient Governments Bargain Over?

The details of specific aid-policy compromises vary widely. However, at a fundamental level, donor agencies and recipient governments bargain over three things: (1) the amount of aid; (2) technical control over how the aid is spent; and (3) policy influence over reform (see table 2.1). The goal of aid policy bargaining is to maximize the utility of the two parties—that is, to find a compromise that satisfies the needs and desires of each to the fullest extent possible.

Donor agencies and recipient governments have similar preferences in regard to aid volumes. Recipient governments prefer to maximize the amount of aid received, and donor agencies prefer to distribute the maximum amount of aid

TABLE 2.1 Preferences of donor agencies and recipient governments

GOAL OF BARGAINING COMPROMISE IS TO MAXIMIZE THE UTILITY OF BOTH PARTIES. THE TWO PARTIES BARGAIN OVER:			
	AMOUNT OF AID	TECHNICAL CONTROL	POLICY INFLUENCE
RECIPIENT GOVERNMENT	Prefers to maximize the amount of aid received	Prefers to maximize the amount of discretionary spending at its disposal	Prefers to minimize donor's influence over domestic policy/reforms
DONOR AGENCY	Prefers to distribute the maximum amount of aid it is authorized to allocate	Prefers to maximize its say over how aid funds are spent (and the ability to involve third parties)	Prefers to maximize its influence over domestic policy/reforms

they are authorized to allocate. Aid agencies have little incentive to withhold money made available to them (Svensson 2003, 2006). Unspent funds are likely to be interpreted as evidence that the aid money is not needed (Ostrom et al. 2002), and considerable stigma is often attached to a reduction or, even worse, the closing of an aid program in a recipient country (Fisher 2013). Alternatively, being perceived as efficient and effective at disbursement leads to promotion. At SIDA, for example, donor officials signal performance in terms of the number of projects signed and amount of funds disbursed (Ostrom et al. 2002).

In regard to technical control and policy influence, donor agencies and recipient countries have different preferences. The recipient government, not surprisingly, prefers to maximize the amount of discretionary spending at its disposal. If offered the choice, a recipient government will undoubtedly prefer to have aid money transferred into its own budget, rather than have aid money transferred to an NGO or to a stand-alone project unit overseen by the donor. Even if the money would eventually go toward the same thing—for example, antiretroviral therapy for HIV/AIDS patients—all governments would prefer to have more discretionary funds at their disposal.

On the other hand, donor agencies prefer, all thing being equal, to maintain a say over how aid money is spent. Donor agencies want to make sure that aid money is spent in line with their policy preferences and is not siphoned off in corrupt practices or spent on undesirable goods like weapons. Therefore, donor agencies prefer to maintain technical control over aid dollars. Only then can they guarantee that aid funds are being spent according to their wishes. In cases where donor agencies cannot distribute the aid themselves, they do not necessarily have a preference for whether the aid goes through the government or through third parties like NGOs, as long as they can verify that the money is being spent properly and according to their agency's preferences.[6]

Recipient governments and donor agencies also have different preferences regarding policy influence. In contrast to technical control, policy influence refers to the economic and political direction of the country, rather than how individual aid dollars are spent. While recipient governments prefer to minimize donor influence over domestic policy, donor agencies prefer to maximize their influence, seeking to extract as much reform from their aid money as possible. Recipient countries prefer to minimize donor interference, because it decreases reform pressure and allows them more space to act according to their own preferences. Even if the recipient government does not necessarily disagree with the reforms being requested by donor agencies, it would still prefer to make such reforms on its own terms. Even when the Ghanaian government did not disagree with the World Bank on the types of economic reforms needed during the structural adjustment era, it still sought to pursue these reforms at its own speed (Whitfield and Jones 2009).

Alternatively, donor agencies prefer to maximize their say over domestic policy issues. Donor agencies desire influence over domestic policy for many reasons. They may, for example, seek to exert influence over domestic policies that affect the donor country's security or geopolitical interests, using their leverage as an aid donor to pressure the recipient government to crack down on terrorism or to enact a trade policy that is more favorable to domestic business interests. The Reagan administration, for example, funneled millions of aid dollars into El Salvador, Honduras, Guatemala, the Philippines, Indonesia, and Zaire, because these governments were fighting threats from the Left that the administration wanted to actively discourage (Radelet 2006b). Donor agencies also desire influence over recipient governments because such influence is perceived as being instrumental in making sure that development initiatives are successful. Donor agencies desire influence because they want to make sure that, for instance, if they build a health clinic in Uganda's Gulu district, it is properly staffed and has access to an adequate supply of medicines.

New bargaining compromises between recipient governments and donor agencies emerge as each party tries to achieve a more preferential bargaining compromise in line with its preferences. A donor agency may be willing to give more technical control to recipient governments if it is promised more policy influence. Similarly, recipient governments may be willing to forgo technical control if they are promised more aid. At times, the interests of the parties may conflict, but the interests of the two parties are not necessarily zero-sum. Both sides have particular interests, which they seek to maximize as much as possible. Maximizing one's interests, however, does not necessarily have to come at a cost to the other party.

Donors and Recipients Have Trouble Making Credible Commitments

If aid delivery mechanisms are the result of a negotiated compromise, it logically follows that such compromises are contingent on donor agencies and recipient governments keeping their part of the bargain. This raises the question: how credible are the commitments of donor agencies and recipient governments?

Scholars have long used guns and butter as stand-ins for how much a country invests in defense (guns) and civilian goods (butter), so let's think about these disparate priorities in relation to aid policy bargaining. Imagine a scenario where a donor agency and a recipient government are bargaining over where the government spends $5 million in revenue, $3 million of which is promised by international donors. While the recipient government prefers to spend more money on guns, the donor agency prefers the government to spend more money on butter. A compromise is therefore reached where the government gets to spend a bit of money on guns in exchange for also spending money on butter. Problem solved.

Or is it? Unfortunately, there is typically no guarantee that either party will uphold its end of this compromise. Donor agencies cannot be sure that the recipient government will actually uphold its commitment to buy a thousand tons of butter and only four thousand AK-47s. If the recipient government decides to buy less butter and more guns (either with aid money or because domestic revenue was freed up because of the availability of donor money), donor agencies are placed in the tricky situation of supporting initiatives that run counter to their preferences and may entail backlash from funders (i.e., taxpayers) back in the donor country. This is exactly what happened, for example, in 2010, when it was discovered that Malawi purchased a $13.26 million presidential jet. While it was not alleged that aid funds were actually used to purchase the plane, the availability of aid funds presumably freed up domestic resources, which were then used to make the purchase.[7]

Likewise, and equally important, the recipient government has no guarantee that the donor agency will actually deliver on its promise to provide $3 million in aid to purchase the butter. Perhaps the donor will change its mind and want the government to buy sugar instead of butter, or perhaps the money to buy the butter will dry up altogether owing to a financial crisis in the donor country, as was the case in the Netherlands in the late 2000s. If this happens, the recipient government will be forced to either dip into its own reserves, which may be very limited, or to renege on its promise to provide its population with a thousand tons of butter.

Recipient Commitment Problems: Aid Fungibility and Moral-Hazard Problems

The problem that aid is spent on things other than what a donor agency intends is acute, because foreign aid is largely fungible (Deverajan and Swaroop 2006).[8] As a senior World Bank economist famously put it, aid fungibility is "when we think we're financing a power plant, and we're really financing a brothel" (quoted in Easterly 2010). Aid fungibility occurs if a government would have undertaken a donor-financed project in the absence of that financing. As a result, the inflow of donor funds relaxes the government's budget constraint and allows the government to spend the money it intended to spend on the donor's project somewhere else. Thus, even if money is targeted toward a specific goal or project, the aid transfer allows the government to buy other things, which may or may not be in line with the preferences of donors (e.g., a presidential jet). A 2010 study of the health sector caused quite a scandal by suggesting that for *every* dollar given in aid, a recipient government shifts between $0.43 and $1.14 of its own spending to other priorities (Lu et al. 2010).

Even without getting into the gray area of fungibility, however, there is ample evidence that recipient governments often back down on their commitments. Perhaps the best example here is structural adjustment. The scope and nature of structural adjustment programs have been heavily critiqued as being heavy-handed and damaging to the poor.[9] Such critiques are important, but what is most interesting for our purposes is the observation that policy conditionality—or the tying of foreign aid to specific targets or reforms (Collier 1997)—was in practice difficult to enforce. Powerful institutions like the World Bank and the IMF were not able to guarantee that recipients desperate for financing actually carried out promised reforms. Why?

As Mosley, Harrigan, and Toye (1995) point out, structural adjustment would not have been needed if the World Bank and the borrower already agreed on the type of reforms that were necessary. Ironically, this meant that "those least in need of the policy reform medicine swallowed it more readily, while those most in need (on the Bank's criteria) swallowed very little at all" (Mosley, Harrigan, and Toye 1995, 1:41). Recipient countries were able to get away with not implementing reforms, because policy conditions were often not enforced. If a government did not meet the conditions of the loan or grant, donor agencies, instead of withdrawing aid, simply put together a new package, allowing the recipient country to avoid making difficult reforms. This created a moral-hazard problem,[10] in that even countries with no serious intention of fulfilling the conditions were tempted to formally accept a conditionality-laced loan in order to access much-needed financing (Azam and Laffont 2003; Burnside and Dollar 2000; Collier 1997; Dollar and Svensson 2000; Hudson and Mosley 2001; Killick 1998).

A classic example is Kenya. Despite Kenya's poor track record of implementation, the IMF and World Bank gave it *twenty-one* adjustment loans between 1980 and 2000, providing aid to support an identical agricultural policy reform on *five* separate occasions and asking the government at least *six* times to increasing the amount of funds available for road maintenance (Easterly 2003a, 37). In 1995, the *Economist* wrote about this sequence of event as follows: "Over the past few years Kenya has performed a curious mating ritual with its aid donors. The steps are: one, Kenya wins its yearly pledges of foreign aid. Two, the government begins to misbehave, backtracking on economic reform and behaving in an authoritarian manner. Three, a new meeting of donor countries looms with exasperated foreign governments preparing their sharp rebukes. Four, Kenya pulls a placatory rabbit out of the hat. Five, the donors are mollified and the aid is pledged. *The whole dance then starts again*" (quoted in Pedersen 1996, 436; author's emphasis). Research has thus far emphasized the impact of moral-hazard problems on aid effectiveness and regime survival.[11] However, the failure of recipient governments to enact promised reforms also suggests an underlying commitment problem in the bargaining compromises reached by donor agencies and recipient governments. Recipient governments promise to undertake future reform with little intention of or incentive to actually carry out the reform.

Donor Commitment Problems: Credible Threats and Credible Promises

Recipient governments are able to make promises that they have little intention of fulfilling, because donor agencies are not able to make credible threats to suspending aid if recipients fail to meet the conditions of aid (Bearce and Tirone 2010; S. Brown 2005; Dunning 2004). Political interests in maintaining good relations with a recipient government often trump desires to punish recipients for failing to meet aid conditions—or indeed even a country's own national laws. The 1961 U.S. Foreign Assistance Act, for example, requires aid to be suspended following a coup d'état, but implementation of the law is iffy at best. In 2013, the military ousted Egypt's elected president, Mohamed Morsi, in a coup, yet aid continued to flow. At the time, a spokesperson for the Obama administration said, "It would not be in the best interests of the United States to immediately change our assistance program to Egypt."[12]

In addition to political pressures not to suspend aid, donor agencies also face a variety of institutional incentives not to suspend aid (Swedlund 2017a). Suspending aid means that development programs have to be stopped midstream. Not only is this often undesirable from a developmental perspective; it is practically difficult to do in cumbersome, bureaucratic organizations like aid agencies (S. Brown 2005). Knowledge has to be filtered up and then acted upon. Suspensions can also put future aid dollars in jeopardy. As Ostrom et al. explain, "A nearly universal pressure exists within almost all development agencies . . . to spend the money that is allocated in one budgetary cycle, as parliamentarians are likely to interpret unallocated funds as evidence that their funds are not needed" (2002, 70). Suspending aid can even be personally costly for donor officials, as "people get promoted by disbursing money, not withholding it" (Collier 2007, 109).

Donor agencies also have a hard time making credible promises. As Pomerantz (2004) puts it, donors are constantly "moving the goal posts" on recipient governments, changing the criteria by which aid is disbursed. This happens for several reasons. First, aid agencies like DFID or SIDA have a great deal of discretion over how aid is delivered, but donor politicians largely make aid allocation decisions. As new governments come to power in donor countries, priorities shift and donor agencies are forced to realign. In the case of U.S. aid, for example, two new initiatives—the United States President's Emergency Plan for AIDS Relief (PEPFAR) and the Millennium Challenge Cooperation (MCC)—are associated with reductions in absolute spending on long-standing programs managed by USAID (Bhavnani, Birdsall, and Shapiro 2004). Second, priorities change as donor officials rotate in and out of different recipient countries. Donor officials typically stay in a given recipient country for only two to four years, meaning that recipient governments are continuously being forced to readjust to new personalities and new ways of doing things. Finally, donor agencies face an incentive to try to extract as much reform in exchange for aid dollars as they can. Donor officials want to show supervisors and taxpayers that aid dollars were well spent. The more they can show for aid dollars, the better. This incentivizes donor officials to continue to add conditions to aid policy compromises well after they have been informally or formally agreed upon.

For recipient governments, the value of the aid declines if the donor agency cannot credibly commit to its release. Developing-country governments rely on aid funds for survival and, for a variety of reasons, find it valuable to be able to deliver butter or other goods provided by aid—education and health care, for example—to their constituents, even if they would have preferred to buy guns. If a donor agency cannot actually deliver on its aid promise, the recipient government is placed in the tricky situation of not being able to provide for its constituents' needs and perhaps of having to renege on its promises. In 2013, Ugandan president Yoweri Museveni highlighted this paradox of aid in a speech to the United Nations: "In our struggle for socio-economic transformation, our biggest problem was funding. . . . Initially, as we struggled for minimum economic recovery, we had to depend on external funding. Although useful, *this external funding was limited, slow in coming, not always focused, and erratic*" (Museveni 2013, author's emphasis). Aid that is more predictable is simply more valuable for recipient governments (Arellano et al. 2009; Bulíř and Hamann 2006; Hudson 2015; Celasun and Walliser 2006, 2008).

How Do Commitment Problems Affect Aid Policy Bargaining?

During their negotiations with one another, donor agencies and recipient governments are presumably not meeting for the first time and are well aware that it is difficult for the other party to make a credible commitment. How might this affect not only choices in aid delivery mechanisms, but also the sustainability of aid policy compromises over the long term? To help us answer this question, it is useful to turn to theories of institutional economics, and in particular the work of Douglass North, whose research helps us to understand not only how parties innovate to help solve commitment problems, but when and if those innovations are likely to be sustainable.

Donors and Recipients Innovate in Order to Overcome Commitment Problems

According to North, institutions are the humanly devised constraints that shape human interactions both formally and informally; that is, institutions are the "rules of the game" (North 1990, 3).[13] They may be created or may evolve naturally, but either way institutions serve as the framework for human interaction, governing what is permissible and what is not. In the context of aid policy bargaining, the compromises reached by donor agencies and recipient governments can be thought of as institutions, in that they order the interactions between the two parties. The efficiency of an institution is determined by three factors: (a) the motivations of players,[14] (b) the complexity of the environment, and (c) how well the players are able to decipher and order their environment. These three variables influence how easy it is to measure and enforce the two parties' commitments to each other.

When an income flow is predictable, rights to an asset are easy to assure. However, "when the income stream is variable and not fully predictable, it is costly to determine whether the flow is what it should be in that particular case" (North 1990, 31–32). The result is that both parties will try to capture some of the income, and significant resources will have to be devoted to measure and monitor the costs of agents. Consequently, transaction costs—or the costs associated with the measurement and enforcement of agreements—will be high (North 1990, 15). Institutions, by way of three structural characteristics—informal constraints, formal rules, and enforcement—can limit the behavior of actors, leading to lower transaction costs and more efficient institutions of exchange.

According to North, parties have a strong incentive to strike a bargain. However, compliance is always a potential problem. When parties anticipate this ex post facto problem, they will attempt to alter the incentives by devising institutions that promote compliance with agreed-on bargains (North and Weingast 1989, 806). Williamson writes: "Transactions that are subject to ex post opportunism will benefit if appropriate actions can be devised ex ante. Rather than reply to opportunism in kind, the wise [bargaining party] is one who seeks both to give and receive 'credible commitments.' Incentives may be realigned and/or superior governance structures within which to organize transactions may be devised" (1985, 48–49). That is, institutions change and evolve as parties seek to reduce transaction costs by fostering more credible commitments.

In the context of aid policy bargaining, this would imply that because donor agencies and recipient governments anticipate the *ex post* problem that the other party might not live up to its side of the agreement, they will attempt to devise institutions that help to limit this problem *ex ante*. In other words, donor agencies and recipient governments innovate to help solve commitment problems in aid policy bargaining.

There is plenty of evidence that both parties do this. In its budget calculations, for example, the Ugandan Ministry of Finance discounts all aid commitments by roughly 30 percent.[15] In other words, the government explicitly plans to get less aid money than donors commit to providing. In the 1990s, the ministry faced the recurring problem that aid totals were less that what were promised, leaving gaps in the national budget. This made it difficult to draft a viable budget. The discounting of aid is unpopular with donors (it makes them look bad) but is seen as necessary to account for the fact that the government rarely gets what it has been promised. Similarly, donor officials often make two schedules when planning a project—a "formal" schedule and a "real" schedule, as they expect delays in the achievement of particular milestones (Pomerantz 2004).

My argument is that the *ex post* problem of credible commitments not only causes donors and governments to take actions like discounting aid predictions and scheduling in extra time, but more fundamentally affects the types of agreements reached by donor agencies and recipient governments. To explain how this might play out in practice, let's return to the guns-and-butter scenario. In this hypothetical situation, a donor agency (the European Commission, for example) wishes to maximize the amount of aid that is spent on butter, while the recipient government (Burundi, for example) wants to maximize the amount of aid that is spent on guns. As a result of their previous interactions, the donor official—who has been in the country for three years—knows to be conservative in disbursements in order to make sure that not too much aid money is diverted to guns. Likewise, the donor official's counterpart in government, who has worked at the Ministry of Finance for over a decade, knows to be conservative in estimates of aid revenue.

The situation looks very different, however, if the two parties are able to make more credible commitments. If the EC is able to credibly promise that $3 million in aid will actually be delivered to buy the butter, Burundi's budget is relaxed. The government might then feel free to make plans to invest any surplus from domestic tax revenues in the purchasing of sugar. To get this guarantee of aid funds, the Nkurunziza government may be willing to give the EC something that it desires—for example, the ability to influence where the butter is actually disbursed, which the EC could use to ensure that the butter goes to those most in need, instead of to party loyalists. Even if the government of Burundi would prefer to minimize donor influence, it might be willing to offer the EC more say over the details of the agreement if it knows that the commitment to deliver $3 million in aid is actually credible. If the EC is given more influence over the terms of the agreement, it may in turn feel more comfortable disbursing the aid in a manner more favorable to the government—for example, through general budget support—because it would feel more confident that Burundi would actually follow through on its commitment to distribute the butter provided by the aid to the neediest members of the population.

The second scenario actually leaves *both* the donor agency and the recipient country better off. The EC is able to disburse more butter, while Burundi, in addition to getting more butter, also gets the ability to purchase some sugar. The negotiated compromise does not come about because of a change in either party's preferences (that is, the government did not stop preferring to buy guns, nor did the donor agency stop preferring to buy butter). Instead, the new arrangement came about because the promise of more credible commitments enabled the emergence of a new, more preferable bargaining compromise between the two parties.

To Be Sustainable, Aid Policy Compromises Must Be Self-enforcing

Unfortunately, however, according to North, even if the bargaining compromises are advantageous to both parties, if they are not enforceable, they will not be sustainable over the long term. According to North, efficient institutions are "self-enforcing" when the major parties to the bargain have an incentive to actually abide by the bargain after it is made. As long as conditions approximate a zero-transaction-cost model, the long-run path is efficient, and institutions that foster credible commitments emerge. However, examples of zero transaction costs are rare:

> If the markets are incomplete, the information feedback is fragmentary . . . and transaction costs are significant, then the subjective models of actors modified both by very imperfect feedback and by ideology will shape the path. Then, not only can both divergent paths and persistently poor performance prevail, the historically derived perceptions of the actors shape the choice they make. In a dynamic world characterized by institutional increasing returns, the imperfect and fumbling efforts of the actors reflect the difficulties of deciphering a complex environment with the available mental constructs—ideas, theories, and ideologies. (North 1990, 96)

In other words, in contexts of complex, impersonal exchange, *there is no guarantee* that efficient institutions will emerge. If institutions are not self-enforcing or patrolled by a third party, it is impossible to prevent reneging. As a result, over time, commitment problems will undermine the sustainability of institutions, even if they are advantageous to both parties.

As applied to our butter-and-guns scenario, this means that even if a negotiated compromise is advantageous for both the EC and the Burundian government, if it is not self-enforcing, it is unsustainable. Donor–government relations take place in complex environments with many competing interests, and there is no third party to enforce the agreements between donor agencies and recipient governments. If the EC decides it wants the money to go toward buying flour instead of butter (perhaps because European farmers have a bumper crop of wheat that year), there is little the government of Burundi can do, save for throwing the EC out of the country, thus forgoing any future aid (not to mention severing an important diplomatic relationship). The EC has more leverage. It could suspend aid if the Burundian government buys more than four thousand AK-47s. However, we have already seen that, in practice, donor agencies have a hard time making credible threats to suspending aid when conditionalities are not met.

As it is applied to aid policy bargaining, North's theory thus has two practical implications. First, if an institutional innovation promises to help with commitment problems, it should be attractive to both parties and therefore more likely to be adopted. Second, and most important, the sustainability of an aid delivery mechanism depends on its ability to incentivize donor agencies and recipient governments to actually abide by their commitments. If an institutional innovation is not able to deliver on its promise to enable more credible commitments, then the negotiated compromise—no matter how promising and appealing it is to both parties—will eventually fall out of favor and have to be renegotiated. That is, even if the government of Burundi and the EC negotiate an agreement that is advantageous to both parties, the sustainability of the policy compromise rests on promises both sides have a hard time keeping.

STUDYING THE DANCE

Research Design, Methodology, and Historical Context

How did I go about studying how donor agencies and recipient governments negotiate the delivery of aid? In this chapter, I outline the methodological tools and strategies I used to gain insight into the development dance. How I carried out the analysis and why I chose the countries I did are just as important as the empirical findings. Without a sound methodology, we cannot be assured that the results are reliable and valid. This chapter also includes historical background on the countries where I carried out fieldwork, background that is vital to fully understand my empirical findings.

My empirical approach relies largely on in-depth fieldwork conducted in Ghana, Uganda, Tanzania, and Rwanda between 2009 and 2015.[1] To understand how exactly aid policy bargaining works in each of the four countries of the study, I interviewed more than 150 donor and government officials, including ambassadors, heads of national banks, permanent secretaries, mid-level civil servants, and civil society organization (CSO) leaders. I read countless policy documents, meeting minutes, and monitoring and evaluation reports and attended meetings between the two parties whenever possible. At times, I was simply a "fly on the wall," observing the more informal interactions between government and donor officials over lunches and in their offices. I also carried out joint workshops in Ghana and Tanzania, where I facilitated a discussion between donor and government officials about the challenges in the aid relationship and how we might overcome them. Collectively, these experiences allowed me to observe firsthand how donor and government officials engage with one another at the recipient-country level.

In addition to in-country fieldwork, I conducted a survey of heads of cooperation (HoCs) working for twenty-three different donor agencies in twenty countries across sub-Saharan Africa. Over one hundred high-level donor officials working for bilateral and multilateral development agencies, such as USAID, the French Development Agency (AFD), and the African Development Bank (AfDB), in countries such as Liberia, Mauritania, and Zambia completed my questionnaire. Data from the survey provide us with additional insights into how senior donor officials working at the recipient-country level view the activities and motivations of the donor agencies they work for and extend the insights of the study beyond the four country contexts. To my knowledge, it is the first survey of its kind, and thus represents a unique source of data.

Research Design and Methodology

The story of how donor agencies and recipient governments negotiate the delivery of foreign aid is far from linear but instead is full of twists and turns. As a result, examining its accuracy and relevance requires us to dive into the complex processes of bargaining and negotiation between donor agencies and recipient governments at the recipient-country level. To gain this in-depth perspective, I compiled case studies of donor–government relations and aid policy bargaining in four country contexts: Ghana, Rwanda, Tanzania, and Uganda. My methodological approach allowed me not only to observe how donor–government relations have evolved over a specified period of time, but also to investigate why changes in aid delivery practices occurred in the first place.

Process Tracing

In the case studies, I rely on a tool called process tracing (e.g., Bennett and Elman 2006; Bennett 2010; Checkel 2008; George and Bennett 2005; Bennett and Checkel 2014). True to its name, process tracing emphasizes causal processes, attempting to connect X to Y by exploring the causal chain between the variables of interest. Similar to how a detective would solve a criminal case, process tracing helps us connect the dots between our variables of interest.

Importantly, process tracing has built-in strategies for handling more complicated relationships. In the complex world of political interaction, it is very hard to be confident that one variable (such as a country's military strength) causes another (such as aggression). Process tracing deals with this problem by allowing for the description of more complex relationships, such as multiple causality, feedback loops, path dependencies, and tipping points (Bennett and Elman 2006; Falleti

2006), all of which may characterize donor–government relations. Instead of testing the relationship between two variables, process tracing isolates a causal relationship by focusing on identifying the mechanisms, or the "component of a causal process that intervenes between agents with causal capacities and outcomes" (Bennett and George 2001, 139). The approach leverages the data points between time A and time B to explain the relationship (or lack thereof) between the variables of interest.[2]

In the research design, variation comes from changes over time and from differences between donor agencies, rather than from differences between the individual country cases. Some donor agencies began to increasingly disburse aid via budget support in the 2000s, while other donor agencies remained wedded to project-based aid. The EC, the Scandinavian states, the Netherlands, the United Kingdom, Canada, and the World Bank, for example, all enthusiastically adopted budget support. Alternatively, the United States, Japan, France, and the IMF never fully embraced budget support (Whitfield and Fraser 2009a). Differences in patterns of adoption across otherwise very similar donor agencies makes it possible to assess whether changes in donor–government relations across time result from changes in the aid delivery mechanisms or something else. It also helps to provide qualitative insight into donor agencies' motivations and considerations when deciding to adopt or abandon budget support, helping to clarify the direction of causality. The analysis of cases in multiple countries was included to reduce context dependency, or the likelihood that the results are valid only in one country.

Data Collection

STUDYING THE DANCE UP CLOSE: IN-COUNTRY FIELDWORK

My primary activity while in the field was semi-structured interviews with donor representatives, government officials, representatives of local and international nongovernmental organizations and think tanks, and independent consultants. In total, I personally conducted more than 150 interviews across the four countries. Owing to return trips (and persistence), I was able to interview a wide selection of key stakeholders on both the donor and the government sides in each country. In all countries, interviewees included heads of cooperation and other senior donor staff, as well as senior government staff involved in donor–government relations, including permanent secretaries, heads of national banks, and department heads. (For a complete list of the interviews conducted for the project see appendix 1.)

For the interviews, I developed an interview protocol, or a common set of questions, that I asked each interviewee. This helped not only to guide my conversations, but also to ensure that I posed the questions in a consistent way across the different persons I spoke with. In order to make sure that I did not overlook topics and themes that were not accounted for in the protocol ahead of time, I took the license to deviate from the protocol when interesting topics arose or when the interviewee was an expert on a particular subject. For example, if a respondent worked in the health sector, I asked about the functioning of that particular sector and about how donors and government worked together (or did not work together) to solve challenges facing the health sector. In order to achieve a more nuanced understanding, I also frequently asked interviewees to expand on a particular historical event or scenario that they mentioned in response to one or more of my questions.

Interviews generally lasted around an hour but lasted anywhere from thirty minutes to over three hours. For purposes of confidentiality and to allow my informants to be able to speak freely, the names of my interviewees are withheld. For the same reasons, I do not attribute quotes and statements to specific donor agencies but refer instead to the speaker as a bilateral or multilateral donor official, civil society representative, consultant, or government official.[3]

To help triangulate the data collected during fieldwork, I also collected and analyzed hundreds of primary documents, including key aid documents and declarations by the four recipient governments and the many donor agencies active in the four countries. Whenever possible, I also examined meeting agendas, minutes, and PowerPoint presentations, as well as documents specific to identified programs of interest. Many of these documents were collected online prior to or after the field visit, but informants also frequently gave me documents while I was in the field. Some of these documents were publicly available, while others were not. I was, for example, given workings drafts of policy documents that were still marked up with in-text comments. At times I also relied on monitoring and evaluation reports to verify findings. However, these were never used as the sole confirmation of a finding.

BROADENING THE SCOPE: SURVEY OF HEADS OF DEVELOPMENT COOPERATION

With only four case countries, it is important to have a way of ensuring that the findings are generalizable, or valid across an even wider range of countries. Therefore, in addition to the case studies, between March 2013 and July 2014 I also carried out a survey of donor officials working for all the major bilateral and multilateral development agencies across twenty countries in sub-Saharan Africa. While some of the countries sampled, such as Liberia and Sierra Leone, received extremely high amounts of foreign aid as a percentage of their national income, others, such as Togo and Kenya, received much lower amounts of aid (see appendix 2 for a description of the sample). This helps to ensure that the findings are reflective of a range of possible aid relationships.

The survey targeted heads of (development) cooperation, commonly referred to as HoCs.[4] The HoC is the person responsible for an aid agency's development portfolio, or the agency's combined set of projects and programs in a given recipient country. This position is distinct from that of an ambassador. While the ambassador is responsible for the political relationship between the two countries, the HoC is responsible for development cooperation and the disbursement of aid. The HoC is the key negotiator with the recipient government about matters related to foreign aid and is therefore in the best position to tell us about donor–government relations and aid policy bargaining at the recipient-country level.

In total, 114 HoCs representing twenty-three different donor agencies participated in the survey, for a response rate of 53 percent. The survey took respondents approximately twenty minutes to complete and was made available for respondents via the online survey platform Qualtrics. Respondents in Francophone countries were given the opportunity to complete the survey in either French or English. Potential respondents were told upfront that all data collected would be anonymized and not associated with either their name or their agency's name. The survey asked the HoCs to answer a variety of questions related to their agency's activities in the recipient country. A full survey protocol can be found in appendix 3.

What Should We Expect to See in the Data?

If the theoretical framework proposed in chapter 2 is correct, what should we expect to see in the empirical data? In other words, what are we actually looking for in the case studies and in data from the survey? To answer this question, it is useful to return to the theoretical framework I outlined in chapter 2.

My argument is that the sustainability of an aid delivery mechanism depends on its ability to foster credible commitments from both donor agencies and recipient governments. In other words, for a donor agency like DFID and recipient government like Uganda to continue to use a particular aid delivery mechanism, they need to be able to trust that the other side will fulfill its promises. This argument is based on the core assumption that aid policy is the result of mutually cooperative bargaining between donor agencies and recipient governments, where the end result is a negotiated compromise. Empirically, to justify this assumption, in the country case studies, we need to see evidence that both parties see the necessity of working together, even if the relationship is fraught with challenges and frustrations. In particular, we should see evidence that donor officials place a strong priority on their relationships with their recipient-government counterparts. We should thus see evidence that not only are donor officials willing to engage in substantial dialogue and discussion with recipient governments, but also that the agreements reached between donor agencies and recipient governments are compromises, rather than being unilaterally imposed by donor officials.

In this bargaining relationship, donor agencies and recipient governments depend on the other party upholding its promises. However, if donor agencies and recipient governments suffer from commitment problems, as I argue they do, we would expect that both find it difficult to uphold their side of the negotiated compromise. In the country case studies, we should therefore see evidence that it is difficult for both donor agencies and recipient governments to uphold their promises to one another and that each party lacks the ability to enforce the other party's commitments. We should also see evidence that commitment problems are a source of frustration for both donor agencies and recipient governments. That is, it is not enough that commitment problems exist; there has to be evidence that both sides see commitment problems as hindering their negotiated compromises with one another.

Finally, and most important, if commitment problems constrain the bargaining compromises reached by donor agencies and recipient governments, we should see evidence of two predictions: (1) donor agencies and recipient governments are drawn to institutional innovations that promise to help reduce commitment problems, and (2) if an institutional innovation does not incentivize donor agencies and recipient governments to abide by their commitments over the long term, it will eventually fall out of favor. I evaluate these two predictions by looking at the shift toward and away from budget support in each of the four countries of the study. If my theoretical framework is valid, we should first see evidence that budget support was appealing to donor agencies and recipient governments because it promised to reduce commitment problems. Commitment problems do not need to be the only motivating factor to take up budget support. However, if budget support was, for example, perceived as undermining the credibility of either donor or recipient commitments, this would falsify the theory. Second, and most crucial, we should see evidence that budget support is on the decline, because one or both of the parties could not uphold their commitments over the long run. Here the source of the commitment problem may be entirely exogenous to the negotiated compromise. What matters is that the policy compromise that enabled budget support to emerge was eventually undermined by the difficulty one or both parties had in upholding their commitments.

Why Sub-Saharan Africa?

In no other region of the world is foreign aid more important than sub-Saharan Africa (Riddell 1999). Despite attention-grabbing cases like Afghanistan or

Iraq, as a region it is sub-Saharan Africa that receives the largest share of official development assistance (ODA). Between 2001 and 2005, 35 percent of ODA went to Africa. In contrast, the next largest regional recipient of ODA was South and Central Asia, at 15 percent of global ODA. During the same period, which includes the height of the wars in Afghanistan and Iraq, the Middle East received only 14 percent of global ODA (IDA 2007). In this way, African development darlings are the key sites in which to understand donor–government relations.

As table 3.1 demonstrates, in comparison to other low-income countries, the four countries of the study (along with Mozambique) received the highest amounts of budget support in the world between 2005 and 2010 (OECD 2011).[5] In three of the four countries of the study, budget support constituted more than 10 percent of public expenditures. I selected these four countries not just because they received large amounts of budget support, however. As will become clear through the case histories, in different ways these countries represent the African states at the forefront of the debates on "ownership" and aid effectiveness in recent years. They therefore serve as key sites in which to observe donor–government relations and aid policy bargaining. At the same time, the strength of their economies and their political histories are quite different. Ghana, for example, has enjoyed a relatively stable two-party democracy

TABLE 3.1 Budget support volumes as a percentage of public expenditure

DIRECT BUDGET SUPPORT	2005	2007	2010	AVERAGE
Ghana				
Total volume (USD millions)	295.84	377.63	602.69	
as % of public expenditure	8.78	6.54	7.81	7.71
Rwanda				
Total volume (USD millions)	198.47	213.39	368.75	
as % of public expenditure	32.53	24.81	24.58	27.31
Tanzania				
Total volume (USD millions)	573.29	745.43	832.80	
as % of public expenditure	18.37	20.94	13.37	17.56
Uganda				
Total volume (USD millions)	391.28	435.46	372.32	
as % of public expenditure	20.92	19.62	10.31	16.95

Data Sources: OECD Paris Survey on Aid Effectiveness, World Development Indicators, and IMF World Economic Outlook Data.

Note: All public expenditure amounts were translated from local currency rates to USD using the midpoint exchange rate between the local currency and USD for December 31 of the year prior to the year concerned. The exception is Ghana; owing to a replacement of currency in mid-2007, the exchange rate of July 1, 2007, was used for calculating the 2005 and 2007 figures.

since the nineties, graduating to lower-middle-income status in 2011. Rwanda, on the other hand, has been dominated since the 1994 genocide by a single party and, despite strong growth rates over the 2000s, continues to face very high rates of poverty. If the findings are similar across the different cases, we can be more assured that the results are not dependent on particular contextual factors, but rather reflective of broader trends.

What about the choice to focus on low-income countries that have histori-cally received large amounts of foreign aid and budget support? Might the results change if we look to middle-income countries that are less dependent on foreign aid, or countries that have historically received less preferential treat-ment by donors? Perhaps. For a variety of historical and contextual reasons, some recipient countries have more negotiating capital than others (Whitfield 2009a). The strength of the government vis-à-vis the donor agency is likely to affect the precise outcomes of specific aid negotiations. It does not, however, change the overall argument of the book, which is that aid delivery mechanisms are sustainable only when recipient governments and donor agencies both trust that the other side will uphold its promises. Although the precise impact of commitment problems might vary across countries (and across time), the basic problem that donor agencies and recipient governments lack confidence in the other party's promises should be a constant across all countries that receive foreign aid.

I chose to focus on low-income, aid-dependent countries because it is here that aid negotiations have the biggest impact on the lives of everyday people. This does not mean, however, that I ignored how variations between different country contexts may affect how the argument plays out in individual countries. My survey, for example, includes respondents working in countries with variable levels of aid dependence. Additionally, over the course of my fieldwork in Ghana, the country shifted from being classified as a low-income country to being classi-fied as a middle-income country. At several points throughout the book, I discuss how this change in status affected Ghana's relations with donors. Finally, in the concluding chapter, I address how aid from China and other "nontraditional" donors, as well as the discovery of significant deposits of natural gas and oil in Ghana, Uganda, and Tanzania, is affecting donor–government relations across the three countries (also see Swedlund 2017b).

Below I provide a historical overview of the four countries in which I car-ried out fieldwork for this study. The goal of these summaries is to provide the reader with the necessary background for the empirical chapters that follow. In these brief synopses, I pay particular attention to two things: (1) key political and economic variables that may influence donor–government relations in the recipient country, and (2) key events and features of the aid system important to donor–government relations in the country. These summaries are not meant to be a comprehensive history but rather a summary of highlights pertinent to the subjects of this study, and are reflective of the situation, as I understand it, as of early 2016.

Ghana

Ghana's postindependence years were politically turbulent. Following independence from Britain in 1957, the country was led by the dynamic Kwame Nkrumah, an influential Pan-Africanist and founding member of the Organization for African Unity, the predecessor to the African Union. Nkrumah was officially elected president in 1960 but six years later was deposed in a coup d'état, setting off a string of political violence in Ghana. In less than twenty years, the country experienced five coups d'état, with power alternating between military and civil governments.

In 1981, Jerry John Rawlings, a flight lieutenant in the Ghanaian Air Force, ascended to power in what would be the fifth and final coup in Ghana. Upon coming to power, Rawlings suspended the constitution and banned political parties. A decade later, however, Rawlings ushered in the Fourth Republic, establishing a new constitution based on multiparty elections. Since 1992, and unlike any of the other countries in the study, Ghana has seen an alteration of power between two political parties: the National Democratic Congress (NDC) and the New Patriotic Party (NPP).[6] A contested presidential election in 2012 led to fears of increased tensions, but such fears were not realized. In April 2013, the Supreme Court of Ghana took up the issue in a nationally televised court case widely watched by the Ghanaian public. By August 2013, the dispute had played out peacefully via the appropriate official institutions.

Like many African economies, in the seventies and eighties Ghana faced a series of economic crises, with its growth rate falling, on average, 0.3 percent annually between 1970 and 1981 (Whitfield and Jones 2009). Previous devaluations of the country's currency had made the IMF deeply unpopular with the Ghanaian public. Nevertheless, in 1983, the worsening economic situation eventually pushed the Rawlings government into negotiations with the IMF and the World Bank.

The economic reforms put into place in the eighties resulted in macroeconomic stability and high growth rates (Aryeetey and Tarp 2000), leading the IMF and World Bank to promote Ghana as a success story. However, during the lead-up to the 1992 elections, the country's structural adjustment program went off track. Spending on the constitutional referendum, election promises, and the elections themselves ballooned the national budget (Whitfield and Jones 2009).

In the nineties, Ghana had a harder and harder time pushing back at the increasing number of incursions made by donors. The shift to multiparty democracy meant that the government was increasingly reliant on aid dollars to fulfill campaign promises and to stay in power. At the same time, during this period, many foreign donors began opening country offices in Accra, increasing reform pressure (Whitfield and Jones 2009). The rise in oil prices, combined with a decline in the world prices for cocoa, gold, and timber, in 1999 only further solidified Ghana's reliance on foreign aid.

In 2000, elections in Ghana brought a new government led by John Kufuor and the NPP to power. In an attempt to manage the economic crisis he had inherited, Kufuor opted to take part in the new Heavily Indebted Poor Countries (HIPC) Initiative. In order to access the substantial debt relief offered by HIPC, the government was required to draft a poverty reduction strategy paper (PRSP) for approval by the boards of the World Bank and IMF. This meant the National Development Planning Commission had to figure out a way to align the requirements of the HIPC program with a constitutional mandate regarding national development strategies that was already in place.[7] Following an interim report in 2000, the first PRSP in Ghana was officially launched in February 2003.[8] Ghana quickly qualified for full debt relief and therefore was under no obligation to produce a follow-up report. However, by this time the development plans put in place in the nineties were out of date. Therefore, instead of going back to an old plan or embarking on a new process, the Kufuor government opted to produce follow-up PRSPs in 2006 and 2010.[9]

Given the importance of foreign aid to the Ghanaian economy, the government has long tried to coordinate development assistance, establishing an International Economic Relations Department in the Ministry of Finance and Economic Planning (MoFEP) in the mid-1990s (Whitfield and Jones 2009). In the early and mid-2000s, efforts to coordinate development assistance were intensified, resulting in a sprawling aid architecture system. At the top is the Consultative Group (CG), a high-level group made up of heads of missions and representatives of the MoFEP, which sometimes includes representatives from an umbrella working group of CSOs. The CG's annual meeting was at first largely a pledging session for aid volumes; however, over time, it has become a high-level forum for reviewing the PRSP results, external resource flows, and the commitments made by both donors and the government (Akwetey 2007).

Under the CG is the Multi-donor Budget Support, or MDBS, Programme, which was established in 2003 under strong leadership from the World Bank (Tsekpo 2008). The MDBS is governed by a framework memorandum first signed in June 2003 and updated in May 2008. Donor agencies form the core members. However, the group is also composed of six observers, including the

MoFEP and the National Development Planning Commission.[10] The group is governed by a rotating troika system consisting of a current, incoming, and outgoing chair. Feeding into the MDBS core group are sixteen sector groups chaired by the relevant government agency or ministry and cochaired by an elected or appointed donor lead in that sector.

There is the sense that development aid is on its way out in Ghana. In 2007, the government officially announced the discovery of commercial quantities of oil in the Gulf of Guinea, roughly sixty-three kilometers off the Ghanaian coast.[11] Along with oil revenues has come increased foreign direct investment (FDI); FDI increased over nineteen-fold between 2000 and 2015 and is by far the highest of all the countries in this study (see table 3.5 in the annex at the end of this chapter). On November 5, 2010, the Ghana Statistical Service announced an upward revision of Ghana's total GDP by more than 60 percent, propelling the country from low-income status to lower-middle-income status literally overnight. With this revision, estimates of GDP per capita doubled from $550 to $1,100 (current USD) (Jerven and Duncan 2012). The event, which was widely covered in the international press, set shock waves throughout the development community and led African development expert Todd Moss to write (2010) on the Center of Global Development blog pages, "Boy, we really don't know anything."[12]

For donor agencies, the change in status indicated that they were no longer engaging with a lower-income country highly dependent on foreign aid. ODA as a share of GNI decreased from a high of 16.3 percent in 2004 to 3.1 percent in 2014 (see table 3.7 in annex). For some, the upward revision in Ghana's national income also means a change in the type of aid they can offer, as middle-income countries qualify for fewer grants and more concession loans. Shortly after the revision the Consultative Group took it upon itself to develop a "compact" charting the future working relationship between donor agencies and the government. The document, which was heavily pushed for by donor agencies, has the explicit goal of reducing aid dependency by 2022 (Republic of Ghana 2012). Nonetheless, foreign aid remains highly salient in Ghana. In 2014, Ghana received the equivalent of forty-two dollars per citizen in ODA from its foreign aid donors (see table 3.8 in annex). And, in 2015, Ghana was forced to turn to the IMF once again after it failed to raise the necessary capital on the international market.

Tanzania

Unlike in any of the other countries of the study, a single party—the Chama Cha Mapinduzi (CCM)—has dominated the Tanzanian political context since independence, earning the CCM the distinction of being the longest-standing political party on the African continent. Following the declaration of the republic in 1962, CCM leader Julius Kambarage Nyerere became president of Tanzania. Nyerere governed for more than thirty years, retiring in 1985.[13] Since Nyerere's time, CCM candidates have dominated national elections.

For its first thirty years, the CCM was the only legally permitted party in Tanzania. This changed in 1992 when, under Tanzania's second president, Ali Hassan Mwinyi, the constitution was amended to allow multiparty democracy. Since the first multiparty elections in 1995 (which the CCM candidate Benjamin Mkapa won), limited political competition has emerged in Tanzania. The 2015 presidential elections are widely seen as being the most competitive in the nation's history. Nonetheless, ultimately, the CCM candidate, John Magufuli, won with 58 percent of the vote against the opposition Edward Lowassa, a former CCM party member who defected from the party after failing to be selected as its candidate in the election (Commonwealth of Nations 2015).

The CCM under Nyerere was originally a proponent of African socialism, advocating for a system of collective agriculture known as *ujamaa*. In the seventies and eighties, several factors undermined Nyerere's vision, including the oil crises in the seventies, the collapse of export commodity prices (in particular coffee and sisal), drought, and the onset of a war with Uganda in the late 1970s.[14] Despite the worsening economic situation, strong domestic support for his vision and financial support from the Scandinavian countries allowed Nyerere, for a time, to hold off pressures from the IMF and the World Bank to embrace a more neoliberal economic agenda. This changed, however, in 1983. Following another downturn in the economy, the Scandinavian countries realigned themselves behind the IMF and World Bank. With aid totals dropping sharply, the government opened secret negotiations with the IMF, and Nyerere made plans to retire (Harrison, Mulley, and Hotom 2009).

Subsequent presidents, starting with Mwinyi in the mid-eighties, have embraced a more pro-market, neoliberal approach to economic development. Negotiations regarding necessary reforms have been contentious, however. In the early nineties, there was a standoff between donors and the government of Tanzania over macroeconomic management and the perception by donors that corruption had increased (Daima and ODI 2005).[15] While the World Bank and the IMF were content with the implementation of a set of IMF-approved economic reforms, bilateral donors dug in their heels, demanding action on corruption (Harrison, Mulley, and Hotom 2009). To help end the standoff, the Nordic countries, led by Denmark, assembled a set of independent advisers—the so-called Independent Monitoring Group—led by Professor Gerry Helleiner of the University of Toronto.[16] The resulting document, commonly referred to as the Helleiner Report, devised a plan for improving donor–government relations and is the basis for aid relations in Tanzania to this day (Wohlgemuth 2006).

By the late 1990s, Tanzania had amassed significant debt, making the potential debt relief on offer via the new HIPC program highly appealing. Enrolling in HIPC meant that Tanzania was required to draft a PRSP. The task of drafting the first PRSP was contracted out to Professor Sam Wangwe, a member of a tightly networked group of pro-reformers who emerged from the University of Dar es Salaam in the late 1990s and were popular with donors. Throughout the process, donors maintained strong oversight, controversially insisting that the government add a section abolishing school fees for primary education and even redrafting the final document in Washington after concerns about quality were raised (Harrison, Mulley, and Hotom 2009). The first Tanzanian PRSP was approved in 2000 and was the first PRSP to go before the boards of the World Bank and IMF. Subsequent PRSPs, commonly referred to as the MKUKUTA I and II in reference to their Swahili acronym, were approved in 2005 and 2010.[17]

Since 2000s, the Tanzanian economy has grown consistently at over 6 percent (see table 3.4 in annex). Along with growth has come a rise in FDI, which increased more than fourfold between 2000 and 2015 (see table 3.5 in annex). In recent years, FDI has been spurred by natural gas discoveries. Natural gas was first discovered in Tanzania in the 1970s on a small island, Songo Songo, off the mainland. But recent finds in the Ruvu basin close to the capital city of Dar es Salaam have pushed estimates of natural gas to over fifty trillion cubic feet in total (Reuters 2016). Owing to uncertainties over the evolution of prices and production, it is difficult to translate estimated reserves (which are expected to continue to rise) into clear numbers. However, finds in the Ruvu basin alone, which currently are estimated at 2.7 trillion cubic feet, were valued at over $8 billion in 2016 (Burgess 2016). Given the potential for earnings, a number of international investors have lined up to cash in. In 2012, British Gas alone announced plans to invest over $15 billion over the coming decade (Neureiter 2012).

Tanzania has long been a "development darling," receiving a great deal of attention and financing from international donors (Edwards 2014b; Harrison, Mulley, and Hotom 2009). Throughout the 2000s, Tanzania received much more aid than Ghana, Uganda, or Rwanda. In 2013 alone, Tanzania received close to $3.5 billion in ODA, more than twice the amount of any other country in the study (see table 3.6 in annex). As it is also the most populous of these countries, this is perhaps to be expected. However, at over $51 per citizen in 2014, ODA per capita is also higher than in either Ghana or Uganda (see table 3.8 in annex).

Given the importance of aid in the Tanzanian economy, it is perhaps not surprising that the government has invested quite a lot in ensuring that the type of aid it receives meets certain standards. The government, for example, took the time to translate the 2005 Paris Declaration into Swahili, widely distributing it among government departments. It also took the time to develop a Joint Assistance Strategy for Tanzania (JAST), which was approved in 2006 by the Tanzanian cabinet (United Republic of Tanzania 2006a). The JAST is a follow-up to a previous assistance strategy published in 2002,[18] and provides a medium-term framework for enhancing aid effectiveness and operationalizing the Paris Declaration at the country level. Nineteen donor agencies (plus the government) signed a memorandum of understanding committing to uphold the principles of the JAST (United Republic of Tanzania 2006b).

The donor community in Tanzania currently organizes itself under the name Development Partners Group (DPG). First established in 2004, the DPG has a secretariat within the United Nations Development Programme (UNDP) and is cochaired by the UN resident coordinator / UNDP representative and a rotating bilateral donor (by convention the budget support chair). The DPG is composed of seventeen bilateral and five multilateral agencies (counting the UN as one agency), and its main group, composed of HoCs, meets every month. In addition several subgroups focus on specific sectors or themes related to the MKUKUTA.

On top of the DPG structure, which is made up exclusively of donor agencies, there is a set of joint donor–government structures. At the top is the Joint Coordination Group (JCG), which draws its membership from permanent secretaries and HoCs. Several sector working groups support the JCG, and there are also four so-called cluster groups, organized according to the major themes of the MKUKUTA, and a special working group for public expenditure. This vast network of coordination structures indicates the immense amount of time that has gone into aid coordination in Tanzania.

The JAST (as well as its predecessor) indicates a strong preference by the government of Tanzania for budget support, which began in Tanzania in its current incarnation in 2001. Budget support in Tanzania is organized through a GBS Secretariat hosted and staffed by DFID. As in Ghana, the group is cochaired by a troika system—or three rotating donors who serve as the current, outgoing, and incoming chairs. In 2013, three multilateral donors (the EC, World Bank, and AfDB) and nine bilateral donors (Norway, the UK, Japan, Sweden, Denmark, Ireland, Canada, Germany, and Finland) were providing budget support (either sector or general) to Tanzania.[19] However, in late 2014, budget support totals took a nosedive in Tanzania following a scandal in the energy sector that implicated several top-level officials (see chapter 6). While some donors have indicated a willingness to restart budget support, there is currently a great deal of uncertainty about the future of the aid delivery mechanism in the country.

Uganda

Uganda has been marred by political strife and conflict over the past sixty years.[20] From independence, the country was led by Milton Obote, first as prime minister and then as president after he unilaterally abolished traditional kingdoms and proclaimed the country a republic in 1966. In 1971, Idi Amin deposed Obote in a coup, and proceeded to govern the country with an iron fist for the next eight years. During his reign, Amin forcibly removed the South Asian population from Uganda and used mass killings to maintain his grip on power, resulting in the death of an estimated three hundred thousand Ugandans (Kasozi, Musisi, and Sejjengo 1994).

Amin was ousted from power in 1979 during the Uganda-Tanzania War, leading to the return of Obote, who ruled until being deposed by General Tito Okello in 1985. However, General Okello was himself overthrown only six months later by the National Resistance Army (NRA), led by Yoweri Museveni, in the Ugandan Bush War (Museveni 1997; Kasozi, Musisi, and Sejjengo 1994; Sathyamurthy 1986). Since his rise to power over thirty years ago, Museveni has faced challenges from rebel groups, including the infamous Lord's Resistance Army, led by Joseph Kony. His hold on power is now, however, considered relatively stable.

Originally lauded by the media and the international community more broadly as one of Africa's new generation of leaders, Museveni has persisted as his international popularity declined over the years. Under the so-called Movement system, political parties were prohibited in Uganda for the first nineteen years of Museveni's rule. In 2005, the moratorium on political parties was lifted. At the same time, the constitution was amended to allow Museveni to run for an additional term. In February 2016, Museveni won yet another term in a controversial election in which opposition groups faced significant intimidation.

After the devastating years of Idi Amin, Uganda's economy started to rebound in the late 1980s and early nineties. After assuming power for the second time in 1980, Obote was forced to turn to the World Bank and the IMF, negotiating an economic reform package in 1981 in which the country devalued the Ugandan shilling in exchange for substantial donor support. The program, however, collapsed in mid-1984. The subsequent NRA government first attempted to implement a series of economic reforms without support from the international financial institutions; however, when these reforms failed, the government was forced once again to turn to the IMF and the World Bank. Between 1987 and 1996, Uganda was seen as one of the few adjustment success stories in sub-Saharan Africa (along with Ghana). The economy grew, and inflation decreased. However, at the same time, external debt skyrocketed, forcing the government to implement a series of debt reduction programs in the mid-nineties (Baffoe 2000).

Uganda's experience with the HIPC program is particularly interesting, as it was Uganda's Poverty Eradication Action Plan (the PEAP), originally drafted in 1996, that reportedly inspired the World Bank and the IMF to begin to require HIPC countries to draft a PRSP (Ernst 2011). A widely told joke at the Ugandan Ministry of Finance goes, "The World Bank saw what we were doing and wrote down a description of the PEAP process. They sent that back to DC where people changed the initials from PEAP to PSRP. Two years later other Bank staff visited us to teach us about the Bank's amazing new process—the PRSP."[21] It was indeed a revised version of the PEAP, approved by the World Bank and the IMF in 2000, that served as the country's official PRSP (Republic of Uganda 2000), with a follow-up being approved in 2004 (Republic of Uganda 2005). Given its leading role in the creation of the PSRP process, Uganda was the first country to qualify for debt relief under both the first HIPC and the Enhanced HIPC Initiative in 1998 and 2000—and did not have to go through the standard six-year review process (Kuteesa and Nabbumba 2004). In 2008, the National Development Plan (which is not an official PRSP) replaced the PEAP, placing a greater focus on growth (Republic of Uganda 2010).

In more recent years, Uganda's GDP grew at an average of 6.5 percent between 2000 and 2015 (see table 3.4 in annex). Still, at $1,670 in 2015, GNI per capita is much less than what it is in Ghana and Tanzania (see table 3.3 in annex). Although FDI has increased almost sevenfold since 2000, net inflows of FDI are still much lower in Uganda than in either Ghana or Tanzania, reaching just over $1 billion in 2015 (see table 3.5 in annex). Nevertheless, net inflows of FDI are predicted to increase in the coming years because of the discovery of oil in the Albertine Graben on Uganda's western border with the Democratic Republic of Congo. While many have long speculated about the presence of crude oil in Uganda, the potential for commercial oil production was not officially confirmed until 2006.[22] As of 2012, the oil fields are estimated to contain deposits of around 2.5 billion barrels, with some suggesting that such amounts could rise to 6 billion barrels once the Albertine Graben basin and others are further explored (ActionAid Uganda 2012).

In 2014, Uganda received an estimated $1.6 billion in net ODA, second only to Tanzania in terms of total aid amount received (see table 3.6 in annex). Between fiscal year 2007/8 and 2011/12, the Ugandan Ministry of Finance estimates, contributions to the total national budget by development partners averaged 25.8 percent, with more than 70 percent of the development budget being provided by donors (Republic of Uganda 2013). More recently, however, foreign aid as a percentage of the national economy has been declining. In 2014, ODA as a share of GNI was only 6.2 percent, down from a high of 16.4 percent in 2006 (see table 3.7 in annex).

Efforts to coordinate and harmonize development assistance in Uganda began as early as the PEAP, which included a section titled "Partnership Principles." In this section, the government of Uganda outlined how it wanted to receive development assistance and asked donors to collaborate within the PEAP framework. Some claim that this is the first time any recipient country had required donors to work in a framework (Ernst 2011). In 2005, efforts to coordinate aid assistance were taken a step further with the establishment of the Uganda Joint Assistance Strategy,[23] which lays out a vision for how donor–government relations should proceed in the country.

Despite these early steps, the aid architecture is less formalized in Uganda than it is in Ghana, Tanzania, or Rwanda. Beginning in the late 1990s, the government and the World Bank began hosting an annual, high-level meeting between donors and the government. However, the last of these meetings was in 2003. There is a donor-only group similar to the DPG in Tanzania. The group, which came into existence in 2003, goes by the name the Local Development Partners Group and meets approximately every month. The World Bank chairs the group and also supports a small secretariat.[24]

In contrast to the other countries, Uganda did not have a distinct budget support group until the late 2000s. Prior to this, budget support in Uganda was organized ad hoc by the individual donors, or via the World Bank's budget support mechanism. However, in 2009, development partners came together to create a separate multi-donor trust fund (also managed by the World Bank), titled the Joint Budget Support Framework (JBSF). The goal of the JBSF was to harmonize funding from the World Bank with the budget support instruments of the EU and the UK. The JBSF began with twelve partners in 2010 but declined to nine partners by 2012, and in the fall of 2012 budget support (both sector and general) was suspended to Uganda following a major corruption scandal in the Office of the Prime Minister (see chapter 6).

Rwanda

Rwanda's recent political and economic history is dominated by the legacy of the civil war and subsequent genocide in the early nineties. In 1990, the Rwandan Patriotic Front (RPF), a Tutsi rebel group, invaded the country from the north, setting off a civil war that would see a series of escalations and de-escalations over the subsequent four years. In April 1994, a fragile peace was disrupted when the plane of the then Hutu president, Juvénal Habyarimana, was shot down, sparking a genocide in which between eight hundred thousand to one million Tutsis and moderate Hutus were killed. The mass slaughter was brought to a halt one hundred days later when the RPF took the Rwandan capital Kigali in July 1994.[25] Since that time, RPF general Paul Kagame has led Rwanda, first from behind the scenes and then as president following the country's first postwar elections in 2000.[26] In late 2015, a highly controversial and widely condemned constitutional amendment extended presidential term limits, giving Kagame the right to run for reelection until 2034 (Uwiringiyimana 2015).

Supporters of Kagame and the RPF, which include high-powered allies like Bill Clinton and Tony Blair (Sundaram 2014), emphasize the massive socioeconomic transformation that the country has undergone since the mid-nineties. Since 2001, the economy has grown at an average rate of close to 8 percent (see table 3.4 in annex). Between 2006 and 2013/14, poverty rates in Rwanda dropped by more than 17 percent (NISR 2014), and the country has made a dramatic rise on the International Finance Corporation's Ease of Doing Business Index. In 2009, the World Bank branded Rwanda as the world's leading economic reformer (World Bank 2009). Although significantly lower than in Ghana or Tanzania, GNI per capita in Rwanda has more than doubled since 2000 and is now comparable to average incomes in Uganda (see table 3.3 in annex).

Critics of Kagame, such as Human Rights Watch and Amnesty International, emphasize that such economic advancements come at the expense of civil and political liberties, and a tendency to exclude dissenting voices from the debate (Straus and Waldorf 2011; Swedlund 2013b). Such criticisms have only grown in strength and number since the recent change in presidential term limits. Scholars and practitioners alike are also critical of Rwandan involvement in neighboring Democratic Republic of the Congo, accusing Kagame and the RPF of unauthorized military activities, fostering instability and conflict, and illegally extracting large amounts of natural resources, such as coltan (columbite-tantalite) and gold (e.g., OHCHR 2010).

Like Ghana, Uganda, and Tanzania, Rwanda opted to participate in the HIPC initiative in the early 2000s in order to access debt relief. Although Rwanda clearly "owned" the PRSP process, external advisers largely wrote early drafts, and citizen participation was minimal (Hayman 2009a). Following an interim report in 2000 and a Participatory Poverty Assessment, the country's first PRSP was finalized in June 2002, with follow-ups, the Economic Development and Poverty Reduction Strategy (EDPRS) I and II, being published in 2007 and 2013 respectively.[27] Thematically, the PRSP process in Rwanda builds on the government's Vision 2020, which outlines Rwanda's objective to become a middle-income country by 2020 by transitioning from subsistence agriculture to a knowledge-based society.

More so than in other countries in this study, Rwanda's recent growth is closely linked to foreign assistance. Prior to the genocide, donor engagement in Rwanda was limited, given the country's small size and minor role in global politics. Following the genocide, however, countries such as the United Kingdom, the Netherlands, and the United States began to take a bigger interest in Rwanda, replacing France and Belgium as the top aid givers (Hayman 2009a). Rwanda has few sources of domestic revenue. The country is not known to possess any significant deposits of crude oil or natural gas, and at the end of 2009 there were only an estimated 34,193 taxpayers in Rwanda (Rwanda Civil Society Platform, and Network of International NGOs 2010). As a result, despite strong rhetoric by Kagame and a "legacy of bitterness" brought on by donors' inaction during the genocide period (Hayman 2009a), Rwanda is highly dependent on foreign aid. At 13.3 percent in 2014, ODA as percentage of GNI is by far the highest of all the countries (see table 3.7

in annex), as is ODA per capita. While Ghana, Uganda, and Tanzania all received between $40 and $50 per citizen in foreign aid in 2014, Rwanda received more that $90 in aid for each member of the population (see table 3.8 in annex).

Given its high rates of aid dependence, it is somewhat counterintuitive that Rwanda has some of the strongest institutions for aid bargaining (Whitfield 2009a). This is likely due, at least in part, to the fact that Rwanda's ambitious plans for socio-economic transformation sit well with international donors, who also nurture a collective guilt over inaction during the genocide period (Reyntjens 2004). Over the course of the mid-2000s, Rwanda implemented several aid management tools, which are widely considered to be best practices by development practitioners. A key example is the Rwandan Aid Policy, which was endorsed by the cabinet in July 2006 and outlines how the government would like to receive development aid (Republic of Rwanda 2006). The aid policy provides guidance on the roles and responsibilities of both the government and donors in aid management and was followed up in 2011 with an Aid Policy Manual of Procedure (Republic of Rwanda 2011a). Another widely lauded initiative is Rwanda's Division of Labour, which requires donor agencies to limit their activities to three sectors (Republic of Rwanda 2010a).

Like the other countries, Rwanda has an expansive aid architecture. All donors are eligible to participate in the Development Partners Coordination Group (DPCG), which organizes both an annual meeting and an annual retreat. In addition, thirteen sector working groups, organized around the themes of the EDPRS, feed into the DPCG. What is unique about Rwanda is that all these coordination bodies are cochaired by a government representative and a donor representative. The DPCG is cochaired by the permanent secretary of the Ministry of Finance and Economic Planning and the resident representative of UNDP, while sector working groups are cochaired by the relevant line ministry and a donor working heavily in that sector.

As I will discuss in more detail in chapter 6, budget support was suspended in 2012 following allegations of Rwandan government support to the Congolese militia group M23. Before it was suspended, budget support in Rwanda was organized via the Budget Support Harmonization Group (BSHG), which used to meet twice a year and was also cochaired (Swedlund 2013a, 2014).[28] The Rwandan government's response to the suspension was to suspend the budget support group. While donors are very frustrated with this decision, the government remains absolute on its position. Without budget support, there will be no BSHG.

Data Annex

Data source for all tables: World Development Indicators (2015). Data is current as of December 2016.

TABLE 3.2 GDP at market prices (constant 2010 USD billions), 2000–2015

	2000	2001	2002	2003	2004	2005	2006	2007	2008	2009	2010	2011	2012	2013	2014	2015
Ghana	18.4	19.1	19.9	21.0	22.2	23.5	25.0	26.1	28.4	29.8	32.2	36.7	40.1	43.0	44.8	46.5
Rwanda	2.7	2.9	3.3	3.3	3.6	3.8	4.2	4.5	5.0	5.3	5.7	6.1	6.7	7.0	7.5	8.0
Tanzania	16.5	17.5	18.8	20.0	21.6	23.4	24.5	26.5	28.0	29.5	31.4	33.9	35.6	38.2	40.9	43.7
Uganda	9.9	10.4	11.3	12.1	12.9	13.7	15.2	16.5	17.9	19.2	20.2	22.1	23.1	23.9	25.0	26.3

TABLE 3.3 GNI per capita, based on purchasing power parity (constant 2011 international dollars), 2000–2015

	2000	2001	2002	2003	2004	2005	2006	2007	2008	2009	2010	2011	2012	2013	2014	2015
Ghana	ND	ND	ND	ND	ND	ND	2638	2683	2859	2924	3036	3324	3472	3725	3724	3839
Rwanda	792	826	916	910	957	1008	1076	1133	1221	1262	1318	1385	1463	1488	1556	1617
Tanzania	1471	1491	1590	1640	1717	1798	1863	1936	1984	2028	2089	2190	2215	2314	2395	2467
Uganda	1045	1050	1116	1150	1180	1211	1303	1373	1446	1501	1527	1622	1632	1629	1641	1670

TABLE 3.4 Annual percent growth of GDP, 2000–2015

	2000	2001	2002	2003	2004	2005	2006	2007	2008	2009	2010	2011	2012	2013	2014	2015	AVERAGE
Ghana	3.7	4.0	4.5	5.2	5.6	5.9	6.4	4.3	9.1	4.8	7.9	14.0	9.3	7.3	4.0	3.9	6.2
Rwanda	8.3	8.7	13.5	1.5	6.9	6.9	9.2	7.6	11.2	6.3	7.3	7.9	8.8	4.7	7.0	6.9	7.7
Tanzania	4.9	6.0	7.2	6.9	7.8	7.4	6.7	7.1	5.6	5.4	6.4	7.9	5.1	7.3	7.0	7.0	6.6
Uganda	3.1	5.2	8.7	6.5	6.8	6.3	10.8	8.4	8.7	7.3	5.2	9.7	4.4	3.3	4.8	5.0	6.5

TABLE 3.5 Foreign direct investment, net inflows (BoP, current USD millions), 2000–2015

	2000	2001	2002	2003	2004	2005	2006	2007	2008	2009	2010	2011	2012	2013	2014	2015
Ghana	165.9	89.3	58.9	136.8	139.3	145.0	636.0	1383.2	2714.9	2372.5	2527.4	3247.6	3294.5	3227.0	3363.4	3192.3
Rwanda	8.3	4.6	2.6	4.7	7.7	10.5	30.6	82.3	103.3	118.7	42.3	106.2	159.8	257.6	291.7	323.2
Tanzania	463.4	388.8	395.6	364.3	226.7	935.5	403.0	581.5	1383.2	952.6	1813.2	1229.4	1799.6	2087.3	2044.6	1960.6
Uganda	160.7	151.5	184.6	202.2	295.4	379.8	644.3	792.3	728.9	841.6	543.9	894.3	1205.4	1096.0	1146.6	1057.3

TABLE 3.6 Net ODA received (constant 2013 USD millions), 2000–2014

	2000	2001	2002	2003	2004	2005	2006	2007	2008	2009	2010	2011	2012	2013	2014
Ghana	866.8	1015.8	1037.5	1300.4	1676.3	1358.8	1421.7	1228.1	1315.9	1657.5	1761.9	1780.7	1801.6	1329.4	1119.0
Rwanda	518.0	498.3	561.2	454.4	595.4	681.5	686.9	762.8	945.1	976.4	1082.5	1250.7	888.5	1085.9	1024.0
Tanzania	1608.4	1976.8	2031.2	2324.9	2172.2	1789.2	2189.5	3048.6	2376.7	3121.1	3109.2	2414.4	2841.8	3430.6	2629.3
Uganda	1355.1	1340.8	1124.6	1336.8	1186.9	1424.1	1817.4	1848.9	1669.9	1887.1	1770.7	1562.5	1655.7	1700.5	1622.0

TABLE 3.7 Net ODA as a share of GNI, 2000–2014

	2000	2001	2002	2003	2004	2005	2006	2007	2008	2009	2010	2011	2012	2013	2014	AVERAGE
Ghana	12.4	12.3	11.4	13.2	16.3	10.9	6.1	4.7	4.6	6.1	5.3	4.7	4.5	2.9	3.1	7.9
Rwanda	18.7	18.5	21.9	18.5	23.8	22.6	19.6	19.2	19.6	17.7	18.2	19.9	12.3	14.7	13.3	18.6
Tanzania	10.6	12.7	11.9	15.0	14.1	9.0	10.1	13.3	8.6	10.4	9.5	7.3	7.3	7.8	5.6	10.2
Uganda	14.0	14.5	12.0	16.1	15.7	13.6	16.4	14.4	11.7	10.2	8.5	7.9	7.2	7.0	6.2	11.7

TABLE 3.8 Net ODA received per capita (current USD), 2000–2014

	2000	2001	2002	2003	2004	2005	2006	2007	2008	2009	2010	2011	2012	2013	2014
Ghana	31.8	33.2	34.7	48.4	68.1	53.8	56.6	51.7	56.5	66.7	69.5	72.2	70.4	50.8	42.1
Rwanda	40.1	36.6	42.5	38.6	55.5	64.1	65.3	76.2	95.7	93.1	100.2	119.6	81.2	98.0	91.2
Tanzania	31.3	36.5	35.4	46.8	46.7	38.4	46.8	68.0	54.4	66.3	64.8	51.8	58.0	68.3	51.1
Uganda	35.9	33.5	28.6	38.1	44.8	42.5	54.7	57.9	52.9	55.7	50.9	45.9	46.4	46.5	43.2

MAY I HAVE THIS DANCE?

Donor–Government Relations
in Aid-Dependent Countries

At the recipient country level, what do donor–government relations actually look like? How do donor and government officials interact with one another on a daily basis? Although the literature on foreign aid is vast, we actually have little empirical analysis on what donor agencies and recipient governments bargain and negotiate over on a daily basis, particularly across multiple countries and years. In this chapter, my goal is to provide the reader with a window into donor–government relations in each of the four country case studies. To those working in the field of international development, these observations should feel recognizable and familiar. The chapter demonstrates that, despite many twists and turns, there is an underlying logic to donor–government relations that cuts across particular country contexts and affects how aid is actually delivered in recipient countries.

Donor–government relations look astonishingly alike across the individual country settings. In part this is because the cast of characters is very similar. On more than one occasion, I was surprised to meet the same donor official in multiple countries. Donor officials move from country to country every two to four years, and at times I happened to catch a donor representative in the last days of his posting in one country and in the first days of his posting in another. The main reason for similarities across the cases, however, is that the goals of the two parties are largely the same no matter the context. In developing countries, for both diplomatic and developmental reasons, donor agencies seek to

FIGURE 4.1 It takes two to tango

exert influence over domestic policy issues. Recipient governments, on the other hand, seek to maximize foreign aid revenues but minimize the interference by donors in their internal affairs. While the specifics of each party's demands vary in important ways (both across countries and across time), the basic interests guiding the interaction are the same.

In this dance between donor agencies and recipient governments, there is a lead: the donor. Still, both parties are integral to the success of the dance (see figure 4.1). Despite a great many changes and frustrations on both sides, donor agencies and recipient governments remain locked in a complicated and continued state of negotiation, in which each side is trying to pursue its interests relative to its negotiating capital. In such situations, it is mutually advantageous for the recipient government and the donor agency to collaborate. However, there are clear frustrations on both sides.

The Dance: Policy Dialogue

At the recipient-country level, donor agencies and recipient governments are continually engaged in what is now commonly referred to as "policy dialogue." Although there is little consensus on the exact meaning of the term, respondents

> ## Box 4.1 What is the policy dialogue?
>
> For us, policy dialogue here, or anywhere elsewhere we operate, is very much about *sitting down with government* with the other stakeholders as well and being able to *discuss* the policy in any particular sector or more broadly and where things are going, how they're getting there.
>
> —Bilateral donor official, September 26, 2013, Uganda
>
> It's a *conversation* between the government and donors about policy, about what government's planning to do and how they're planning to do it. Ideally, [*chuckle*] policy dialogue is a two-way conversation, with people listening on both sides.
>
> —Bilateral donor official, June 5, 2012, Tanzania
>
> High-level *dialogue on the policy, the direction that government is taking*, the policies that are going to be implemented or being implemented in order to move into that direction.
>
> —Government official, April 25, 2013, Ghana
>
> Italic emphases added by the author.

across all four countries emphasize that a policy dialogue is a discussion or a conversation between donor agencies and the recipient government (see box 4.1). As one respondent explained, the policy dialogue is a way to monitor progress, to raise key issues of concern, and more generally to work with the government to see what possible measures could be taken to help solve issues of concern,[1] like low rates of electricity provision in the rural parts of the country, or high tariffs on imported goods. Areas of concern are generally identified by donor agencies, but solving them requires buy-in from the recipient government. As a result, donor agencies seek to engage in policy dialogue with the recipient government.

What are donor agencies and recipient governments hoping to achieve with the policy dialogue? And what is their incentive to engage in the policy dialogue? Development practitioners frequently refer to three distinct dialogues with the recipient government: a political dialogue, a policy dialogue, and a technical dialogue. In practice, differences between these three dialogues are often arbitrary. However, conceptually, the objective of each is distinct. The political dialogue focuses on diplomatic and geopolitical issues, while the technical dialogue is focused on more practical, disbursement-related topics and project implementation. Occupying the fuzzy middle is the policy dialogue. The policy dialogue focuses on big-picture development issues, such as the country's plan for combating poverty or improving the delivery of health services.

The policy dialogue provides a space for donor agencies to discuss development policies and practices with the recipient government. The policy dialogue is not just about working with the recipient government to deliver goods and services to beneficiaries. Instead, it is about having an opportunity to contribute to the discussion about *how* such goods and services are delivered to beneficiaries. The policy dialogue is about having a say over larger, cross-cutting issues, such as governance, that affect the success of not only donor programs and the efficiency of aid money but also the effectiveness of the recipient government's broader development agenda.[2] In regard to education, for example, this might involve questions of how much to invest in primary, secondary, or tertiary education. Or it might involve discussions about the content of curriculum, and how such curriculum should be developed.[3] Within the policy dialogue, donors use the promise of aid funds to gain leverage over domestic policy issues they care about. That is, they use the promise of aid dollars to lobby for reduced disparities in access to a basic education by asking the government, as they did in Ghana, to invest more resources in historically deprived regions.

Key priorities vary among individual donor agencies. For example, in many African countries, the majority of USAID money goes to health (and in particular to combating HIV/AIDS).[4] Therefore, health policy is likely to be a priority for the agency. But when interests overlap, donor agencies often work together on common themes in order to increase the pressure on recipient governments to implement desired reforms.

The Dance Floor: The Aid Architecture

How and through what means do recipient governments and donor agencies engage in policy dialogue? The short answer is, continually, in many different ways and at many different levels. As I briefly alluded to in chapter 3, over time complicated aid architectures have developed in each of the four countries of the study. These structures have emerged out of the need to have coordinated interactions between not only donors and the recipient but also between different donor agencies. However, the underlying objective of the aid architecture system is to facilitate interactions—both formal and informal—between donor agencies and the recipient government.

Broadly speaking, we can think of the aid architecture as being composed of three levels, which mirror the three different types of dialogue. Again, the divisions between the political, policy, and technical levels can be somewhat artificial. Political and policy issues are discussed at all levels, as are to some degree technical issues. However, making conceptual distinctions among these three levels helps to illustrate the complicated web of structures that have, over time, been established across all four countries in order to help manage foreign aid and donor–government relations.

First, the diplomatic or political level is where the president or prime minister (or both) and cabinet members engage in dialogue with ambassadors and senior donor staff on big-picture topics. Such discussions formally take place in the context of an annual to semiannual meeting between donors and the recipient government. These meetings—held in high-end hotel conference centers—are large events, with two hundred or more participants. Typically, they are more pomp and circumstance than substance.[5] However, they can be important for building relationships. Donor agencies often formally announce their annual aid pledges at these meetings, flying in high-level officials from abroad to make the announcement and garnering the event attention in the national newspapers. In return for these aid pledges, recipient governments promise to make big-ticket reforms, such as improving public financial management or increasing political representation.

Second, there is the operational level, which focuses on policy. Discussions at this level might include the composition of the national budget or the annual development plan.[6] In theory, the crux of the policy dialogue takes place here. In each of the four countries of the study there is a development partners group, which meets regularly (typically once a month). In contrast to the high-level meetings described above, these meetings involve senior donor staff (instead of ambassadors). They take place in boardrooms over tea and coffee and generally involve twenty-five to thirty participants (the number varies based on the number of active donors in the given recipient country). These meetings are more frequent and more intimate.

Just how permanent a fixture government officials are in such meetings differs from country to country. In Rwanda, the Development Partners Coordination Group (DPCG) is cochaired by the UN representative and the minister for finance and economic planning. Thus, meetings always involve both donor and government stakeholders. However, in other countries, there are "donor only" coordination groups. For example, in Tanzania, the Development Partners Group (DPG) is cochaired by the UN representative, along with a bilateral donor agency (usually the chair of the budget support group). Government officials often attend the first half of the group's monthly meeting to discuss special issues. However, their presence is by invitation, and about halfway through the proceedings the government representatives depart so that donor officials can discuss common responses to issues "without the interference of the government."[7] This, of course, changes the tenor of the meetings, putting the government in the position of an invited guest rather than a partner in the planning and implementation of the group.

Third, there is the technical or sector level. Groups at this level are charged with discussing the more nuanced details of development cooperation. Each of the countries of the study has its own complicated web of sector groups, which—typically in conjunction with the relevant line ministry—are charged with developing sector-level policy and coordinating discussions about topics and issues relevant to that specific sector. For example, in a given recipient country, the health sector working group might debate the merits of a push or pull method of delivery for prescription drugs, while the agriculture working group may discuss what type of irrigation systems are needed for different regions of the country. Discussions at this level generally draw heavily on sector experts and often include NGOs and foundations working in the sector. For example, in Uganda the health sector is heavily reliant on faith-based groups, which in some areas of the country are the only providers of health services. Thus, the Catholic, Protestant, and Muslim Medical Bureaus are an important part of the dialogue at the technical level.[8] Ideally, technical groups feed into the higher-level groups, but how successful they are in doing so varies widely.

In each country of the study there is also a budget support working group, which is charged with coordinating issues related to this specific aid modality. Because of the unique nature of budget support, this group (intentionally) straddles the boundaries between the political, policy, and technical. On both the donor and government sides, so-called technical staff are charged with implementing budget support. However, budget support meetings generally draw high-level staff from both the government (permanent secretary or the minister of finance and sometimes even the president) and the donors (ambassadors and heads of cooperation). As will be discussed at length in chapter 6, this is a major part of the appeal for donor agencies.

The Stage Managers: External Finance Units

Over the years, recipient governments have taken note of the need to engage with their foreign aid donors in a more regular and systematic way. In all four countries of the study, a specialized unit or department exists within the ministry of finance that is charged with the sole task of managing "external finance"—that is, foreign aid. These units are organized in slightly different ways across the four countries, but all have the same task—to manage foreign donors and the aid they bring with them.[9] Because of the importance of development aid to the budgets of each of the recipient countries, these units are important players within the ministry of finance in all four countries.

In Tanzania, for example, the External Finance Department consists of a staff of more than forty. The unit was first created in 1973 (Wohlgemuth 2006). It is headed by a commissioner for external finance and consists of four units: Bilateral Cooperation, Multilateral Cooperation, Regional Cooperation, and Aid Coordination. In the bilateral and multilateral units are several "desk officers" who act as liaisons with particular donor agencies, giving every donor agency a contact point at the ministry. Depending on the size of the donor agency, a desk officer may be responsible for anywhere from one to three donor agencies. In the other units, the staff is responsible for specific tasks, such as serving as liaison with the general budget support group or managing a database for donor disbursements.[10]

Across all four countries of the study, donors have at various times and in various capacities provided financial support to these units. For example, Rwanda's External Finance Unit was at first funded by a basket fund operated by the United Nations Development Programme (UNDP) and was originally housed in the UN offices and staffed by UNDP personnel. The unit is now integrated within the Ministry of Finance. However, it still receives financial and technical support from UNDP. Donor agencies have been willing to provide financial support to external finance units because they see it as advantageous to have strong, capable counterparts in government.

While the heavy reliance of each of the countries on foreign aid certainly suggests the need for external finance units, the existence of these units is somewhat remarkable, given what is often limited capacity within ministries in low-income countries. The fact that recipient governments would be willing to assign anywhere from five to forty people in contexts where talented personnel are hard to come by indicates the importance they place on their relationships with donors—and on the money it brings in.

The Tune: National Development Plans

What are the substantive issues around which the policy dialogue is organized at the recipient-country level? In theory, in all four countries of the study, the policy dialogue is organized around the country's national development plan. Such plans, which generally cover around five years, are designed to provide a road map for medium-term development in the recipient country. In each of the countries of the study, the national development plan determines the number and themes of the working groups, which (in theory) feed into the national policy dialogue.

In each of the countries, the national development plan and the body that is responsible for drafting the plan have a relatively specific history. For example, in Ghana, the national planning process is determined by the constitution, which was drafted in 1992. The constitution calls for the establishment of a National Development Planning Commission governed by a board. The board is responsible to the president, who appoints most of the members.[11] In Tanzania, the planning department has a longer history, given the legacy of socialism. Over the years, there has been tension between the Planning Commission in the president's office, which has historically been in charge of planning, and the planning department in the Ministry of Finance, which has more recently (particularly during the HIPC years—see below) taken up planning tasks.

Despite these important contextual differences, beginning in the late 1990s, national development plans across the four countries began to take a more uniform shape, as all four governments opted to enroll in the HIPC initiative. Opting into the program, which offered significant debt relief (see table 4.1), meant that the government was required to draft a poverty reduction strategy paper (PRSP) for approval by the boards of the IMF and the World Bank. While PRSPs were supposed to be "owned" by recipient governments, the need to meet the specific requirements of the program and to get the boards' approval meant that donor involvement in the drafting process was very heavy.[12]

After fully qualifying for debt relief under the HIPC program, all four countries have attempted to (re)establish some sort of authority over national development plans, often to the frustration of donors. A source of contention across all four countries is that while PRSPs focused largely on poverty and social sectors, new development plans—developed much more independently by recipient governments—focused much more explicitly on economic growth and the productive sectors. This shift often worries donor officials, who are concerned that recipient governments might neglect social services and poverty reduction, which are key priorities for donors.

A good example here is Tanzania. In 2010, the country passed its third (and final) PRSP, the MKUKUTA II, which was supposed to run until fiscal year 2014/15 (United Republic of Tanzania 2010). However, in 2012, Tanzania returned to its socialist roots and drafted a Five-Year Development Plan (United Republic

TABLE 4.1   HIPC milestones and debt relief obtained

Ghana
Decision point: February 2002   **Completion point**: July 2004
Debt relief obtained (as of December 2012): $7.4 billion

Rwanda
Decision point: December 2000   **Completion point**: April 2005
Debt relief obtained (as of December 2012): $1.3 billion

Tanzania
Decision point: April 2000   **Completion point**: November 2001
Debt relief obtained (as of December 2012): $6.8 billion

Uganda
Decision point: February 2000   **Completion point**: May 2000
Debt relief obtained (as of December 2012): $5.5 billion

Note: Debt relief obtained is reported in nominal terms and represents assistance delivered under the HIPC initiative and the MDRI 2.

Source: HIPC documents and World Bank and IMF staff estimates (reported in World Bank and IMF 2013, 25).

of Tanzania 2012). This meant that for two years there were *two* medium-term development plans—one produced by the Ministry of Finance, and one produced by the Planning Commission in the president's office. The drafting of the five-year plan was rather baffling and frustrating to donors, who expressed that they did not know which plan they should align with, and that the sudden creation (at least to them) of the new plan was a violation of their agreement with the government of Tanzania. Donor officials were frustrated because they interpreted the new plan as a violation of agreed-on commitments.

To make matters even more complicated, in 2013 Tanzania began instituting a program titled "Big Results Now." The so-called BRN program is not a national development plan but rather an approach imported from Malaysia by senior Tanzanian government officials that identifies a limited set of priority areas.[13] These priority areas are then workshopped in intensive retreats involving key stakeholders that last for several days. The overarching goal of the BRN program is to generate innovation and a deep commitment to the focus areas. While donor officials have participated in the BRN workshops (at the behest of government officials), it is clear that the Tanzanian government drove the adaption of the program, whose staff report directly to the president (see, for example, Janus and Keijzer 2015).

Over time, several donor agencies agreed to support the BRN initiative. However, support from donors was not immediate, and several donor officials expressed to me their concern about the approach, emphasizing that key sectors for donors (such as health) are not included. According to some, support from donor agencies has in part come about because of a feeling among donor officials that they have little choice but to support the initiative.[14] As a donor official explained,

> Officially we're still after MKUKUTA, but in practice, we are all focusing on the BRN. . . . Many sectors have been left out. We still don't know whether or not they will be included, and we don't know how to deal with the cross-cutting issues. . . . I think we were all rather skeptical in the beginning. . . . But there was no other way than supporting at least verbally and confirming that we would be willing to look at our own portfolios and see how we could . . . support government in the implementation of the BRN because . . . they're really pushing for it.[15]

In other words, despite their hesitations, donors felt compelled to support the initiative, because they wanted to be part of the debate.

Tanzania's experience with HIPC, the Five-Year Development Plan, and the Big Results Now initiative highlights a key feature of the policy dialogue between donor agencies and recipient governments. Donor agencies use aid money (in this case the promise of substantial debt relief) to allow them to insert themselves into the debate and put key issues on the table. However, recipient governments often thwart such efforts, sometimes rather unexpectedly. When this occurs, donor agencies have little choice but to figure out a way to remain engaged in the policy dialogue.

Why Do Donors and Recipients Partake in the Dance?

The complicated network of dialogues, working groups, and informal interactions described in the previous section requires an immense amount of work by both donor and government officials. It can also be a major source of frustration. Across the four countries of the study, respondents frequently complained that the aid architecture was "heavy" and that the transaction costs of the policy dialogue for both donor agencies and the recipient government are high. One respondent in Tanzania, for example, reported that in the previous year he and his colleagues counted *190 meetings* related to the policy dialogue that they were required to attend.[16] Why would recipient governments and donor agencies be willing to invest so much in building such complicated systems? Why don't donor agencies simply demand that the government adopt the policies that they favor?

At the recipient-country level, donor agencies and recipient governments are dependent on one another. The power dynamics between donor agencies and recipient governments are far from equal; as a senior Tanzanian government official put it, "It is not a relationship between two equal partners. The conversation on the giving side is backed up by money. The conversation on the receiving side is motivated by the needs."[17] However, despite donors being the dominant party in the bargaining relationship, each party is essential to the other's success. Accordingly, even though both are deeply frustrated with their dance partner, they keep showing up on the dance floor.

The Partner: Recipient Governments

The incentives for the recipient government to engage in a policy dialogue with donor agencies are relatively straightforward. In countries where domestic revenues are low, foreign aid is a vital part of the national budget. Particularly in certain sectors, such as health or education, recipient governments rely on the influx of foreign aid dollars to provide basic goods and services to their population.

This does not mean, however, that these governments are entirely passive recipients. In fact, government officials often engage in an intense back-and-forth with donor officials. Discussing Tanzania in particular, one respondent explained that recipient countries are "very experienced in getting aid. They know their donors, they know how to work with them, and also persuade them."[18] As another put it, there are ways of "resisting policy infringement from the hand that gives."[19]

Take as an example negotiations over performance assessment frameworks, or PAFs. PAFs emerged in the context of general budget support in order to allow for a more structured assessment of the government's progress on a set of commonly agreed-on indicators. PAFs are organized slightly differently in different countries (and have changed in their design over the years; see chapter 6). However, the basic principle is that donor and government officials agree on a set of targets and reforms, which the government commits to undertaking in exchange for the release of budget support. After a certain amount of time, typically a year, the indicators are assessed and aid is disbursed accordingly.

PAFs are a very clear example of donor agencies using aid funds to buy influence over domestic policies they care about. Donors promise aid money, if the recipient government completes the agreed-on reforms. Ghana's 2010 PAF, for example, was composed of thirty-nine targets, each tied to a specific policy objective.[20] Of these thirty-nine targets, twelve were identified as triggers; that is, the disbursement of aid that year was tied to their fulfillment. These twelve triggers asked the government to complete a very specific task like establishing and implementing an electricity automatic tariff adjustment mechanism in exchange for promised aid funds (Republic of Ghana 2010a).

The PAF asks recipient governments to commit to certain actions in exchange for aid money, but aid donors do not exclusively dictate its content. In each of the countries, the development of a PAF is a long and sometimes contentious process. A good example is the negotiations that took place regarding the 2012 PAF in Ghana, when donors and the Ghanaian government had a vocal and public disagreement about whether the county's PAF should include actions requiring parliamentary approval (see box 4.2). In particular, there was contention over whether the PAF should require the passage of an oil revenue management bill. While donors argued that including the bill in the PAF was necessary to ensure the government was committed to sound fiscal management, the government countered that passing a bill is not within the control of the Ministry of Finance and Economic Planning (MFEP), the agency that ultimately signs and commits to the PAF on behalf of the government. Therefore, the government argued that it would be unreasonable to ask the MFEP to commit to actions that it does not have a final say over.[21]

From the perspective of staff members working at the MFEP, it was absurd that donors wanted them to promise that specific legislation would be passed. Legislation, after all, is parliament's prerogative. At most, Ministry of Finance

Box 4.2   Negotiation of the 2012 Ghanaian Performance Assessment Framework

We have big trouble every year, and especially in 2012, to agree on the PAF on time. . . . The problem is that the quality of the indicators proposed is not always what we expect. It's either not ambitious enough, not strategic enough, not focused enough.
—Multilateral donor official, April 10, 2013, Ghana

Over about a month, two months, we do a back and forth, back and forth, until we get what we think is a doable list that government is comfortable with and that also satisfies the needs of our various headquarters. . . . The triggers are the more difficult aspect of it, because *government aims to select the easiest*, to be assured of a disbursement. Which is rational. While [*development partners*] *aim to put government through its paces.*
—Bilateral donor official, April 11, 2013, Ghana

In some cases *development partners are very unreasonable*, very unreasonable in the sort of things they want to push. . . . I say, "I cannot do this. I will not be able to, because you will come back to assess me. And in your assessment you are not flexible." So why should I take on something that I, glaringly and obviously, know that I cannot achieve?
—Government official, April 24, 2013, Ghana

Italic emphases added by the author.

staff can promise to submit legislation to the cabinet for approval and perhaps guarantee that parliament will at least vote on the bill. As one government representative emphasized with considerable gusto, an executive agency cannot push a bill through the U.S. Congress. What donors are asking for is undemocratic.[22] On the other hand, donor officials tended to see the unwillingness of government officials to commit to such triggers as evidence that their counterparts were not fully committed to meaningful reform. In other words, they saw it as evidence of a lack of a strong commitment.

The Lead: Donor Agencies

If negotiations with their counterparts in government can be so frustrating, why would donor officials engage in them to begin with? Foreign aid is after all a "gift" given to developing countries (Furia 2015). The donor officials I interviewed spent countless hours trying to track down their government counterparts, collecting business cards, mobile numbers, and tidbits of personal information all in hopes of increasing their access to key government officials. They bragged about having good connections with the government or lamented the difficulty of working with their counterparts in government. Why is cultivating strong relationships with recipient-government officials so important to donor officials?

Quite pragmatically, the policy dialogue is simply part of a donor official's job description. Noting first that perhaps she should not be so sympathetic to donor officials, a government official in Ghana explained that when you are the head of cooperation at a development agency, you are constantly being asked by your superiors, "What are you bringing back to headquarters? How often do you see the minister of finance . . . ? What do you discuss?" Donor officials need to be able to report that they had a productive and meaningful conversation with the recipient government. Ideally, they should also be able to report that these meetings took place at the highest level. It is much more powerful for donor officials to be able to say that "I met with the president and we discussed X, Y, Z" than to say, "I just had a meeting with the director for multilaterals who says, blah blah blah."[23] Accomplishing this requires a good working relationship with the recipient government.

But why is it that people back in the donor agency's headquarters care so much about a strong, working relationship with the recipient government at the recipient-country level? As I will discuss more in chapter 5, a strong working relationship is seen as necessary for gauging a government's commitment to particular initiatives. As a donor official working in Rwanda noted, acting as liaison with the government is necessary, because they "need to know what the government is thinking."[24] As a respondent in Ghana further explained, because aid must be monitored, policy dialogue is regarded by her agency as necessary for disbursement; it is part of her due diligence.[25] For donor agencies, a productive dialogue with the recipient government increases the likelihood that their development initiatives will be successful. This is why donor agencies have offices in recipient countries to begin with. If interacting with recipients was not considered important, donor agencies could simply disburse the money from the donor's headquarters in Washington, Brussels, or London.

In one way or another, donor officials almost always have to work with government counterparts to disburse aid. Of the approximately $2.5 billion received by the government of Tanzania over the course of the 2012–2013 fiscal year, approximately $1.96 billion was given to the government. This means that nongovernmental funds accounted for only one-fifth of the country's ODA that year. Even if we look only at project aid, which was roughly $1.5 billion, over $1 billion of it went to the government (United Republic of Tanzania 2014, 8). In the words of a Ugandan donor official, "You do it with government [in] one way or another."[26] If you are a donor official working for a donor agency that has promised to provide foreign aid to a recipient country, the recipient government is a stakeholder and thus must be dealt with—whether you like it or not.

Still not convinced that the government is really a key stakeholder for donor officials? After all, it could be that donor officials simply pretend to consider the government as an important stakeholder for the sake of appearances. Data from my survey of donor officials suggest that this commitment is not just rhetoric. Under the condition of anonymity, I asked respondents to rank particular stakeholders in order of importance for determining their agency's country-level strategy or its key strategic priorities in the recipient country.

Given the dominant assumption that aid is driven by the strategic considerations of donor countries, I expected donor officials to overwhelmingly report that their home ministry or agency's headquarters was far and away the most important stakeholder. However, instead survey respondents indicated that the most important stakeholder was the recipient government (see table 4.2). On average, respondents ranked the recipient government above all other stakeholders, including their home ministry or agency's headquarters and their agency's mission or country office.

Not all donor agencies give equal weight to recipient governments. Respondents working for multilateral agencies, as well as agencies that provide budget support, are slightly more likely to rank the government as a more important stakeholder, for example. Nonetheless, across the sample, which includes donor officials working for twenty-three different donor agencies, respondents report that the recipient

TABLE 4.2 Recipient governments are the most important stakeholder in the formation of donors' country-level strategies (N = 111)

RANK	STAKEHOLDER	MEAN RANK (SD)
1	Government of [country]	2.4 (.16)
2	Your home ministry and/or agency's headquarters	3.1 (.23)
3	Your agency's mission or country office	3.4 (.21)
4	Multilateral donors (including the European Commission) in [country]	5.2 (.18)
5	Bilateral donors in [country]	5.1 (.15)
6	Civil society in [country]	5.6 (.21)
7	Domestic public opinion in your home country or in your agency's member countries	6.4 (.20)
8	International civil society	6.7 (.19)
9	Domestic business interests in your home country or in your agency's member countries	7.1 (.05)

Source: Author's original data. Respondents were asked, "How are your agency's country-level sector priorities formed? Please rank the following stakeholders in order of how much influence they have over your agency's country-level strategy in [Country]."

government is a key stakeholder in the formation of their agency's country-level strategies. Eighty-three percent of respondents ranked the recipient government as one of the top three stakeholders in the formation of their country-level strategies.[27]

Perhaps also surprising to those who assume that donor policy is decided entirely back in donor countries, respondents ranked other donors—multilateral and bilateral—and civil society in the recipient country as more influential in the development of their country-level strategy than public opinion and business interests in their home country. Collectively, the results indicate that country-level strategies are powerfully shaped by the recipient-country context.

Limited Donor Influence

If donor agencies hold most of the negotiating power, why don't donor officials simply dictate to the recipient government the conditions of their aid? Despite their presumed weight in recipient countries, throughout my interviews donor officials frequently reported that influence over important domestic policies is actually rather difficult for them to exercise (see box 4.3). Donor officials

---

Box 4.3   Limits of donor influence in recipient countries

It's even limited for us what we can influence in terms of policy dialogue. We can only maybe plant the seeds, but if anybody in the government doesn't want to do something, they're not going to do it.

    —Multilateral donor official, October 2, 2013, Uganda

We can say we have policy influence, but I think we often overplay that, and *it's not been to the extent that perhaps we would have wished for.* And also that, perhaps, it's not been grounded in the kind of the reality of the context in which we find ourselves.

    —Bilateral donor official, September 26, 2013, Uganda

We try to do it together, but we go and we seek. We try to go to the highest level. It's *difficult to get meetings* with the politicians.

    —Bilateral donor official, May 23, 2012, Tanzania

We're not the government. *We cannot steer the country.* We cannot tell another sovereign country what to do.

    —Bilateral donor official, September 26, 2013, Uganda

         Italic emphases added by the author.

repeatedly referred to the finessing required by their position, emphasizing that donor–government relations is not a donor-dictated game. While it is aid money that brings everyone out to play, pacing and skill are required to keep the game going satisfactorily.

The reasons for donors' perceived lack of influence are likely manifold. But at a basic level, donor influence is limited because donors' wishes and demands are only one part of the forces at play in a recipient country. As a donor official in Tanzania explained, "We can go in and play hardball with them. . . . But he's got seventeen other pressures on him which moderate whatever he promised to do with us."[28] Even if a government is committed to a reform, competing domestic pressures can always undermine commitments. Recipient governments are not unitary actors; even if one part of the government is committed to making a reform, not all relevant agencies and departments may be on board, thus hindering implementation.

For a reform to be successful, there almost always has to be both technical and political support.[29] Politicians are prone to making grand promises, for which there may or may not actually be money to implement.[30] To demonstrate his commitment to primary education (and possibly to drum up a few votes for the party), the minister of education, for example, may commit to building a hundred new classrooms in rural areas. However, if the Ministry of Education does not actually have the budget to pay for these classrooms, the minister's commitment means relatively little. On the other hand, even if the money is there, if the minister is not committed to building the classrooms, they may never get built. For these reasons, donor agencies are constantly engaging in a "two-level game,"[31] talking to both the technical and political levels.

In practice, it is often difficult for donor officials to know what is politically possible in a recipient country (see box 4.4).[32] As a Tanzanian respondent noted, donor officials "are really good at being experts in pounding the table and telling the government what they should do. But we're not that expert in understanding why it is they aren't doing what we think they should."[33] As another respondent cynically put it, donor officials "never seem to know who is in charge."[34] Recipient governments rarely if ever explicitly communicate their boundaries.[35] As a result, donor officials are frequently left to make an educated guess as to when and where donor officials are actually committed to a desired reform. In making this decision, donor agencies have an information disadvantage and often find it hard to motivate governments to take corrective action. As Hyden writes, "They are faced with a true moral hazard; i.e., they are ready to give the government the benefit of the doubt, hoping that it will take corrective action on its own" (2008, 272).

Box 4.4   Difficulty understanding the local political context

Politics are very, sometimes very informal, very centralized, and it's very unclear why decisions are made, despite all the pretense of formality of reporting and everything. So, I mean, reading the newspapers can be very confusing in this country; *you never know [chuckle] what's happening.*

— Multilateral donor official, September 23, 2013, Uganda

I would say [it is] *almost impossible for the average development partner to really understand how the Tanzanian system works.* They tend to have two different spheres of actions. There is the internal one where no *mzungu* [foreigner] is allowed.

— Multilateral donor official, May 29, 2011, Tanzania

We're not politically attuned in general, and there's lots and lots of nuances that we have no idea about in the Tanzanian context—people who are related to each other or went to school together or are from the same ethnic group or were connected twenty-five years ago in the founding of the political party. There's multiple, multiple layers.

— Bilateral donor official, July 4, 2012, Tanzania

You have to understand when an argument is not an argument, but a pretext or something. This is some sensitivity you have to develop. . . . But at some point *you just have to understand there are other issues they don't want to tell you.*

— Bilateral donor official, September 26, 2013, Uganda

Italic emphases added by the author.

A Negotiated Compromise

In this chapter I demonstrated the complex bargaining processes that go on every day in Accra, Kampala, Kigali, and Dar es Salaam. In these spaces of negotiation, donor and government officials do not meet as equals.[36] However, the two parties are mutually dependent. Donor agencies and recipient governments rely on one another in countless ways. Thus, despite the considerable frustrations on both sides, the two parties remain locked in a complicated dance.

At the recipient-country level, donor agencies and recipient governments are both trying to maximize their preferences. This provides a strong incentive to continue to engage with one another. While government officials rely on the aid money provided by donor agencies, donor officials remain reliant on the recipient government to continue and indeed to succeed with their operations in the recipient country. As one donor official in Uganda put it, "You need to make it work."[37] This need to make it work means that donor agencies and recipient governments are constantly engaging in a back-and-forth where the end result is not a perfect reflection of *either* side's preferences but rather a negotiated compromise.

5

A HALFHEARTED SHUFFLE
Commitment Problems in Aid Policy Bargaining

At the recipient-country level, donor agencies and recipient governments are engaged in a complicated dance in which the end result is an aid policy compromise. For both, a great deal rides on these agreements. But how likely is it that each side will keep its part of the bargain? Let's imagine, for example, that a donor agency has promised $10 million to support the building of a toll road from a recipient country's national airport to the capital city. The toll road is badly needed to ease congestion and decrease the costs of exports and imports. In return for the aid money, the recipient government has promised to fairly compensate those who will be relocated because of the new road, as well as to successfully complete the project and eventually pay back the loan. How likely is it that each side will be able to fulfill its commitments?

In the case of the fictional toll road, the donor agency relies on the recipient government to manage the relocation process. This could pose a number of both political and practical challenges for the recipient government, as it requires the relocation of citizens who presumably would rather stay put. In addition, the donor agency is relying on the recipient government to manage the procurement and tendering process; but what if the recipient government lacks either the capacity or the political will to complete or maintain the road?

To complicate matters even more, what if, after a year, the donor agency decides there has not been enough progress on the project, or that it would rather spend the money on another infrastructure project, like the building of a dam for hydroelectric power? Agreements between donor agencies and recipient governments are typically not legally binding, and even if they are, a large project, such as the building of a road, will require many different smaller agreements (with different contractors) over a multiyear period. In practice, there is often very little to keep the donor agency from backing out of a commitment (either fully or partially), except for goodwill.

In this chapter, I provide evidence of commitment problems on both the donor and the recipient sides, demonstrating that the difficulty each has upholding its promises over the long term is a constant source of frustration for both donor agencies and recipient governments.

Credibility Problems and Why They Matter
Recipient Commitment Problems

Readers are not likely to find it surprising that recipient governments do not always do what they are asked to do. According to a respondent in Uganda, this drives donors "crazy": "[The government agrees] to do things, and then they turn them down, they can't do them at all. I mean they sit with each other and say, . . . 'We will pass this law.' It is never passed. 'We will strengthen this department.' It is never strengthened. So many things. I think that drives [donors] mad."[1] When asked what frustrates donors most about the way the government operates, a donor official in Ghana similarly explained that sometimes it feels like government officials are less committed to reform than they as outsiders are. Here she noted that every year some of the triggers for budget support do not get implemented until a month before they will be assessed. This is immensely frustrating for her, because these triggers and priorities are supposed to be "owned" by the government. From her perspective, completion at the final hour suggests that the government is implementing the reform only because of development financing (which of course might be the case). She believes that the government should be inherently committed to the reform and should not need to be further incentivized by donors.[2]

For donor officials, a big part of their job is figuring out what recipient governments are actually committed to. As one donor official put it, "You need to pick and choose and try to find where the commitment of the government lies."[3] However, even when a donor agency believes that the government is actually committed to a particular reform, efforts to foster reform often fail. This was the case, for example, in Tanzania when donors—especially the World Bank—put a great deal of emphasis on business reforms in the mid-2000s. According to a donor official, who even after several years remained frustrated about the events that had transpired, the government was saying to donors, "We are interested. We want to improve business environment. . . . We want this." However, at least from the perspective of this particular donor official, the Tanzanian leadership simply did not move on the agreed reforms. This was incredibly irritating to him, because he genuinely believed the government was committed to reform in this area.[4]

Most donor officials recognize that many of the areas where they want to see reform are challenging for the government. They also understand (at least in theory) that change will not happen overnight. They do, however, expect realistic, credible commitments. Using the example of subsidies, which is often a hot topic with donor officials, one respondent in Ghana explained that what they really want from the recipient government is credible figures. If the president is up front about the political difficulties of removing subsidies and provides a reasonable time frame and targeted reduction, donors might be disappointed that things won't change as quickly as they would like, but the government's commitment to reform is taken seriously. However, when the real figures are suppressed and the challenges for implementation are not transparently presented to donor officials, "nobody takes you seriously."[5]

CORRUPTION

For many donor officials, one of the key ways in which trust in a recipient government's commitments is undermined is corruption. Donor officials working at the recipient-country level regularly have conflicted feelings about corruption. On one hand, many recognize that corruption is often endemic in the places where they are working (and sometimes also in their home countries). They therefore see it as all but inevitable. On the other hand, corruption undermines the success of their aid programs and can create major problems for their agency. Therefore, corruption is seen by donor officials as a violation of the government's commitment to development and can at times be taken rather personally.

This is what happened in 2012 when the Ugandan auditor general discovered that over $11 million of donor money in an account set up in the Office of the Prime Minister to support a peace and reconciliation program in Northern Uganda had been siphoned off. Donor response to this corruption case was significant, not to mention swift; over $300 million in aid (most of it budget support) was suspended. Response to the corruption case was in part so strong because donor officials took the discovery personally. Not only did the scandal involve a program designed for the poorest of the poor; it also involved an institution (the Office of the Prime Minister) and a government official (Amama Mbabazi) that donor officials had deemed trustworthy.

For donor agencies, corruption, in contrast to other more abstract political transgressions like political repression, has a direct effect on their agency's development portfolio (Swedlund 2017a). Corruption, particularly when it explicitly involves donor money, makes it very difficult for the donor agency to justify development expenditures back home. In this way, it can directly jeopardize the donor agency's presence in the recipient country. Responding to the scandal, the former EU ambassador to Uganda, Roberto Ridolfi, said, "How can I now go back to Europe and ask for aid for Uganda ... ? The recent corruption scandals are a breach of trust between the country and its development partners" (quoted in Jeanne and Njoroge 2012). Corruption puts aid budgets at risk, which puts donor officials' jobs at risk. Accordingly, donor officials take it quite seriously.

How a recipient country deals with corruption is not, however, always a source of friction between donor agencies and recipient governments. In Rwanda, the government's tough stance on corruption has won it many supporters in the development community. Despite increasing accusations of political repression (e.g., Straus and Waldorf 2011), many donor agencies remain committed to providing aid to Rwanda. This can, at least in part, be traced back to a sense among donor officials that the government has a strong commitment to reform, which includes a zero-tolerance policy on corruption. Such a sentiment is clearly reflected in the vocabulary used to describe the regime, which includes frequent references to the "political will" of the government. The belief that the Rwandan government takes corruption seriously gives the government credibility in the eyes of many donor officials.

SPEED OF REFORM

Most donor officials recognize that reform takes time and is not always easy. However, professional incentives to produce (and demonstrate) results regularly clash with realities on the ground, leading to frustration. Delays in reform may come about for a variety of reasons (which will be addressed more explicitly toward the end of the chapter). But whatever the reason for delay, a slow pace of reform is not in line with the organizational incentives of donor agencies, which need to be able to demonstrate results to funders—that is, donor countries and their taxpayers.

Aid agencies reward employees according to their ability to distribute funds and to successfully complete projects in a timely and efficient manner. Donor officials are usually posted to a country for between two to four years. At the end of their posting, they need to have something to show for their time in the recipient country. At the same time, each year the donor agency is given a budget, which it needs to spend. As a donor official in Tanzania explained, "All these donors here, they want to show some projects are happening, right? They want project documents to be approved soon, they want the appraisal committees to be happening on a timely fashion, and then they want the money flowing and they want the reports that it was spent."[6]

Organizational pressure to show results can lead to what one respondent called a "tin ear" in figuring out what will likely succeed and what will likely fail, because it means that donor officials may not read between the lines or simply ignore signs that a recipient is not fully committed to an initiative.[7] Recipient governments rarely explicitly say no to donor officials, as they do not want to do anything to disrupt their relationship with the donor agency. This does not mean, however, that recipient governments are always completely on board with a reform, and it certainly does not mean that they will be able to successfully implement it. In order to access financing, recipient governments might agree to a reform that they have little intention of actually carrying out. Recipient governments might also agree to a reform that they believe is necessary, only to discover that they lack the political clout to be able to implement it. Often, despite warning signs that commitment is lacking or that change is likely to be difficult, donor representatives forge ahead with a reform program, because it is in their professional interest to be able to claim that reform is ongoing.

For donor officials, the perception that reforms are moving slowly often translates into a more general impression that the government is not actually committed to reform (which of course might be the case). According to a donor official in Tanzania, for example, "The greatest frustration is that too little of our counterparts in government have a thorough commitment to attaining results as quickly as possible."[8] During my conversations with donor officials across all four countries of the study, I regularly got the impression that respondents believed that they, as foreigners engaged in development cooperation, are more committed to socioeconomic reform than their counterparts in government are.[9] At times these claims are laced with a heavy dose of paternalism (which of course is infuriating to recipient counterparts).[10]

Donor officials were often quick to point out exceptions to this generalization. In each country, donor representatives regularly mentioned a small group of domestic "reformers" (with the same names coming up over and over).[11] However, overall, and not without reason, donor representatives are frequently highly pessimistic about the credibility of their counterparts' commitments. Recipient governments frequently have a variety of competing pressures, and donor agencies are not necessarily their first priority—particularly if the recipient believes that aid dollars are not actually contingent on fulfillment of the agreement.

Donor Commitment Problems

While it may not be surprising that it is often difficult to get recipient countries to commit to reform, readers may find it less obvious that donor agencies also find it difficult to make credible commitments. After all, these are relatively advanced bureaucracies representing highly developed countries; problems such as corruption and capacity should be less of an issue. There is, however, an abundance of evidence suggesting that donor agencies have a very difficult time upholding their commitments to recipient governments, and that this poses a significant challenge for recipient governments.

MOVING THE GOALPOSTS

A key frustration for recipient governments is that donor agencies are incessantly "moving the goalposts" (see box 5.1). Recipient governments regularly feel that they do not know where they stand with donors, or feel that they meet the conditions of the aid, only to be presented with another set of conditions. According to Pomerantz (2004), the perception of changing conditions and evaluation criteria is incredibly damaging to reliability, and hence to trust between donor agencies and recipient governments.[12]

Recipient-government officials rely on aid dollars to plan their budgets and implement development projects within their borders. A shift in donor priorities and agendas means that the recipient government has to modify its spending plans based on the whims of donors, reallocating its own resources where possible to cover gaps in financing left by shifting donor priorities or by cutting planned programming altogether. For example, owing in part to the emphasis on achieving the Millennium Development Goals (MDGs) by 2015, over the past decade many donors have heavily invested in the social sectors—for example, health

---

Box 5.1   Donors move the goalposts

Donors can be *pernickety, fickle, unpredictable, can change the goalposts*, can quite often come in and insist on their parallel systems, transaction costs being quite high, [so] that there is probably a dearth of mutual accountability

—Bilateral donor official, September 26, 2013, Uganda

Lack of patience, *lack of strategic patience* [by donors . . .] I'm not talking of . . . electoral cycles, so a new government every four years, but I'm talking a little bit more about another cycle which this is the cycle of, at the global level of development thinking and which influences the focus and the priorities of development partners and *which always comes quicker than a government can adapt to*, because the government needs to adapt.

—Bilateral donor official, March 23, 2012, Tanzania

And the problem is that . . . policy frameworks are shifting every five to eight to ten years . . . For a certain approach, you really need a longer time to build and to improve the effectiveness of a tool.

—Bilateral donor official, May 29, 2012, Tanzania

Italic emphases added by the author.

and education. However, recently the flavor of the month has shifted toward trade, infrastructure, and energy. In the Netherlands, for example, the minister for international development is now the minister for foreign trade and development cooperation. Consequently, if recipient governments want to maintain current services, they will need to allocate more of their own funds toward the social sectors. As one respondent explained, changes in the normative priorities of donors make it difficult for the recipient country to "steer a stable course."[13]

Moving the goalposts is not just about changing normative commitments to a particular development path. It is also about adding or changing the conditions for disbursement after a negotiated compromise has already been reached. For example, when asked about what frustrates the government about the way donor agencies work, a donor official in Uganda replied "changing the goalposts," explaining that this is hard on recipient governments because "you can't tell them that . . . if you do your homework, you will get X amount of money." Instead, the message is, "If you do your homework, you might get it, but we're not sure yet."[14] Similarly, a donor official in Tanzania noted, "I think sometimes the government feels that even though they do everything they're supposed to do, we don't."[15]

This was certainly what the Ghanaian government felt in regard to the procurement act that was passed in 2003. According to Ministry of Finance representatives, who are still frustrated many years later about how events played out, it was donor agencies that pushed for the law. The draft was shared widely with donors prior to its passage. Yet, after it was passed, according to a respondent, the law suddenly was "not good enough for donor agencies to use themselves."[16] As a result, the Ministry of Finance must continue to use the procurement regulations of individual donors. This is extremely time-consuming for a government department that is already struggling with capacity problems. Thus, not surprisingly, it has resulted in a great deal of frustration from government officials, who consider it a large (and avoidable) burden. From the perspective of government officials, the procurement law is simply another example of donor agencies breaking their commitments by moving the goalposts after they were mutually agreed upon: "You [donors] practically drafted this document. *You gave us the input, and now you're telling me the act is not okay?* What is wrong? Why didn't you tell me the truth before? Okay, so that gets my nerves. . . . This document came from you guys. You sat down when it was a bill. We shared it with you. We gave you the document, we disseminated it. We had meetings. We presented it to you. And now we have a problem here."[17]

AID PREDICTABILITY

As the former minister of finance in Rwanda, Protais Musoni, explained in a public speech to development partners, "The important issue is not only the amount of aid allocated to a particular project or programme but the predictability of the financing given." According to Musoni, the worst-case scenario is that "a programme commences, the offices are set up, advocacy and training is underway, but the finances for actual implementation are delayed." As a result, "the beneficiaries' expectations and hopes have been raised and then there is no resulting action. This undermines the population's faith in both government and donors, and the process of poverty reduction" (Musoni 2003).[18] When aid constitutes a significant proportion of the national budget, which is does in all four countries of the study, even a small degree of aid unpredictability can pose a big problem for recipient governments.

Recipient governments often explicitly emphasize the importance of aid predictability in official documents. The Ugandan National Development Plan, for example, articulates that "being able to predict aid disbursements with respect to volume and timing is essential for the management of public finances and for planning and implementation of Government programmes" (Republic of Uganda 2010, 70). Similarly, the Ghana Aid Policy rationalizes the existence of the policy by noting that "since the early years of independence, Ghana has been a beneficiary of external assistance. Though external aid plays a significant role in the Ghanaian economy, it has been fairly unpredictable and/or not delivered effectively and efficiently" (Republic of Ghana 2010b, 14).

According to a small but growing scholarship from economists (Arellano et al. 2009; Bulíř and Hamann 2008; Hudson 2015; Celasun and Walliser 2006, 2008), recipient governments are right to be concerned about aid volatility and predictability. Kharas (2008), for example, estimates that the deadweight loss associated with aid volatility—or the degree to which aid fluctuates over time—ranges from 15 to 20 percent of a country's programmable aid. According to his estimations, this means that aid volatility causes a $16 billion loss in aid globally, *each year*. Given global poverty rates, this is a huge amount of aid dollars that are—according to his calculations—largely being wasted.

Compounding problems of aid volatility are problems of aid predictability, or the difference between expected disbursements and actual disbursements.[19] Looking specifically at the four countries of the study, according to estimates by Celasun and Walliser (2008), the absolute value of commitment minus disbursements was, on average, equal to or greater than 2 percent of each country's GDP between 1995 and 2005 (see table 5.1). This represents a huge sum of money for cash-strapped governments. Across the four countries of the study, 2 percent of GDP translates into between $411 million and $704 million (constant 2010 prices) *per country* in undistributed ODA for 2005 alone. Sometimes these gaps are made up for in subsequent years. But even when commitments are smoothed to represent a three-year moving average, aid unpredictability remains very

TABLE 5.1   Deviations of gross ODA commitments from disbursement, averages, 1990–2005 (in percentage of GDP)

		ANNUAL COMMITMENTS		SMOOTHED COMMITMENTS	
	NET AID TRANSFER	COMMITMENTS MINUS DISBURSEMENTS	ABSOLUTE VALUE OF COMMITMENTS MINUS DISBURSEMENTS	SMOOTHED COMMITMENTS MINUS DISBURSEMENTS	ABSOLUTE VALUE OF SMOOTHED COMMITMENTS MINUS DISBURSEMENTS
Ghana	9.3	–0.5	2.0	–0.9	2.4
Rwanda	26.0	–0.2	3.1	–2.1	6.8
Tanzania	12.8	0.4	3.2	–0.2	1.7
Uganda	14.4	0.3	2.1	–0.5	2.3

Source: Celasun and Walliser 2008, 558. Smoothed commitments equal the three-year moving average of commitments (the average of the current and past two years) minus disbursements.

high in all four countries of the study, with Rwanda—the most aid-dependent state—being the most extreme example.

Aid volatility and aid (un)predictability are problematic, because they can result in a number of adverse effects, such as lower rates of investment, increased vulnerability to shocks, less efficient government budgeting, and ultimately lower levels of growth (Lensink and White 2001; Celasun and Walliser 2008). In Ghana, for example, Tuffour explains that throughout the 1990s, both commitments and disbursements were volatile, with disbursements as a proportion of total commitments ranging from between 29 percent and 81 percent and averaging about 64 percent. Because of shortfalls in the budget due to unpredictable aid, the Ghanaian government was forced to increase domestic borrowing and draw on its reserves, making "dependence on development aid more and more precarious" (Tuffour 2005, 3). If a recipient government doesn't receive aid funds as promised, it may be required to take out more loans (often at a substantial cost), or simply not pay its bills. Starting or scaling up new development projects would also be unwise, if funding is not guaranteed.

It is not just aid shortages, however, that can be detrimental to the recipient country's economy; aid windfalls can encourage spending on government consumption rather than investment (Celasun and Walliser 2008). If a government is not able to accurately plan for incoming sources of revenue, whether they are higher or lower than predicted, it is unlikely to use the resources efficiently when they do arrive. As a donor official in Ghana put it, if a recipient country gets $50 million on the last day of the year, what is the country supposed to do with it?[20]

In practice, what habitually happens is that makeshift and poorly designed initiatives are quickly thrown together so that the donor agency is able to disburse the funds and the recipient government does not lose out on aid dollars.

For example, during a lunch appointment with a member of staff in the External Finance Unit in Tanzania, my lunch date spent a good part of the meal hastily trying to put together a million-dollar package of support to the national statistics office. He had been informed of the availability of the funds only the day before, and the money had to be disbursed by the close of the fiscal year—which was in less than four hours. This situation is not exceptional. Ostrom et al. (2002) report that within the Swedish Development Agency, up to 40 percent of the year's disbursement takes place in the final two months of the budget cycle.

You might be wondering whether aid predictability is a consistent problem across all donor agencies, or if there are particularly egregious offenders. At the recipient-country level, individual donor agencies do develop different reputations regarding predictability. I told you in chapter 2 that the Ugandan government discounts all aid promises by around 30 percent. Reportedly, the Ministry of Finance used to calculate different discount factors for individual donor agencies based on how successful an agency was at delivering promised aid dollars.[21] This suggests that the *degree* to which donor agencies have trouble following through with their commitments varies across agencies (and likely also over time).

That being said, data from my survey suggests that aid predictability, particularly over the medium term (one to three years out), is a persistent challenge in the aid relationship—both across countries and donor agencies. When asked about their agency's actual disbursements in comparison to agreed amounts last year, 35 percent of respondents reported that their agency's actual disbursements were either lower or higher than previously agreed-on amounts (see table 5.2). In other words, for more than a third of the agencies included in the sample, the amount of foreign aid disbursed in the previous year was different from the amount of aid their agency had promised to the recipient country.

Even more troubling is the predictability of their agency's future aid amounts, as reported by respondents.[22] The most common response was that amounts

TABLE 5.2 Predictability of aid disbursements last year

LAST YEAR, MY AGENCY'S ACTUAL DISBURSEMENTS . . .	% (FREQ.)
were lower than agreed amounts in [country].	24 (24)
were roughly equal to agreed amounts in [country].	65 (65)
were higher than agreed amounts in [country].	11 (11)

Source: Author's original data. Respondents were presented with the question "Which of the following best describes your agency?" and then asked to select one of the following options: "Last year, my agency's actual disbursements were lower than agreed amounts in [Country]"; "Last year, my agency's actual disbursements were roughly equal to agreed amounts in [Country]"; or "Last year, my agency's actual disbursements were higher than agreed amounts in [Country]." (N = 101)

were predictable one year in advance (40 percent), with an additional 18 percent and 13 percent reporting they can predict for two years and three years, respectively (Swedlund 2015). This means that approximately a third of respondents reported that their agency can accurately predict by only *six months or less* the amount of aid they will disburse. This is hardly enough time for recipient governments to accurately plan for future budget cycles.[23]

When asked about how difficult it is for their agency to provide promised aid on time and to give accurate predictions one year and three years in advance, the results are even more striking (see figure 5.1). Over two-thirds of respondents (67 percent) reported that it is difficult for their agency to disburse promised aid on time, while 65 percent reported that it is difficult to give accurate predictions of aid disbursements even one year in advance. When asked about accurate predictions three years in advance, the number reporting that it is difficult to predict aid jumps to over *90 percent*. Only 9 out of 103 respondents reported that it was not difficult for their agency to give an accurate prediction three years in advance of how much aid they planned to disburse.

These results underscore the difficulty recipient governments have in planning for aid dollars. Recipient governments are often expected to be grateful for whatever aid dollars eventually flow their way. But if recipients do not know when

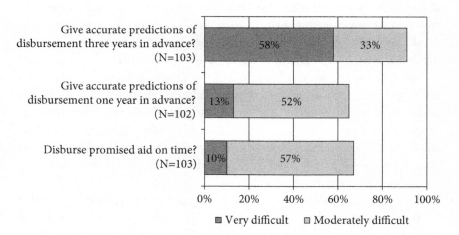

FIGURE 5.1 Donors struggle to provide predictable aid. Respondents were asked, "In [country], is it difficult for your agency to: (a) disburse promised aid on time? (b) give accurate predictions of disbursements one year in advance? (c) give accurate predictions of disbursements three years in advance?" and asked to choose from the following options: very difficult—moderately difficult—not difficult.
Source: Author's original data.

or indeed if aid money will actually arrive, it is unrealistic to expect that they will consistently be able to spend the funds wisely. At the same time, if aid is not guaranteed, it is unreasonable to expect recipients to carry out promised reforms in order to access aid dollars. Why would a recipient government carry out challenging and potentially politically costly reforms to access aid money, if there is no guarantee that aid dollars are actually linked to the implementation of such reforms?

Why Can't Donors and Recipient Governments Credibly Commit?

Why is it that donor agencies and recipient governments have such a hard time keeping their promises to each other? If both donor agencies and recipient governments recognize the challenge that commitment problems pose to the bargaining relationship, why do both sides have such a hard time upholding their side of the agreement?

One possible explanation is that neither side actually cares about development; hence the agreements are little more than formalities. While not unreasonable to consider, there is actually little reason to assume that altruism is entirely absent from development aid. We know that other priorities, such as security and the economic interests of the donor country, often take precedence over development motives (see, for example, Lancaster 2007; Lundsgaarde 2012; Milner and Tingley 2013). However, between donor agencies, who are charged with distributing aid, and recipient governments, who have at least a nominal interest in providing services for their population, there is little reason to think that altruism is entirely absent. At the recipient-country level, donor agencies and recipient governments spend countless hours negotiating such agreements; thus, all things being equal, there is little reason to think that both sides would not want the agreements to succeed. Why is it then that commitment problems are so rampant in development cooperation?

According to institutional economists, institutions are inefficient when they are unsuccessful in solving transformation and transaction costs. According to North (1990), solving transformation and transaction costs will be more difficult if there are (a) competing and multiple interests, (b) if the environment is particularly complex, and (c) if it is difficult for the other party to measure and/or enforce commitments. In the case of foreign aid, not only are there multiple and competing interests in a complex environment, but neither side has the capacity to measure or enforce the other's commitments. This undermines the efficiency of foreign aid institutions, because it increases transformation and transaction costs. Even if commitment problems are widely recognized by donor and government officials, development practitioners are often powerless to prevent these problems from undermining the negotiated compromises reached by the two parties.

Competing Interests in a Complex Environment

In this section I focus on three factors that make it difficult for donor agencies and recipient governments to make credible commitments: politics in the recipient country, politics in the donor country, and bureaucratic hurdles. This discussion is not intended to capture all the reasons why it might be difficult for donor agencies and recipient governments to make credible commitments. Instead, my goal is to demonstrate the extreme inefficiencies present in development cooperation through a few key examples.

POLITICS IN THE RECIPIENT COUNTRY

In developing countries, "upward" accountability to donor agencies is often stronger that "downward" accountability toward citizens (Bräutigam 1992; Martens 2002; Wenar 2011). Nonetheless, recipient governments still face a variety of competing domestic pressures that can undermine their ability to make credible commitments to donor agencies. In particular, political pressures related to the desire of the recipient government to stay in power often compete with the commitments to reform they have made to donor agencies.

A good example is the case of Uganda, where President Yoweri Museveni has taken to the creation of districts in recent years. In 2002, there were 56 districts in Uganda; by 2010 this number had risen to 111 (plus the capital city of Kampala).[24] As one respondent explained, district creation does not make sense from a developmental perspective, because it poses difficulties for the delivery of goods and services; however, from the perspective of the ruling party, it makes perfect sense: "From a political perspective, it's the best investment that you can do to maintaining power. You buy off people, divide and conquer."[25] Thus, despite donors demanding that the government stop creating districts—and a promise by the president in that regard—there is little reason to believe that the moratorium on district creation will hold, if further decentralization is seen to be politically advantageous.[26]

Exactly how domestic politics in recipient countries influence the credibility of commitments will vary across different time periods and contexts. However, a commonality across all the cases is that donor–government relations are often strained during election years. During these periods, the political climate is particularly charged, as the ruling party is often in a fierce battle to retain power. It is therefore not surprising that several respondents noted that "hiccups" between donor agencies and recipient governments occur more frequently in election years.[27]

In particular, donor officials frequently mentioned being frustrated with "off-budget" spending during election years. For donor agencies, the recipient country's budget is a public statement about where the government's priorities lie. At the same time, it is also indicative of how committed the government is to development and sound fiscal management. It is for this reason that donor agencies find it so desirable to be involved in budget preparations, and often advocate for a certain percentage of the budget to be spent on development initiatives (in contrast to, for example, the military). Donor agencies want to make sure that more money is spent on butter than guns.

For donor officials, off-budget expenditures constitute a violation of the recipient government's commitment to spend their money in a particular way, and can therefore lead to their agency delaying the disbursement of aid funds. For example, for many donor agencies, a positive report by the IMF's Policy Support Instrument (PSI) program is required to disburse certain types of aid, such as budget support. High rates of off-budget spending during an election year can lead to a poor PSI report, resulting in delayed aid funds and strained relations between donor agencies and recipient governments.

For an illustration, let's return to Uganda. In fiscal year 2010/11, an election year, the budget outturn—or how much the government actually spent that year—reached 114.5 percent of the approved budget. This high outturn was largely caused by supplementary requests amounting to 27.7 percent of the approved budget, which was far higher than in previous years.[28] In particular, spending on defense reached an excess of 280 percent, while service delivery sectors (e.g., health and education) received only between 85 and 95 percent of promised allocations (World Bank et al. 2011).

Particularly for donor agencies providing budget support, the high budget outturn was problematic and viewed as a violation of the Ugandan government's commitments. In response, they issued a joint statement chastising the government for not sticking to its commitments. In the statement, the budget support group made clear that any shifts away from poverty-reduction efforts are supposed to be *jointly* agreed on by donors and government. They saw the excessive spending during the election year as a violation of their agreed-on commitments.[29]

POLITICS IN DONOR COUNTRIES

It is not just politics in recipient countries, however, that can affect the efficiency of institutions of foreign aid. Politics in donor countries also powerfully affect the ability of donor agencies to make stable, long-term commitments. A donor official in Rwanda, for example, noted that although aid predictability is a great goal for development partners to be working toward, her donor agency is constrained in its ability to actually deliver aid as promised, because in practice other things often take precedence. Her agency cannot just say that it needs to continue to disburse aid because it is necessary to be predictable. While she understands the importance of aid predictability, the concept is not sellable back home.[30] A donor official in Uganda put it more succinctly: "We're political entities, we're subject to political pressure, we're subject to the whims of our ministers."[31]

The global financial crisis of 2007–2008 meant the many donor agencies had to tighten their belts, backing out of prior commitments. Perhaps the best example is the Netherlands, which began instituting drastic cuts to its foreign aid budget in 2011. In that year alone, aid budgets were slashed by €400 million, and the number of partner countries—that is, countries receiving bilateral aid from the Dutch government—was more than halved, from thirty-three to sixteen. In 2012, it was announced that the aid budget would be cut by an additional €3.25 billion over the next four years. In total, this meant that the Dutch foreign aid budget would be cut by over 25 percent in just five years (Spitz, Muskens, and Van Ewijk 2013).

While all the countries in the study felt these cuts, Tanzania was the hardest hit. In 2011, Tanzania was the eighth-largest recipient of Dutch aid and received close to €89 million in bilateral assistance from the Netherlands (Spitz, Muskens, and Van Ewijk 2013). That same year, however, Tanzania was dropped from the list of Dutch partner countries, and by the end of 2013, bilateral cooperation between Tanzania and the Netherlands was phased out.[32] Although this change in policy had nothing to do with events in Tanzania, it clearly had important ramifications for the government's budget. Despite promises by the Dutch government to not reduce aid to Tanzania in 2011/12, budget support to Tanzania was cut by 12 percent just two weeks before Tanzania unveiled its national budget that year (Mande 2011). Since then, Dutch development cooperation has slowed to a trickle in Tanzania.

BUREAUCRATIC HURDLES

While the institutions of foreign aid are no doubt powerfully shaped by politics within both recipient and donor countries, it would be a mistake to assume that political calculations and interests are the sole reasons why donor agencies and recipient governments find it difficult to uphold their commitments. The two parties also face much more mundane bureaucratic hurdles, which can undermine the credibility of their promises to each other.

In recipient countries, for example, it is very clear that capacity is frequently an issue. Even if there is broad-based support for an initiative, if the capacity to carry out reform is not there, the reform is unlikely to get implemented. As one Tanzanian respondent noted, although the issue of capacity in development is cliché, it is a big problem.[33] Several donor officials pointed out that while they have a dedicated staff to interface with their counterparts in government, recipient countries have much more limited staff. As a donor official put it, the donor agency has a "staff dedicated to policy dialogue. . . . They want to talk. . . . That's what their job description says, 'You need to talk to governments.' And they want to have meetings with government, and government is probably saying, 'We don't have that luxury.'"[34]

Recipient governments are not just interfacing with one donor but many. While there are dedicated units in each one of the countries' ministries of finance to deal with donor agencies (see chapter 4), the capacity of government to manage donors and all their demands is typically very strained. Often a single policy officer is charged with coordinating the aid from two to three different donor agencies. For example, in the External Economic Relations Unit within the Ministry of Finance in Ghana, one individual is in charge of foreign assistance from the United States and Canada, while another is in charge of aid from Japan, China, and Korea. As a respondent pointed out, recipient countries must manage many different contractual commitments, all on a shoestring budget: "We are so many around the table, coming with many different issues . . . maybe also some difficulties to cope with. . . . They want money. So, they are ready to take some commitments, but then, once it comes to implement them, they are a bit blocked because of so many things. *They are lost in all these contracts that they have signed with us, and then, they have limited capacities.*"[35]

In practice, it is often difficult to know whether a slow pace of reform is caused by capacity challenges or something else. Perhaps limited capacity is simply a convenient cover, allowing a recipient government to take the money but not implement the reform. While it would be difficult to deny that recipient governments sometimes use limited capacity strategically, it is also hard to deny that capacity is not an acute challenge for recipient governments. Even if staff numbers are sufficient (which they frequently are not), basic office skills, such as computer literacy, are often in short supply. Additionally, efficient and effective government employees are frequently poached by donor agencies promising better salaries and working conditions, as well as more opportunities for advancement.

Another bureaucratic hurdle impeding credible commitments, this time by donor agencies, is the high rate of staff turnover within country offices. Not only must recipient governments deal with multiple donors; the individuals who are charged with representing donor countries in developing countries regularly change. Donor officials are in a particular recipient country on average two to four years, with some staying for much shorter periods.[36] On average, HoCs who responded to my survey reported holding in their current position for 24.7 months.[37] Relatively short stays in recipient countries by foreign donor officials make it difficult for the recipient government to establish long-term working relationships with donor officials. It also means that as new donor staff comes in and out, recipient governments are forced to readjust to new priorities and new criteria for assessment, as personal preferences, particularly of more senior donor officials, influence what types of programs and projects are selected for funding. As a senior government official in Tanzania put it, we "have made so much mileage, and all the sudden it changes."[38]

Lack of Measurement and Enforcement Capacity

Even if recipient governments face a number of domestic pressures to renege on their promises, it may be feasible for donor agencies to take these pressures into account or force recipient governments to act according to donor demands. After all, donors should possess considerable weight in recipient countries heavily dependent on foreign aid. Similarly, it may be possible for recipient governments to measure donor variability and pressure donors into upholding their commitments, even when there are competing pressures to renege. Unfortunately, however, empirical evidence from across the four country cases suggests that the ability of both parties to either measure or enforce commitments is extremely limited.

MEASURING AND ENFORCING DONOR COMMITMENTS

It is likely unsurprising to readers that recipient governments often have little sanctioning power over donor agencies. As long as recipient governments remain dependent on foreign aid, they remain reliant on donor agencies. As a result, despite their many frustrations with the way donor agencies operate, recipient governments will continue to welcome donor agencies and the funds they bring with them. But can't recipient governments at least measure the volatility of donors' promises in order to try to mitigate some of the most damaging effects by planning ahead?

Recipient countries do try to track donor commitments, attempting to account for them as much as possible. For example, all four countries of the study have implemented electronic aid management systems (to varying degrees of success). These systems ask donor officials to input their expected commitments and actual disbursements anywhere from monthly to yearly, so that the government has a better idea of aid flows.[39] Previously, aid commitments and disbursements were largely captured in complicated Excel charts that could not be updated easily or frequently. However, new online software systems are designed (and marketed to recipient governments) explicitly for the purpose of capturing aid funds.[40]

Rwanda and Ghana have also tried to institutionalize national-level assessments of donors' performance: the Development Partner Performance Assessment Framework (DP-PAF) in Ghana and the Donor Performance Assessment Framework (DPAF) in Rwanda. Both assessments take their inspiration from frameworks used by donor agencies to measure recipient government performance. As a Ghanaian government official explained, donors assess the government when it "coughs" (i.e., constantly). However, before the creation of the DP-PAF, the government of Ghana did not have any means of assessing the performance of donor agencies.[41] These new assessment frameworks, which are aided considerably by the aforementioned aid management systems, provide the government with a tool to assess donor performance, measuring how well donors were able to keep their commitments.

Each year the performance of bilateral and multilateral donors is assessed (individually and collectively) based on a set of indicators designed to measure the *quality* of development assistance. The Rwandan DPAF, for example, establishes targets and then each year gives donors either a passing grade or a failing grade (Republic of Rwanda 2010b, 2011b, 2013a). Tellingly, the assessment criteria are almost all related to the credibility of donor commitments: for example, the percentage of ODA recorded in the national budget; the percentage of ODA disbursed using the government's budget execution procedures, auditing procedures, financial reporting systems, and procurement systems; and the percentage of ODA delivered in the year in which it was scheduled.

The creation of such assessment frameworks demonstrates a desire by recipient governments to improve the creditability of donor commitments. In these assessments, recipient governments grade donor agencies based on how good they are at keeping their promises. The initiative, however, also points to a fatal flaw in development cooperation: recipient governments lack enforcement capacity. Such assessments try to publicly shame donor agencies into upholding their commitments. Sometimes this works. Low scores often embarrassed the donor officials I spoke to. However, at the end of the day, recipient governments have no way of sanctioning a donor agency, if it fails to meet the stated goals. Donor officials may prefer to be assessed positively by the framework (many publicly lauded the initiative). However, there is no direct consequence for failing to meet the framework's standards. Funders (i.e., taxpayers) are generally unaware of such assessments, and even if they were aware of them, we have little reason to think they would care. The average American is more likely to care if

USAID money was stolen or misused than if USAID got a poor score on the Rwandan DPAF.

MEASURING AND ENFORCING RECIPIENT COMMITMENTS

What about the other way around? Are donor agencies able to monitor and enforce commitments by recipient countries? Despite the relative influence that many donor agencies wield in recipient countries, respondents across all four countries stressed that donor representatives are actually quite limited in their capacity to measure or enforce the commitments made by recipient governments.

Over time, donor agencies have increasingly sought to formalize the commitments of recipient governments in measurable frameworks. Donor agencies consider this to be a best practice because it enables them to actually measure the promises made by recipient governments. As a donor official in Tanzania explained, "If you don't have a proper methodology agreed and proper indicators, then you are going to have just terrible arguments about whether it's being met or not or whether it's been partly met or just [being met]."[42]

However, even when measurement is possible, donor agencies often lack the ability to enforce the promises made by recipient governments (see box 5.2). If the government fails to complete the requested action, donor agencies have few options, save for the suspension of aid (either partially or entirely). While potentially a powerful tool for enforcing commitments, suspension is not consistently used as an enforcement mechanism by donor agencies (Swedlund 2017a).

Box 5.2   Enforcement by donor agencies

We're not yet strong enough to force the government to be accountable to us.

—Bilateral donor agency, July 4, 2012, Tanzania

Donors really want the government to achieve certain goals, but then the government actually has its own agenda, . . . And they're basically, "Well, we do what we want to do," . . . So, *what are you going to do about it?* [Donor agencies] really *lack the power to enforce* some measures that they would like to make the government do.

—Bilateral donor official, April 3, 2013, Ghana

A country's government is not going to do what they don't want to do.

—Bilateral donor agency, June 5, 2012, Tanzania

Italic emphases added by the author.

Suspending aid is generally a headquarters, not mission-level, decision. Therefore, the desire to suspend aid may be at times superseded by a political desire by donor politicians to maintain friendly, diplomatic relations with the recipient government. At the same time, donors face pressure to disburse all aid that they have been authorized to allocate (Collier 2007; Ostrom et al. 2002; Svensson 2003, 2006).

This does not go unnoticed by recipient governments, who after all are not new to the aid game. According to a donor official in Ghana, "[the] government recognizes the fact that development partners need to disburse. So, sometimes, they do not do what they have to do, knowing that whatever it takes, aid will be disbursed."[43] As a Ugandan donor official explained, if you work with both carrots and sticks, you have to be able to use both instruments. In practice, however, donor agencies rely mainly on carrots. Giving the example of the education sector, he noted that instead of cutting aid because of poor performance, donors have actually increased the total budget. According to him, this gives the impression that "we give you the money and moreover, because you misbehave, we give you more money." He went on to argue that, in practice, donor agencies lack the political capacity to link disbursements to actual results, noting that "this has been proved in the past. . . . Maybe now they can arrange new systems so that they can be much more effective. But so far, my doubts remain."[44] For foreign aid to truly incentivize a change in behavior, donor agencies must be able and willing to suspend aid when prespecified conditions are not met.

In recipient countries, donor agencies and recipient governments are continuously engaging in a back-and-forth with the goal of reaching an aid policy compromise that maximizes their preferences relative to their negotiating capital. Such aid policy compromises are, however, continually being undermined by the difficulty both sides have upholding their promises. Because donor agencies and recipient governments are often unable to measure, let alone enforce, the other side's commitments, the two sides are forced to take a leap of faith, entering into agreements with each other with little assurance that the other side will actually uphold its commitments. In the next chapter, I consider how this ever-looming threat of commitment problems influences choices in regard to the way aid is delivered, as well as the sustainability of aid delivery mechanisms over the long term.

TRACKING A CRAZE
The Rise (and Fall) of Budget Support

**The plan was, crudely, chuck your money to budget support, close up
new projects, and we'll talk about problems of the day. That was the
concept.**

—Bilateral donor official, June 1, 2012, Tanzania

In the late 1990s and early 2000s, many donor agencies began to embrace a new
way of delivering foreign aid, called budget support. Within just over a decade,
there was close to a tenfold increase in the amount of budget support disbursed
worldwide. In 1990, donors disbursed $11.5 billion in general budget support.
By 2002, this figure had risen to $98.6 billion.[1] Although related to aid delivery
mechanisms used in the past, budget support is unique in that it requires donor
agencies to disburse funds directly into the treasury of the recipient government
without placing strong conditions on how the money is used. In addition, the aid
delivery mechanism includes a strong emphasis on aid coordination and harmonization between donor agencies and the recipient government, asking donor
agencies to disburse foreign aid collectively and according to shared assessment
frameworks. Yet, despite all the hype around budget support, as with so many
different aid delivery mechanisms before it, enthusiasm was short-lived. In 2013,
global totals of general budget support were back down to $10.4 billion. Why
did donor agencies embrace budget support with such fervor at the turn of the
century? And why did enthusiasm around budget support die out so quickly?

The rise and decline of budget support as a popular aid modality represents a
unique opportunity to study the adoption of and shift away from a particular aid
delivery mechanism that is not only innovative but also counterintuitive. Given
poor governance and limited public financial accountability in many recipient
countries, why would donor agencies trust recipient governments with large
sums of aid funds in the first place? And why, after investing so much in building

the structures that facilitated the disbursement of budget support, would donor agencies move so quickly away from this way of delivering foreign aid?

According to the theoretical framework presented in chapter 2, choices in aid delivery are the result of a negotiated compromise between a donor agency and a recipient government. In these negotiations, it is donor agencies that ultimately must sign off on aid disbursements. However, because donor agencies rely on recipient governments for implementation, recipient governments have nego-tiating capital (see chapter 4). In practice, however, it is frequently difficult for donor agencies and recipient governments to actually uphold their side of the bargaining compromise (see chapter 5).

This raises the question: In what ways might the existence of commitment problems affect aid policy bargaining between donor agencies and recipient governments? In this chapter, I empirically examine the rise and fall of budget sup-port as a popular aid delivery mechanism in order to test two predictions regard-ing the impact of commitment problems on the selection and the sustainability of aid delivery mechanisms over time. First, donor agencies and recipient gov-ernments will be drawn to institutional innovations that promise to help reduce commitment problems. Second, the success of an innovation—measured by how long it lasts—depends on the innovation's ability to incentivize donor agencies and recipient governments to actually abide by their commitments.

A New Dance: Why Donors and Recipients Embraced Budget Support

As with the rise (and fall) of aid delivery mechanisms before it, the embrace of budget support by foreign aid donors was influenced by a variety of particular historical and social factors. Budget support came about in the mid-2000s as part of a growing ideological consensus that tackling poverty required donors to give more ownership to recipients. At least in part, this consensus can be seen as a response to a skepticism about foreign aid (e.g., Moyo 2009). To justify aid bud-gets, donors needed to articulate that they had a "new" approach, one that would be more successful than those tried in the past. At the same time, global leaders needed to show progress on the Millennium Development Goals. Achieving the MDGs required an unprecedented amount of aid money, which was promised by a coalition of international donors in 2002 at the Monterrey Conference in Mexico. Budget support, which is a direct resource transfer, allowed donors to quickly disburse large sums of aid funds.

We should not, however, assume that the shift toward budget support was inev-itable. Nothing about these particular historical events required donor agencies to embrace budget support (and in fact not all did). International development practitioners had been advocating for ownership and a more concerted effort on poverty reduction since at least the 1960s (e.g., L. B. Pearson 1969). And as I will discuss in more detail below, budget support entailed a substantial risk for donor agencies.

In this section I argue that budget support was the product of a negotiated compromise between donor agencies and the recipient government, one from which both sought to benefit. Enthusiasm about the aid delivery mechanism rested (rather precariously) on a policy compromise between donor agencies and recipient countries. Donor agencies stood to gain more influence over development policy decision making. Recipient governments were promised firmer goalposts and more predictable aid.

What Was in It for Donor Agencies?

When a donor agency elects to provide budget support, it gives up technical control over how aid dollars are spent. Although donor agencies are often not keen to admit it—at least publicly—donor officials are clearly aware of the potential for budget support to be misused. As a donor official in Ghana put it, "You don't have any control. . . . Once it goes to the budget, if they decide to finance white elephants, there's nothing we can do."[2] As another donor official acknowledged, there is no good answer to the questions "How do you know that the money goes where it should be going, and how do you know it's not being stolen?" "Because budget support is fungible, we wouldn't know if it was our euros or the government's euros that were being stolen."[3] If the financial risk for misuse of funds is high, why is it that so many donor agencies readily embraced budget support at the turn of the century?

For donor agencies to be willing to take on the risks associated with budget support, they must have benefited in some other way. History shows that donor agencies are unlikely to be enticed to take on such a big risk merely because of a shift in normative preferences. Again, donor agencies are largely upwardly accountable to the donor country and its taxpayers. If a donor agency was willing to voluntarily give up technical control over aid funds, increasing the possibility of financial misuse, it must have benefited from the compromise in another way.

My argument is that donor agencies were willing to take on this risk because, in exchange, they were promised more policy influence over domestic decision making (also see Swedlund 2013a). That is, donor agencies traded technical control for increased policy influence. This argument stands in direct contrast to the policy rhetoric around budget support prevalent in the mid-2000s, which emphasized that recipient governments would gain *more* (not less) ownership over domestic policy decision making. It is not, however, inconsistent with anecdotal evidence on budget support, which suggests that donor agencies able and willing to provide budget support enjoy a preferential status in recipient countries (i.e., Gould 2005; Harrison 2001; Hayman 2009a, 2009b; Knoll 2008; Molenaers 2012).

To test the argument that budget support promised donor agencies more pol-icy influence, it is useful to first look to results from my survey of donor officials. When asked about their agency's motivations to begin budget support,[4] close to 80 percent of those sampled indicated that a desire to increase their agency's policy influence over the government was a motivating factor in the agency's decision to begin providing budget support to the recipient government.[5] More-over, when directly asked whether providing budget support increases a donor agency's influence with the recipient government, more than 60 percent of the sampled HoCs answered yes—budget support donors have more influence than non–budget support donors.

HoCs representing donor agencies that currently or have previously provided budget support were even more likely to report that the aid delivery mechanism gives you influence with the recipient government (see figure 6.1). Seventy-eight percent of HoCs representing donor agencies that previously provided budget support (but no longer do) indicated that the modality increases a donor agen-cy's influence with the recipient government. This suggests that HoCs working for donor agencies that have suspended budget support feel the loss of the aid modality now that it is no longer a part of their portfolio.

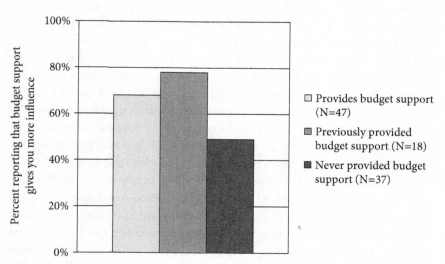

FIGURE 6.1 Budget support gives you more influence with the government. *Source:* Author's original data. Respondents were asked, "In your opinion, do donors that provide budget support have more influence with the government of [Country]?" and asked to select either no or yes.

Why is it that such a high percentage of HoCs believe that budget support increases a donor agency's influence with the recipient government? Interviews with practitioners across the four countries of the study suggest that donor officials believe budget support increases their donor agency's policy influence in three key ways. First, it grants budget support donors a seat at the table. Second, budget support amplifies the voices of donor agencies. Third, budget support provides a license to ask questions about how the government spends not just aid dollars but the whole of its budget (also see Swedlund 2013a).

A SEAT AT THE TABLE

For donor agencies, budget support is "an access ticket."[6] In all four countries of the study, respondents told me that providing budget support gives a donor agency privileged access to the recipient government—that is, a "seat at the table" (see box 6.1). Access comes mainly via specially designed working groups intended to streamline the provision of budget support in recipient countries. However, it can also come about more informally, in the form of access to high-level politicians via unofficial channels. When a donor agency provides budget support, it is invited to join an exclusive and often privileged policy dialogue structure. For donor agencies, access to this policy dialogue is extremely valuable, because it gives them more access to domestic decision makers:

> To put it plainly, if you are doing budget support then you can buy a seat at the table. Aid, to be blunt, is not just about humanitarian assistance; it is about promoting foreign policy of another country. If you are

---

Box 6.1   A seat at the table

What is important for each of those partners which are still giving budget support is the simple fact that *we are part of . . . the highest level policy dialogue, that we're simply sitting at the table,* that we're able to follow discussions, that we will in theory be able to raise our own voice.
> —Bilateral donor official, October 28, 2013, Uganda

When you put a big amount of money on the table, then *you can have a dialogue at the highest level.*
> —Multilateral donor official, October 30, 2013, Tanzania

We want to be at that table. . . . The governments want the money, are happy to take it, and *they're willing to then negotiate with us on policy dialogue.*
> —Bilateral donor official, July 4, 2012, Tanzania

Italic emphases added by the author.

---

working through projects, if you're working through civil society, you're not talking to government. It's like coming to my house and instead of talking to the head of the house, you're talking to the worker or the child. So, the advantage of giving budget support is you're having government-to-government [discussions] ... you're talking to the head of the house, and you are able to push for policies that you think ... will adamantly move the country forward.[7]

Over and over, and across all four countries of the study, respondents emphasized the value of being a member of the budget support working group, often contrasting this select group to the larger—all-inclusive—donor group to emphasize its importance. For example, a respondent in Tanzania explained that the government of Tanzania does not take the inclusive Development Partnership Group (DPG) seriously. It does, however, take the budget support group very seriously, adding that there is resentment of the budget support group from those who are not eligible to participate.[8] Similarly, a donor official in Uganda, whose agency does not provide budget support, explained that it is very difficult for her agency to be outside the budget support framework, noting that budget support donors can set goals and conditionalities for the government. They are able to talk with the Bank of Uganda, the Ministry of Finance, and the Office of the Prime Minister. Budget support donors engage in a great deal of information sharing that her agency is excluded from.[9]

VOICE AMPLIFICATION

Of course, there is little value in being a part of the club if no one is paying attention to what you are saying. According to respondents, providing budget support not only gives you access; it also increases the probability that the government will actually pay attention to what you are saying. In other words, providing budget support amplifies the voices of donor agencies (see box 6.2). If you provide budget support, it is easier to persuade the government to take up a particular reform.[10]

This is particularly appealing for smaller donors, who can use budget support to garner more attention from the recipient government. By providing budget support, smaller donors increase their prominence in the donor pecking order.[11] As one respondent explained, budget support donors "make a small contribution to a big pot."[12] These pooled funds can then be used to nudge recipient governments toward desired reforms, because larger amounts of funds provide an incentive for recipient governments to take the demands of the donors more seriously. As a donor official in Tanzania noted, "We've got a lot more weight than we ever would've had on our own. Instead of $10 million a year it's $500 million a year."[13] Similarly, a respondent in Uganda noted that with budget support—in

---

Box 6.2 Voice amplification

For donor[s], it gives us more of a leverage with government, because as a group, we contribute a sizable proportion of the development budget. *So it makes getting government attention on policy measures we think are important . . . easier.*

—Bilateral donor official, April 11, 2013, Ghana

[With budget support, you] have greater leverage in terms of challenging the government about progress. . . . By putting money in the basket, while you might not be able to determine where it goes, I think *you are gaining power in terms of overall direction of the country.*

—Civil society representative, October 11, 2013, Uganda

While if you and I, representing a donor, we go to the ministry of infrastructure and we agree to build a road, they're very happy, but that's fine. And *if we go to ministry of finance and we give $500 million cash and we ask for something, normally we get it.*

—Multilateral donor official, May 29, 2012, Tanzania

Italic emphases added by the author.

---

contrast to other aid modalities—it is not always about how much money you give, but how active and engaged you are. From a small-country perspective, "how on earth would you get the same kind of traction?"[14] Referencing Germany, which at the time provided a relatively small amount of budget support to Tanzania in comparison to other donors in the country, one multilateral donor official remarked that even though the Germans do not provide lots of money, they "wield a big stick." "Once you are in the [budget support] club, you're in—no matter how much money you contribute."[15]

A LICENSE TO ASK QUESTIONS

Finally, providing budget support gives donor agencies a license to ask questions about a whole host of issues that it would otherwise be difficult for them to comment on. Respondents across all four countries explained that budget support donors are able to exercise influence over a larger set of resources and so-called cross-cutting issues (i.e., topics such as gender or governance that stretch beyond a single sector), which are almost impossible to address with other types of foreign aid. As a donor official in Uganda noted, "It's another nexus in terms of development and dialogue, which you don't have if you just give project aid."[16]

Box 6.3   A license to ask questions

[Budget support] *offers an opportunity to discuss issues which are otherwise difficult to address* ... [i.e.,] corruption, human rights, democracy.... They need to be discussed, and otherwise it's difficult to have a good platform for that.

—Multilateral donor official, April 10, 2013, Ghana

[Budget support] does give you *a different approach to working with government* because you're not focused on just a project, but *you can look at the broader scope*; especially with general budget support, macroeconomic dialogue, [public financial management] dialogue, these are things that are important for every single project you implement with government.

—Multilateral donor official, October 2, 2013, Uganda

[Budget support] allow[s] you *to have discussion about the big picture.* Yeah, the broad direction the government's going. ... It *allows you to actually have a more strategic dialogue* with ... the government.

—Bilateral donor official, June 5, 2012, Tanzania

Italic emphases added by the author.

In particular, donor agencies that give budget support are able to comment on the whole of the government's budget, rather than just on the specific sectors that the donor directly funds through basket or project aid.[17] According to Tuffour (2005), when donor agencies engage in budget support, they become "special taxpayers" that have similar enough interests to use their contributions as leverage for policy changes. Instead of funding a specific project, such as a school or hospital, budget support donors fund the government itself. As a donor official in Ghana explained, this gives budget support donors leverage over budget preparations as a whole. Because they are directly funding the government's budget, it is easier for donor agencies to comment on how public money—not just aid money—is being spent.[18] According to a high-level government official in Tanzania, even though 75 percent of the Tanzanian budget is generated domestically, and only 10 percent of the remaining 25 percent (or 2.5 percent of the overall budget) is provided by budget support, donors providing budget support are "able to influence the prioritization of the allocation of 100 percent of the national budget."[19]

Respondents also repeatedly emphasized that providing budget support allows them to comment on cross-sector issues that cannot be addressed with project aid. A multilateral donor official in Ghana told the story of needing electricity at a school that a donor agency was building. He explained that if you provide only project aid, it is difficult to get such an issue on the agenda. However, budget support allows you to get at cross-sector issues, such as electricity provision, because it provides you with a way to have conversations at a high level.[20] Similarly, a bilateral donor official in Tanzania emphasized that through budget support, donors can look at the bigger picture, scrutinizing the budget in general. Noting that many development issues cannot be solved at the sector level, he emphasized that, via the PAF, donor agencies are able to get at the "apex of issues."[21] According to an independent consultant in Tanzania, previously many donor demands were far-fetched and removed from the project they were funding. However, when the same issues come up under the general budget support (GBS) framework, they suddenly aren't far-fetched anymore. In his words, budget support donors have "gone into the kitchen and want to know how [the] food is cooked."[22]

POLICY INFLUENCE AND THE CREDIBILITY OF AID COMMITMENTS

Why is it that policy influence is so desirable to donor agencies? In aid-dependent countries, shouldn't donor agencies be able to wield a great deal of influence even without providing budget support? Why take on the financial risk of providing budget support?

As I explained in chapter 5, it is often extremely difficult for donor agencies to ensure that the commitments of recipient governments are credible. Recipient governments face a variety of domestic pressures, which can undermine their commitments to donor agencies. In recipient countries, donor officials use policy influence to help them garner more credible commitments from recipient governments. As a respondent working in Uganda explained, budget support created a framework that incentivizes reform on action points and deliverables. In return for budget support, you get an effort by the government to make commitments that are more predictable.[23] As another respondent noted, influence is "not necessarily the power to get them to always do what you want them to do." Instead, it is "about leverage or the ability to put certain things on the table or to get movement on certain key issues that are important to [you]."[24]

According to respondents, budget support was designed to incentivize more credible commitments by recipient governments in three overlapping ways. First, by giving recipient governments more "ownership," budget support attempted to place the responsibility for development clearly with the recipient government, making it easier to hold recipient governments accountable for failures. As a senior NGO leader in Uganda noted, "If you are doing a project . . . government is always going to be saying that 'well, we are not in charge. You're in charge.'"[25] Alternatively, if a donor agency is supporting the recipient government through budget support, responsibility for implementation falls squarely on the government. As is clearly reflected in policy documentation coming out of high-level meetings between recipient and donor countries throughout the 2000s, discussions about "ownership" focused mainly on what donors expected from recipient governments, rather than on what donor agencies might themselves do to foster ownership (see box 6.4). The idea was that by putting responsibility more squarely on the recipient government, recipient governments would be more likely to make commitments that are credible and hence more likely to actually be carried out.

Second, by formalizing commitments into shared frameworks, budget support was designed to get recipient governments not only to publicly commit to reforms but to commit to reforms they actually cared about and would thus be more likely to implement. Consider, for example, the assessment frameworks that guide the disbursement of budget support in all four countries of the study. It would be wrong to assume that these assessment frameworks represent an easing of reform pressure on recipient governments. As one respondent

---

Box 6.4   "Ownership" defined by the Paris Declaration on Aid Effectiveness

Ownership
Partner countries exercise effective leadership over their development policies and strategies and coordinate development actions.

14.   Partner countries commit to:
- Exercise leadership in developing and implementing their national development strategies through broad consultative processes.
- Translate these national development strategies into prioritised results-oriented operational programmes as expressed in medium-term expenditure frameworks and annual budgets.
- Take the lead in coordinating aid at all levels in conjunction with other development resources in dialogue with donors and encouraging the participation of civil society and the private sector.

15.   Donors commit to:
- Respect partner country leadership and help strengthen their capacity to exercise it.

Source: OECD (2005).

remarked, "By linking our own performance projects to the [performance assessment framework] indicators, we're putting even more pressure on government. We're trying even harder to push them for certain reforms."[26] What the assessment frameworks do allow, however, is for the recipient government to be more involved in crafting the indicators on which it will ultimately be assessed. The assumption made by donor officials is that recipient governments are going to be more inclined to actually meet the requirements if they have a hand in shaping them. Donor officials hoped that recipient commitments would be more credible if the government was directly involved in their drafting.

Third, budget support tried to extract sounder commitments from recipient governments by elevating the discussion to a higher level. With project aid, the relevant government counterpart is the germane sector ministry—for example the ministry of health or education. Alternatively, with budget support (even sector budget support), the relevant government counterpart is the minister of finance and the minister's deputies.[27] For donor officials working in recipient countries this is an advantage, not only for status reasons, but because it is assumed that commitments at a higher level have more "sticking power."[28] Commitments undertaken at a higher level are assumed to be more credible. As a donor official in Uganda explained, budget support gives you "buy-in" with recipient governments:

> [Budget support] moves from the technocratic sphere to the political sphere, so, you have an ambassador saying, "Listen, we would like to help you with this, we would like to help you bring road, water, and sanitation to eight hundred thousand Ugandans; we are sure that your government thinks it's a good idea. But if we . . . do that, we [need you to sign] a new water sector program. Of course, you need assurances, because why would you give it as unearmarked funds if you don't have a good dialogue forum to address some challenges that might arise? So diplomatically, it's also, that's part of the extra layer, *it's also about explaining to government what you need, but also what you can provide.*[29]

By elevating negotiations to a higher level, budget support was assumed to make it easier for donors to extract credible commitments from a recipient and to provide a forum for addressing any problems that might arise in the future.

What Was in It for Recipient Governments?

At first glance, the benefits of budget support for recipient governments may seem obvious. Budget support means that aid is going directly into government coffers, giving the government greater technical control over where aid money is spent. This is, of course, extremely valuable to cash-strapped recipient governments, who would no doubt prefer to be able to spend aid dollars themselves, rather than see the funds siphoned off to NGOs or other development contractors.

While this obvious benefit is certainly important and is not to be underestimated, budget support does not come without strings. In exchange for more technical control over aid funds, recipient governments give donor agencies greater access to their internal workings, something that they are not inclined to want to do. Why is it then that so many recipient governments overwhelmingly prefer budget support to other types of aid?[30] What makes technical control over aid funds so valuable to recipient governments?

My argument, based on the four country case studies, is that recipient governments were willing to accept the increased policy influence that came along with budget support because they believed it would help with donor commitment problems. In particular, recipient governments were promised clearer, more credible assessment criteria and more predicable aid disbursements. These commitments were valuable to recipient governments, because they promised to improve the credibility of donor commitments.

FIXED GOALPOSTS

When aid is given in small, piecemeal chucks, as it is with project aid, there is always the opportunity for the donor to introduce new criteria and demands on the recipient government, making it difficult for recipient governments to know how donors will assess them in the future. A core tenet of budget support is that donors have to disburse according to a shared PAF, in which the criteria for disbursement are clearly laid out in an assessment framework that is jointly agreed on with the recipient government. Thus, the recipient government is aware of the criteria for assessment well in advance and can plan accordingly. As one respondent remarked, the "charm of budget support" is "easy-to-formulate conditionalities" that are calculable for the recipient government.[31]

Take the case of Rwanda. Prior to the suspension of budget support, the Rwandan PAF was composed of fifty indicators on the bases of which the government was assessed each year. From these fifty indicators, donor agencies could pick the criteria on which they would disburse budget support for the subsequent year. The PAF was not light on demands for the Rwandan government. The appeal was therefore not that the money came with fewer strings. Instead, what the Rwandan government found valuable about the PAF was that the criteria for assessment were clearly laid out well in advance. In other words, the rules of the game were fixed and predetermined. If a donor agency wanted to add a new indicator to the

PAF, it had to replace one of the existing fifty indicators.[32] Because the previous year's assessment determined the subsequent year's disbursement, the government could calculate in advance what it needed to do to receive the promised aid.

A common set of assessment criteria is particularly valuable when foreign assistance comes from dozens of different donor agencies. More aid typically means more donors, and with an increase in the number of donors also comes an increase in the number of demands and conditions.[33] In policy rhetoric, "transaction costs" is an overused and overstretched term. However, the general message communicated by policy documentation on budget support, as well as by respondents across the four countries of the study, is that the costs of the aid industry are too high for recipient countries, and that budget support was designed to decrease these costs. As one respondent noted, government officials "don't get to work, . . . because it's mission after mission coming and meeting them."[34] While individual donor demands may be reasonable and even tacitly accepted by the recipient governments, at some point the sheer volume can become unmanageable for recipient governments.

Comparing the budget support to an era dominated by project funding, a representative of the GBS Secretariat in Tanzania, for example, noted that "we have to try and remember what it was like before; I wasn't here but it sounds fairly ghastly, [*laughter*] in terms of hundreds of projects all sort of sapping the capacity of the government."[35] According to another Tanzanian official, pet projects by individual donor agencies consume a great deal of time, and before budget support, the budget was "a big mess." Prior to the introduction of budget support, the government did not have control over either inputs or outputs, and it never knew what it would get in terms of aid dollars from year to year.[36] The government prefers budget support because there is a clear agreement on what needs to be done.[37]

Along with the introduction of budget support came a promise to harmonize and coordinate the activities of donors. As a respondent in Tanzania explained, with budget support, "You don't have to run to all different kind of donors doing different projects. . . . You're free to allocate it wherever you want and fill the gap of where you don't get other projects in."[38] As another respondent remarked, "Instead of having fourteen development partners running and signing their own individual agreement or asking for their own individual report or meeting, it can be done in one go."[39] For donor agencies, this is advantageous in that it increases their collective strength vis-à-vis the government; however, it is also attractive to recipient governments, because it promises to streamline donor activities, asking donor agencies to commit to a common set of criteria for the disbursement of funds. This is valuable for recipient governments, because it means aid is calculable in advance.

AID PREDICTABILITY

Budget support also promised to make aid more predictable for recipient governments. Whether budget support is actually as predictable as proponents claim is a separate empirical question. However, what came out quite clearly from my interviews with practitioners on the ground is that greater aid predictability is often used to justify budget support (see box 6.5). According to a donor official in Ghana, "If you want to have a certain stability in your disbursements to a country, [budget support] is an instrument that can help."[40] Similarly, another donor official in Ghana argued that the biggest benefit of budget support for the government is "having an assured, predictable flow of funds to support your budgets."[41]

In contrast to project aid, which is disbursed in small chucks as key milestones in the project are met, budget support is disbursed at the start of the year in a large lump sum.[42] As a donor official noted, with budget support you "don't have all these approval and objection processes and procurement challenges that can slow down disbursement."[43] This is beneficial for the recipient government for several reasons. First, it means that the government benefits from a

---

Box 6.5   Budget support and predictability

[Budget support] *increases the predictability of external resource availability and disbursements* by basing funding decisions on outcomes of a joint review of performance based on a commonly agreed Performance Assessment Framework, which takes place prior to the financial year in which disbursements are to be made. This in turn facilitates more strategic and realistic budget planning, as GBS funds are known in advance.

—Joint Assistance Strategy for Tanzania
(United Republic of Tanzania 2006a, 21)

Multi-donor Budgetary Support (MDBS) is the latest and most challenging initiative. It has 10 DPs [development partners] committed to providing collective support and ongoing budgetary assistance to the Government of Ghana (GoG) to implement the Ghana Poverty Reduction Strategy (GPRS). *A direct benefit is the predictability in donor inflows.*

—Ghana Multi-donor Budget Support Newsletter
(Republic of Ghana 2005, 1)

Italic emphases added by the author.

large chunk of aid, instead of piecemeal disbursements. Second, it means that aid money comes in at the beginning of the year when governments can better plan for it. Third, and most important, it means that once the money has been disbursed, a donor agency cannot renege on its promise to deliver a prespecified amount of aid because of unforeseen events or changes in donor policy that are beyond the control of the recipient government. Once the money is delivered, it is subsumed into the country's national budget, and the recipient government is responsible for spending it. As a result, the recipient government becomes less vulnerable to the whims and changing policies of donor agencies.

A Breakdown in the Compromise

For recipient governments, budget support promised clear, calculable disbursement criteria, which are not only articulated well in advance but are shared across multiple donor agencies. In return, donor agencies were promised more policy influence over domestic policy decision making, providing them an incentive to take on the risks associated with budget support.

For a time, this compromise seemed to be working. Budget support totals were on the rise, and many observers portrayed donor–government relations in the early to mid-2000s as idyllic. However, across all four countries of the study, budget support has gradually fallen out of favor. Changing political realities ultimately undermined the fragile bargaining compromise on which budget support rested.

Over time, donor agencies could not overcome the temptation to change the goalposts, and events largely exogenous to development cooperation increasingly made it more difficult for donor agencies to live up to their commitment to provide a more predictable form of assistance. At the same time, the inability of recipient governments to pass certain reforms, and the emergence of several corruption scandals caused donors to doubt the value of budget support in gaining policy influence. As a result, across all four countries of the study, the precarious compromise on which budget support rested has broken down.

Turning Down the Taps

The heyday of budget support was the early to mid-2000s. In these years, budget support totals were on the rise, and donor–government relations were widely seen as moving in the right direction. However, toward the turn of the century, budget support's "honeymoon phase" began to crash (Republic of Ghana 2008, 4), and budget support totals began to decline. The fact that declines in the amount of budget support took place in all four countries of the study indicates that the shift away from budget support cannot be fully explained by specific events in the individual recipient countries. Rather, it reflects a broader turn away from the aid delivery mechanism.

There are, however, interesting variations in the manner in which the shift took place in the individual countries. In Uganda, budget support was suspended in December 2012 after the auditor general released a report alleging that $11 million of donor funds were stolen from an account in the Office of the Prime Minister that had been set up to fund a peace and reconciliation program in the northern part of the country. As a result, upward of $300 million in budget support—equivalent to 1.3 percent of Uganda's GDP—was suspended (Republic of Uganda 2012). Following the implementation of a set of targets by the Ugandan government, smaller amounts of sector budget support have been reinstated, but at the time of writing, general budget support remains off the table.

In Rwanda, budget support was also suspended in 2012. In this case, the culprit was a UN report accusing the government of supporting a militia group (M23) widely seen as causing instability across the border in the Kivu region of the Democratic Republic of the Congo.[44] As a result of these allegations, several donor agencies cut budget support (as well as military aid) to Rwanda, resulting in a shortfall of approximately half ($55.2 million) of the GBS promised to the Rwanda government that year (Republic of Rwanda 2013b).[45] Since 2013, budget support programs have been tabled by donor agencies active in the country.

In Ghana, budget support continues but has slowed to a trickle. In 2013, donor agencies suspended budget support to the country over concerns about economic mismanagement, particularly large overruns by the government in the budget that year.[46] Over a two-year period, donor agencies withheld approximately $700 million in direct budget support to Ghana, causing a huge gap in the country's national budget (Abbey 2015). Following a more positive assessment of the country's financial situation by the IMF in June 2015, the World Bank, AfDB, and the European Commission reinstated budget support to Ghana (Abbey 2015; Hanna 2015). However, for most bilateral donor agencies, GBS remains off the table, and budget support totals remain substantially lower than in previous years.

In Tanzania, budget support totals have also taken a nosedive. In late 2014, donors suspended over $500 million in budget support to the government after a scandal in the energy sector.[47] Beginning in early 2015, some donors began to unfreeze budget support (Anderson 2014; Ng'wanakilala 2015). However, it is still unclear how much budget support, particularly GBS, donor agencies will be willing to provide to Tanzania in coming years, and—as in Ghana—the total volume of budget support has dropped considerably.

It is not just budget support totals that have plummeted, however. Across all four countries, in conjunction with the decline in budget support totals, we have also seen a decline in a more general sense of goodwill between donors and the recipient government. I witnessed this firsthand over the course of my visits to each county. As I explain in more detail below, as budget support totals declined, both parties became increasingly disillusioned with the strength of the aid relationship. Recipient-country officials began, once again, to complain about the unpredictability of aid, while donor officials became increasingly frustrated about being shut out of domestic policy decision making.

The Enforceability of Commitments

Why is it that we saw a closing down of the budget support taps in the late 2000s across all four countries of the study? Throughout the decade, donor and government officials put a great deal of effort into building structures to support the disbursement of budget support. Why is it then that the tide so quickly shifted away from budget support?

According to results of my survey of donor officials, the shift cannot be attributed to a low rate of support for the aid modality among development practitioners. Despite all the challenges faced by the aid delivery mechanism in recent years, when asked about their personal opinion regarding budget support, close to half of the sample still selected that they believe this aid modality is a good idea (see figure 6.2). HoCs representing agencies that provided budget support were particularly favorable about it; over 70 percent answered that, in their personal opinion, budget support is a good idea.[48]

Similarly, in my discussions with policy makers on the ground, respondents in all the country case studies remained, on average, positive about budget support. Respondents were sensitive to the aid modality's limitations, frequently pointing out, for example, that engaging in budget support was risky for donor agencies. However, they were just as keen to remind me of budget support's benefits, particularly policy influence. Several respondents openly expressed frustration about their agency's shift away from budget support, emphasizing that it was not given enough time to work. For example, a donor official in Tanzania said that "politically, there's a pullback on the part of our government, . . . which I think is wrong. . . . I think we need to give it longer, we need to not abandon the process at this point."[49]

According to the theoretical framework I put forth in chapter 2, the sustainability of an aid delivery mechanism is determined by its ability to foster credible commitments from both donor agencies and recipient governments. For a given aid delivery mechanism to be sustainable past an initial period of

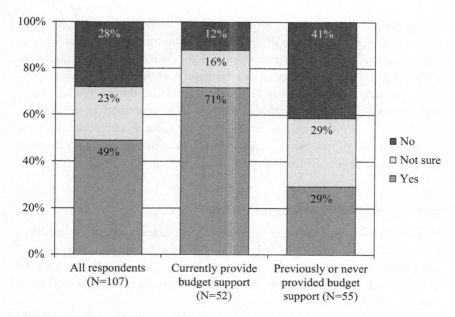

FIGURE 6.2 Percentage of HoCs in favor of their agency providing budget support. *Source:* Author's original data. Respondents were asked, "In your personal opinion, is it a good idea for your agency to provide budget support to [Country]?" and asked to select between yes, no, or not sure.

enthusiasm, the commitments made by both parties need to be self-sustaining (North 1999). In this regard, the aid policy compromises that allowed for the emergence of budget support were *always* precarious. For both parties, there were advantages to the negotiated agreements. Thus, even in the face of scandal, donor and government officials working on the ground are hesitant to abandon the aid delivery mechanism and the advantages it implies. Ultimately, however, the compromise that allowed budget support to emerge was not self-enforcing. Because of the vulnerability of the aid system to commitment problems, over time it became more and more difficult for donor agencies and recipient governments to fulfill their promises to one another. As a government newsletter in Ghana notes, budget support, like all aid modalities, is "a living animal, constantly changing in response to emerging realities" (Republic of Ghana 2008).

SHIFTING THE GOALPOSTS

Budget support was supposed to fix the goalposts across multiple donor agencies, promising more measurable assessment criteria and a decrease in transaction costs, particularly for recipient governments. In each of the recipient countries, optimism around the dialogue structure and the individual country PAFs was originally very high. However, over time, these structures have become more and more overloaded, and pessimism about the ability of donors to live up to their commitments has grown more acute (see box 6.6).

In particular, fixing the goalposts across a number of different donor agencies has proved to be difficult. In practice, and despite what are often good intentions on the part of donor officials, it is difficult to coordinate and harmonize donor agencies—even those willingly engaging in budget support (Bourguignon and Platteau 2015). Across all four countries, respondents repeatedly noted that, despite their best efforts, it was difficult to keep the PAFs from becoming overloaded with narrow and specialized donor demands. Instead of a streamlined document with clear targets and assessment indicators, respondents complained that PAFs became over time a "Christmas tree" upon which donors hung their various demands and pet interests.

GBS is pooled funding. This is what gives donor agencies greater leverage, as it allows them to pressure recipient governments as a collective body. However, narrow donor-specific needs and wishes can easily lead to an abundance of

---

Box 6.6   Moving the goalposts

At stake is the Paris Declaration of 2005, in which donors and recipient countries struck a deal: recipient countries would tackle corruption, strengthen their institutions and take other steps to better manage aid. In return, donors would improve the coordination and predictability of their aid flows and give developing countries greater control over how the money is spent.

Six years later, only one side has kept to its bargain. The O.E.C.D.'s latest monitoring report shows that developing countries have made "significant" progress, particularly in improving their planning and financial management. But donors have disappointed in 12 out of their 13 targets, making significant progress in only one, that of improving coordination between themselves.

So how have they responded? Like a five-year-old losing a kick-around in the park. Rather than trying harder, they change the rules.

—Jeremy Hobbs, executive director of Oxfam International, "Moving the Goal Posts," op-ed, *New York Times*, November 21, 2011

(emphasis added)

requests and demands, which overburdens the dialogue.[50] Importantly, donor officials frequently underscored that they understood it was important to keep donor demands narrow and strategic in order to be able to exercise greater policy influence on the government. Yet, at the same time, many donor officials seemed somewhat resigned to increasing donor demands, repeatedly mentioning variable donor interests as an explanation for the overburdening of the PAF and the policy dialogue more broadly.

Consequently, whether or not budget support has actually led to a reduction in transaction costs for recipient governments is hotly debated among practitioners. Some argue that compared to the alternative, budget support clearly reduces transaction costs for the recipient government. Others argue that the extensive policy dialogue structures that have emerged to manage budget support are often very heavy and merely add to (rather than replace) previous structures.[51] Still others argue that transaction costs decreased for a time but then increased again toward the end of the decade.[52] What is clear, however, is that budget support has not met the expectations of either donor agencies or recipient governments in terms of reduced transaction costs and that, from the recipient government's perspective, the goalposts are anything but fixed.

As a Tanzanian government official explained, over time many donor agencies increased the number of tranches used to disburse budget support in a given year. Instead of giving budget support as a lump sum at the beginning of the year, as originally promised, donor agencies increasingly began delivering budget support in installments often directly tied to performance (so-called performance tranches). At the same time, many donor agencies have opted to give more sector budget support—by its very nature more targeted—and have added more and more conditionalities to its disbursement.[53] As a government official in Tanzania explained to me, all of this demands more meetings and makes it more difficult to implement agreed-on actions on time. The government therefore now often finds itself in the situation where donor agencies continue to add requirements long after such agreements are supposedly fixed. According to a colleague, this means that the type of funding that is currently being offered is not actually budget support, as it was originally agreed. In his opinion, the aid modality is being corrupted as an exit strategy for donor agencies.[54]

AID (UN)PREDICTABILITY

Along with fixed goalposts, recipient governments were promised more predictable aid. In its heyday, aid given via budget support does appear to have been more predictable than other forms of aid. The government of Rwanda reported that in FY 2011/12 (right before budget support's crash), general budget support had a predictability rate of 93 percent, while sector budget support had a predictability rate of 92 percent. Alternatively, project support was only 88 percent predictable, with (financial) project aid provided via loans being only 38 percent predictable (Republic of Rwanda 2013b).[55] Similarly, an evaluation of budget support in Tanzania from FY 2005/6 to FY 2011/12 claimed that annual disbursements from projects and basket funds would have been 20–25 percent less predictable than budget support and much more volatile (European Commission et al. 2013).

However, what development practitioners seemed to underestimate is that, perhaps even more than other aid modalities, budget support is vulnerable to political shifts in donor countries. Budget support may have the advantage of being released in large tranches, but as one development consultant put it, the aid delivery mechanism is prone to "political accidents." Although budget support ratios are generally more predictable, you still have the issue of commitments being honored, because there is no one to *enforce* the disbursement.[56]

This challenge became very clear in the case of the abrupt suspensions in Rwanda and Uganda, which left the governments in an incredibly difficult situation. In the case of Rwanda, grant budget support went from being 91 percent predictable in FY 2011/12 to 49 percent predictable in FY 2012/13 (Republic of Rwanda 2013b, 2013c).[57] In both Rwanda and Uganda, the suspension of budget support left a major financing gap in the government's budget. In some cases, salaries of civil servants went unpaid for several months (Akello and Rugambwa 2013).

Consistent with the core argument of this book, recipient governments portray the suspension of budget support as a violation of the commitments made to them by donor agencies.[58] Shortly after the suspension, the Rwandan Central Bank governor, Claver Gatete, was quoted in the *Economist* as saying that the suspension of funds already promised was a gross betrayal, and that Rwanda has lost its ability to make the best use of foreign assistance (*Economist* 2013). Similarly, in Uganda, government officials expressed widespread frustration about the suspension. Frustration was particularly high because the fraud was discovered and reported to donor agencies by the Ugandan government itself. Many Ugandan government officials therefore believed that they were being punished for upholding their side of the bargain: for working hard to stamp out corruption. As one government official put it, "We were the victims of our own success."[59]

Donor officials argue that these events constituted a breach of the underlying principles of budget support, and as a result, the withholding of aid funds by donor agencies is perfectly legitimate (and within the parameters of the negotiated agreement). However, there is plenty of evidence that maintaining commitments to releasing budget support funds had over time become harder and harder for donor agencies, even without a major scandal. Back in 2012, a donor official in Tanzania complained to me that that each year he fights the battle with his headquarters to live up to their commitments. In theory, budget support is released based on the previous year's assessment. Approximately sixty days after the final report is produced, donor agencies have to commit to providing a set amount of budget support for the coming fiscal year. Therefore "when it comes time to disburse, there shouldn't be a whole lot of other questions."[60] This is, however, rarely how disbursement actually proceeds.[61] In practice, current events frequently interfered with long-standing disbursement promises.

Toward the end of the first decade of the century, it became more and more difficult to justify budget support in donor countries because of several events exogenous to development cooperation. Most significantly, a financial crisis resulted in a tightening of aid budgets across Europe and more demands on donor agencies.[62] As donor countries were forced to tighten their belts, budget support was increasingly put on the chopping block.

In the case of Uganda, for example, it is clear that the European financial crisis exacerbated calls to suspend aid following the discovery of fraud in the Office of the Prime Minister.[63] The majority of the stolen aid funds came from Ireland, which was particularly hard hit by the crisis. For several days after the scandal broke, the Irish papers were filled with news articles and editorials about the missing aid funds. As a respondent noted, the scandal came at a time "where public finances were under such constraints and where aid is such the topic of debate." According to him, whereas in 2003 or 2005 the events would not have made very many waves, the current political context propelled consolidated action.[64]

At the same time, in several donor countries, more conservative governments less favorable to budget support (and foreign aid in general) assumed power. As a result, some donor agencies were forced to withdraw from their budget support commitments for reasons entirely unrelated to the aid modality's performance. For example, despite a critical assessment of the Tanzanian government in 2009–2010, the Netherlands still planned to enter into a new general budget support commitment, because development practitioners still saw the value in the aid modality. However, then a new Dutch government, which was much more critical of budget support, was elected, and the GBS mechanism was suspended. Thus, the decision not to continue providing budget support "was not a consequence of those earlier developments. . . . It was a new decision and based rather on the reassessment of budget support as a modality."[65]

This is not a story unique to the Netherlands or to Tanzania. Respondents in all four countries of the study told a similar tale. Referring to international agreements signed as a follow-up to the 2005 Paris Declaration on Aid Effectiveness, one respondent noted that "the basic problem of Accra and Busan is . . . the erratic behavior of the politicians in the donor countries."[66] Similarly, another donor official said that in the future his agency may not be able to give GBS, "not because we have negative experience or a negative evaluation, but simply because there are other priorities at home that are higher than the GBS."[67] Instead, in the future his agency was likely to offer Tanzania more financing to deal with climate change and money for renewable energy.

It is important to note that donor officials working at the recipient-country level are not only aware of how frustrating the lack of predictability can be for recipient governments, but also recognize that this is backtracking on agreed-on compromises. Speaking about the suspension in Uganda in particular, one donor official, for example, said, "Yeah, they were not happy. . . . It's not predictable. So that means we agree on this reform, and then suddenly something happened, [and] you said, 'No, we suspend the thing.'"[68] Similarly, a donor official in Tanzania noted that the "predictability or commitment must be very, very unclear to governments." He went on to explain that unfortunately aid is "not really linked exclusively or in a very straightforward way to performance. Donor agencies often argue that if a recipient government performs better, it will be rewarded. Some donor officials like to believe this, and sometimes we are able to follow through. However, often it is other things back home that are driving the shifts."[69]

It is also important to underscore that while recipient governments prefer budget support to other aid modalities, this preference is based on donor agencies fulfilling certain promises. Governments are willing to make concessions to donors *in exchange* for budget support. However, as a government official in Tanzania noted, donors cannot stop providing GBS and "expect continual engagement with government."[70] What makes budget support valuable for recipient governments is the presumed degree of predictability. As a donor official remarked in Uganda, without that predictability, the government's willingness to engage in the aid modality decreases. He said that, out of frustration, the Ministry of Finance recently indicated that "if the budget support carries on this unpredictability, you better forget about the budget support."[71] Following the suspension of budget support in Rwanda, the government simply refused to participate in the Budget Support Harmonization Group. Donors strongly protested, saying that they would lose an important forum with government. However, the government's position was absolute: without a guarantee of budget support for the foreseeable future, donors should not expect special access to government.

A LACK OF RESULTS

While donor officials frequently admitted that they were often unable to live up to their promises, they were also quick to point out deficiencies in progress toward reforms by recipient governments, expressing disappointment about what their participation in budget support actually bought them. As a respondent in Tanzania noted, donor agencies had a lot riding on the reforms that they were pushing via budget support, and there was disappointment when such reforms were slow to come about.[72]

Budget support has some important advantages: a seat at the table, a louder voice, and a license to ask questions. However, just like previous aid delivery mechanisms, it lacks strong enforcement mechanisms. As a donor representative in Ghana noted, there is no guarantee of results with budget support (or any aid delivery mechanism, for that matter). You can push an agenda, but then you have to step back and rely on the recipient government to implement it.[73] Budget support can help you to gain traction with a particular reform agenda, but it cannot guarantee implementation.

It is often extremely difficult (if not impossible) for donor officials to measure a recipient government's commitment to enacting agreed-on reforms. Budget support did not solve this issue. Through increased dialogue and political influence, donor agencies hoped to be able to better gauge the government's willingness to take on particular reforms. They also hoped to force the recipient government to make more explicit and public commitments that could be credibly measured. However, even if a recipient government expresses willingness to take on a reform, it may not be able to credibly commit to reform. As a donor official remarked, in the case of Uganda, his worry is not political will but rather political commitment. Discussing corruption in particular, he noted that many in the current government are actually willing to address corruption. However, "when it comes to commit, they will think of the vote."[74] In other words, even if government officials are in favor of reforms, the political obstacles for implementation are often great.

Sustainability in Aid Delivery

You might be wondering at this point whether the policy compromise on which budget support was based was entirely unrealistic to begin with. Given their long track record of working with recipient governments, surely donor officials would not voluntarily put so much faith into recipient governments. Were they really so surprised by the corruption cases or the lack of movement on key reforms? At the same time, government officials were not born yesterday. Surely they understood that the promises made by donor officials under the guise of ownership and aid effectiveness were grandiose and ultimately unattainable.

My argument is not that this is untrue, but rather that, owing to the nature of development cooperation, the two parties need to work together. Donor agencies and recipient governments remain intricately linked—whether they like it or not. Even if donor agencies have the upper hand in negotiations, they rely on recipient governments in order to implement aid programs successfully. For their part, recipient governments heavily depend on the aid money donor agencies provide. The result is that both parties must to some degree take a leap of faith and work together, despite long-standing pessimism about the credibility of donor and government commitments.

It is also precisely because donor agencies and recipient governments have been working together for decades and thus understand how hard it is for the other side to make credible commitments that they are constantly seeking out innovations that promise to help reduce commitment problems—on both sides. These institutional innovations, however, will not be politically sustainable over the long term if they are ultimately unenforceable. Budget support promised each side something it wanted. This was appealing to both parties and hence contributed to the popularity of the aid delivery mechanism at the outset. Because, however, it lacked self-enforcing mechanisms to ensure that each party kept its promises, it was ultimately unsustainable.

Given the frequency of fallings-out between donor agencies and recipient governments, it is not surprising that one often hears donor and government officials speak of "highs" and "lows" in the relationship between donor agencies and a recipient government. In each of the four countries, there are narratives about the current status of the relationship, as well as narratives about high points and low points in the past. These narratives do not appear to be based on any objective feature of the relationship (e.g., aid volumes). Rather they are based on the perception of a strong commitment by the other side at a particular point in time. As a donor official in Tanzania put it, the aid system is based on trust and good-quality dialogue. This means commitments on both sides. "If you don't have this, you get into a very difficult situation."[75] Unfortunately, strong commitments are hard to come by, and trust is often undermined.

7

THE FUTURE OF THE DEVELOPMENT DANCE AND WHY WE SHOULD CARE

> **We are not newcomers, we know the reality. . . . So, we say, "Okay, we agree." But we know we will face difficulties. But we will continue, hoping that someday things will get better.**
> —Bilateral donor official, April 10, 2013, Ghana

In this book, I told the story of the development dance, a seemingly never-ending process of bargaining and negotiation between donor agencies and recipient-country governments. It is a dance that both partners willingly join. But it is a dance that leaves neither side particularly satisfied. Time and time again, donor and recipient government officials enter into new arrangements, adopting new aid policies and practices with the hope that this time their hard-fought compromises will be politically sustainable. However, again and again, both parties are left disappointed, as compromises break down and have to be renegotiated. The breakdown of aid policy compromises is so ubiquitous in development cooperation that most development practitioners see it as an evitable part of the aid system. As one donor official in Uganda told me, "There [will] always be a fallout, and people will always be frustrated on both sides. But then again, what is the alternative? . . . You need to make it work."[1]

In the previous chapters, I looked back in time. In this final chapter, I look forward into the future. I ask what it might take to "make it work." I also ask how my findings might be affected by recent events, including the rise of China as a foreign aid donor and declining rates of aid dependence in some African countries. I do not offer any simple solutions or answers. Instead, I aim to begin a conversation about how we might go about building a system of delivering aid that is more politically sustainable. Above all, I hope to convince you that we need to spend the time and energy to "make it work."

1

Theoretical Findings (and Why They Matter to Practitioners)

This book aims to contribute to our understanding of foreign aid in two key ways. First, quite simply, I have sought to extend our understanding of relations between donor agencies and recipient-country governments. Analyses of donor–government relations are surprisingly scarce and have almost exclusively focused on the problem of delegating aid delivery (i.e., principal-agent problems). My research advances our understanding of what donor agencies and recipient governments bargain and negotiate over and how these negotiations affect choices regarding how foreign aid is actually delivered to beneficiaries in recipient countries.

Second, I have sought to shed light on a pressing question for international development: What determines the political sustainability of aid delivery mechanisms? To the frustration of individual development actors, historically, different aid delivery mechanisms have come into and fallen out of fashion. Not only does this constant reinvention lead to fatigue and feelings of frustration about foreign aid among practitioners and the general public alike, it also means that we rarely have time to evaluate whether a particular way of delivering aid is actually effective before global attention shifts toward the next big thing.

In this book, I have shown that there is an underlying logic to these relentless changes in aid delivery tools. This logic is apparent only if we unpack donor–government relations at the recipient-country level. Because donor and government officials foresee problems with commitment, they will seek out innovations that promise to help with commitment problems. However, if an aid delivery mechanism is not able to efficiently limit commitment problems over the long term—that is, past an initial period of enthusiasm over the negotiated compromise—the aid delivery mechanism is unlikely to be politically sustainable and will eventually fall by the wayside in favor of new approaches and tactics.

Importantly, this means that how aid is delivered is determined not only by what is most effective, but also by the desire to limit commitment problems. If we want to know whether an aid delivery mechanism is likely to be sustained over the long term, we should look not only at whether it actually leads to socioeconomic development. We need to look also at whether it induces credible commitments from both donor agencies and recipient governments. My findings also suggest that until we are able to solve commitment problems on both the donor and recipient sides, we will continue to see fads and fashions in the delivery of foreign aid.

Future research should continue to break open the black box of aid, extending the basic model of aid policy bargaining put forth in this book by addressing important subsidiary questions, such as: How do variations in the design of aid agencies affect the types of aid policy compromises reached by donor agencies and recipient governments? Are certain agencies able to make more credible promises than others, and why? It will also be important to test the theories advanced in these pages to contexts outside Africa. I believe that my core ideas will be broadly applicable to other countries and regions. However, the only way to verify if this is the case is to test my arguments in other regional contexts.

In future research, it will also be important to consider what can actually be done to limit commitment problems in foreign aid. Important questions raised but unable to be answered by my research include: Is there an inherent trade-off between donor and recipient commitment problems? That is, does solving one, lead to the other? What happens if and when donors actually follow through with threats to suspend aid? Can we change the institutional design of donor agencies to help limit commitment problems?

Lessons for Practitioners (and Why They Should Matter to Theorists)

For policy makers, my findings suggest that designing better ways of delivering aid requires us to address not only the difficulty of getting recipient governments to uphold their promises to foreign aid donors, but also the problem of getting donor agencies to live up to their commitments to recipient governments. In other words, it is not just about "building a better mousetrap" for recipient governments (Radelet and Levine 2008), but also about incentivizing donor agencies to live up to their own commitments. As Pomerantz puts it, "Everyone must understand—donors and government alike—that they are playing the same game while on the same team. The rules can't change during the game, and players can't miss practice, be late for the game, or drift on and off the field" (2004, 133). This is, of course, easier said than done.

Over time, donor agencies and recipient governments have made important strides in improving the measurability of both donor and recipient commitments. Initiatives like aid management systems ask donor agencies to make their promises regarding aid volumes explicit to recipient governments. This allows recipient governments to at least measure what they should be receiving in terms of foreign aid dollars. Similarly, assessment frameworks, which explicitly lay out the conditions for the disbursement of aid, formalize both donor and government promises in a way that is measurable for both parties.[2]

What remains a persistent problem, however, is enforcement. Even if donor agencies and recipient governments make a good-faith effort to keep their promises, and even if their commitments are measurable, if they are not enforceable, competing pressures will eventually undermine the commitments made by both sides. Exogenous shocks like a refugee crises in Europe will undermine the commitments made by donors to recipients, and political pressures in recipient countries will continue to overrule the promises made by recipient-government leaders to foreign aid donors.

For aid delivery mechanisms to be self-sustaining over the long term, both parties need to have an incentive to keep their commitments—either because internally they find it more valuable to fulfill their commitments than to pull back, or because enforcement from a third party increases the costs of retracting. It is up to policy makers to innovate in order to solve the problem of enforcement, and it is up to theorists to test whether these innovations actually work.

Is Results-Based Aid Sustainable?

The empirical portion of this book focused on the shift toward and then away from one innovation, general budget support, arguing that the compromise upon which budget support rested was ultimately unsustainable. At the close of this book, it is useful to apply my theory to a more recent innovation, results-based aid (RBA).[3] Just as with budget support, there is a great deal of contestation over what should be classified at RBA, but a defining feature of the approach is that aid is disbursed according to a prespecified "unit price" only *after* specific results have been achieved (Klingebiel and Janus 2014). In Rwanda, for example, the UK's DFID committed to making an annual payment to the government calculated on the number of additional children who take a series of national-level exams.[4] This is not the first time donors have used "ex post conditionality." However, more recently, it has clearly become much more popular—and much more mainstream—to deliver aid in this way.

The shift toward RBA is consistent with my argument that as negotiated compromises break down, donor agencies will be drawn to institutional innovations that promise to help reduce commitment problems in the bargaining relationship between donor agencies and recipient governments. It is also consistent with a historical pattern in which the pendulum has swung back and forth between emphasizing *donor* commitment problems and *recipient* commitment problems. Structural-adjustment policies emphasized recipient commitment problems, attempting to extract reforms from recipient governments via conditionality-laced loans. Budget support took a different approach, easing the formal conditionality requirements in favor of a more predictable flow of aid based on a commitment by donors to not shift the goalposts on recipient countries. With the rising popularity of RBA, the pendulum is swinging back toward a focus on the challenge of getting recipients to uphold their part of the bargain, emphasizing aid in exchange for results.

As a tool of development, RBA has both pros and cons.[5] What is most interesting for our purposes, however, is whether RBA offers a viable solution for reducing commitment problems between donor agencies and recipient governments. The approach tries to remove donor agencies from the messiness of development assistance, rewarding recipients only when they meet the conditions of negotiated contracts. RBA, in principle, binds recipients and donors in a contractual relationship where the indicators and the rewards are explicitly laid out for both parties. In this way, RBA does appear to improve the measurability of both donor and recipient commitments. At the same time, it also appears to make it easier for donor agencies to enforce promises by recipients. Take the program mentioned in Rwanda. In this case, the Rwandan government is rewarded with aid only if the number of students taking the national exam actually increases.

However, the aid delivery mechanism does little to address donor commitment problems. Under results-based aid, the ability of recipient governments to *enforce* the commitments made by donors—either to a specific project or to the aid delivery mechanism more broadly—is still very limited. As with other types of aid, often these agreements are based on memorandums of understanding that are not legal binding. And even if there is a contract in place that guarantees the recipient a certain amount of aid in exchange for a particular result, there is no guarantee that the contract will be renewed. As a result, a recipient cannot be assured that the donor will not shift the goalposts in the future. The recipient is being asked to recalculate its development program in accordance with objectives that may or may not be around for that long. At the same time, because donor agencies face a pressure to disburse, it is also uncertain whether poor performance will actually result in fewer aid dollars. Perhaps the donor will simply opt to deliver the aid in another way if the recipient does not deliver on its promises. A smart government would hedge its bets and invest only minimally in donor demands.

Accordingly, despite measurable results and a tentative enforcement mechanism, the negotiated compromises reached by the two parties are still constrained by commitment problems. If donor agencies want to incentivize recipient governments to put their full force behind the initiative, governments need to be assured that the donor agency is committed to the program for more than a single funding cycle. They also need to know that donor agencies will actually disburse according to the agreed-on conditions. Without these assurances, there is little (external) incentive for recipient governments to truly invest in the desired reforms. It would therefore be unrealistic to assume that aid agencies will be any more successful at coaxing reform out of recipient governments than under previous approaches. This suggests that over time, disappointment in the aid delivery mechanism will likely build, leading the two parties to question its value and to continue to be on the lookout for "new" aid delivery mechanisms that are more efficient at solving commitment problems.

What Happens If the Bargaining Power of Traditional Donors Declines?

As we look into the future, a fundamental question facing donor–government relations in some (although certainly not all) countries in sub-Saharan Africa is whether we are at a critical juncture in which the bargaining power of traditional donor agencies is declining, and, if so, how this might affect relations between the two parties in the future. The theoretical framework I outlined in chapter 2 rests on the basic premise that negotiations between donor agencies and recipient governments are best characterized as being mutually cooperative. It does not assume, however, that the two parties enter the negotiations on equal footing. Donor agencies rely on recipient governments for implementation, while recipient governments rely on donor agencies for survival.

If recipient governments are less reliant on aid funds, they may be able to more effectively push back against donor demands, reducing how much donors are able to ask for in exchange for foreign aid dollars. If this is the case, it will likely become even *more* important for donor agencies to be able to credibly commit to delivering aid as promised. In contexts where donors are less and less salient, to continue to exert influence, donors will need to make their aid more attractive to recipient governments. Increasing the credibility of aid promises is one way to do this.

To consider how this might play out in practice, let's examine two potential alternative sources of revenue for the countries where I conducted fieldwork: development financing from China and revenue from newly discovered natural resources.

China in Africa

In recent years, a great deal of discussion—both in the popular press and in the academic scholarship—has emerged on the growing importance of "nontraditional" donors, particularly China, in Africa (e.g., Alden 2007; Bräutigam 2009; Rotberg 2008).[6] Estimates of the total value of Chinese development assistance to Africa vary widely and are prone to exaggeration.[7] Nonetheless, it is clear that China is heavily investing in at least some parts of Africa. This has led some to predict that the bargaining power of traditional donors vis-à-vis recipient governments is declining (e.g., Mohan and Power 2008; Reisen and Stijns 2011; Woods 2010).

We should be careful about assuming that China is actually drastically changing relations between traditional donors and recipient governments in Africa (Swedlund 2017b). ODA still vastly outpaces official finance from China in most African countries (Dreher et al. 2014; Quadir 2013). Chinese aid also works very differently than traditional foreign aid. Most Chinese assistance goes to Chinese companies engaged in the productive sectors, meaning it is often more comparable to foreign direct investment than traditional ODA (Bräutigam 2011; Kragelund 2008). This means that most African governments court *both* ODA and Chinese financing, seeing them as complements rather than competitors (ECOSOC 2008; Kragelund 2010; Swedlund 2017b).

It is worth, however, briefly exploring why Chinese aid is so appealing to recipient governments. When Chinese aid does compete with traditional foreign aid, for example in the case of large infrastructure projects like dams and roads, it is often more appealing to African governments (Swedlund 2017b). Why is this? My conversations with recipient-government officials in Uganda, Tanzania, and Ghana suggest that Chinese assistance is particularly appealing for reasons consistent with the core argument of this book: Chinese financial assistance is not perceived to suffer from as many commitment problems as traditional development assistance.

Over and over, government officials told me that they prefer Chinese aid because it is perceived to be quicker to materialize and has fewer strings attached. Conceding that interest rates from the World Bank are typically better than those provided by China, one Ghanaian government official, for example, emphasized that the value of Chinese assistance is that the Chinese deliver on their promises. Giving the example of the Bui Dam on the Black Volta river, he explained that the dam was a World Bank project for years but never actually got built. In contrast, after the Chinese took over the project, construction on the dam "started very fast."[8] Similarly, a frequent consultant for the Ugandan government emphasized that the Karuma Dam on the Victoria Nile had been in the works for many years but had never come to fruition. Once the Chinese took over the project, construction quickly began.[9]

As critics rightly point out, Chinese assistance is often much swifter, because it lacks socioeconomic and environmental safeguards required by traditional donors (Alden 2005; Moss and Rose 2006; Taylor 2006; Tull 2006). What matters most to recipient governments, however, is that the project is actually completed—and quickly. It is clearly a dominant perception among many recipient-government officials that the Chinese are much faster than traditional donors at getting things done. One donor official recounted going to the Tanzanian Investment Centre and having it explained to him that, if a traditional donor wants to build a road in 2012, the process needs to start in 2007. If the Chinese are going to build the same road, they start in 2011, and it is finished in 2012. The same official noted that, in Tanzania, the Chinese are proposing to build a natural gas pipeline in three years.[10] With his institution it would take fifteen years—and in the end might not even get built.[11] In recipient countries, there is the clear perception that Chinese development promises are more credible than promises from traditional donors.

Increasing Domestic Revenues from Natural Resources

Another, even more important, source of alternative financing is newly discovered natural resources: oil in Ghana and Uganda and natural gas in Tanzania. In these countries, at least some donor officials fear that current or anticipated revenue from natural resources will, over time, decrease their agency's leverage with the recipient government.

Take for example Ghana, where oil revenues are already flowing, and ODA as a percentage of GNI is rapidly decreasing. In 2004, ODA was over 16 percent of Ghana's GNI. Just ten years later, in 2014, it was only 3.1 percent. As one respondent put it, while aid remains important for capital, "they [the Ghanaian government] could run the country without us."[12] According to some respondents, increased domestic revenue—whether from oil or other sources—is already changing how much leverage donors have over the government of Ghana.[13]

In Tanzania, several donor officials also expressed uncertainty about the future, noting that future earnings from natural gas and increasing net inflows of FDI have the potential to change the dynamics between donor officials and recipient governments. According to one donor official, quite a bit of time remains before the government of Tanzania has enough money to totally replace aid. However, in not so many years, we will see a significant increase in FDI, which will "change a lot of the premises for some of the dialogue and interaction."[14] For another donor official, this coming shift represents a window of opportunity to "out-build systems and strengthen the government stability and get some accountability," because it will become more and more difficult for donor agencies to leverage policy influence in the future.[15]

Even in Uganda, where oil has not yet come on line, and where it is uncertain how much money is at stake, many believe that the promise of oil has made the government less keen to bargain with donor agencies. One respondent, for example, told me that the oil find shifted the dynamics between the government and donor agencies, particularly in light of the 2012 aid suspension. According to him, the government is angry about the suspension and does not want to get back to the way things were before. Oil gives the government the opportunity to move away from a dependency on foreign assistance.[16] In the words of one civil society representative, the promise of oil allows the government to "limp" along without donor money until oil starts to flow.[17]

Ultimately, we should be careful about speculating about what is, after all, a relatively unknown future. China's presence on the continent, at least in regard to aid, is prone to exaggeration, and oil revenues are notoriously volatile. It is also not the first time "Africa's rise" has been predicted, and in many countries—including Rwanda—aid dependence remains very high. After failing to raise the necessary funds on the capital market, Ghana, for example, was forced to take a $918 million extended credit facility loan from the IMF in 2015.[18]

However, whether such changes arrive soon or in the distant future, donor agencies working in these contexts should prepare for a time where aid constitutes a smaller and smaller percentage of national budgets and they have less and less leverage over recipient governments. To stay relevant, donor agencies will need to increase the attractiveness of their aid. My findings suggest that one way to make aid more attractive is to increase the credibility of aid promises. If donor agencies are able to provide foreign aid predictability without moving the goalposts, the assistance offered by donor agencies may continue to be valuable and thus useful for gaining policy leverage—even if it is a smaller and smaller part of national budgets. However, if aid remains haphazard and unpredictable, recipient governments, if given the choice, would be wise to seek greener pastures elsewhere.

Final Remarks

For scholars of foreign aid, my findings suggest that aid policy is the result of a negotiated compromise between donor agencies and recipient governments, in which the agreements reached are constrained by commitment problems. This can affect choices in aid delivery mechanisms, and also means that the negotiated compromises between donor agencies and recipient governments are bound to break down over time. Theoretically, this means that we cannot continue to assume that aid policy is inherently designed to be effective, but rather we must unpack processes of bargaining and negotiation between donor agencies and recipient governments, paying close attention to the constraints faced by both parties.

For development practitioners, my findings suggest that designing politically sustainable aid delivery mechanisms requires us to think through how to concretely address commitment problems in the bargaining relations between donor agencies and recipient governments. Building aid delivery mechanisms that will last beyond an initial period of enthusiasm requires us to design institutions that incentivize *both* donor agencies and recipient governments to live up to their commitments. While this is no doubt likely to be challenging, it is also a way forward. Instead of complacently assuming that fads and fashions will always rule the day, by focusing on designing institutions that explicitly address commitment problems, we can begin the arduous process of building more politically sustainable ways of delivering foreign aid.

For all those who are interested in foreign aid more generally, my findings suggest that aid is always negotiated, and that these negotiations affect the way foreign aid is actually delivered to beneficiaries. If we want to improve the delivery of foreign aid, we have to break open the black box of donor–government relations. We should care about not just where aid is allocated, but how it is delivered and the conditions attached to it. We should also care about whether the agreements between donor agencies and recipient governments are sustainable over time.

APPENDIX 1. LIST OF INTERVIEWS

GHANA	DATE	ORGANIZATION
1	April 2013	Netherlands Embassy in Accra
2	April 2013	World Bank
3	April 2013	African Development Bank
4	April 2013	Embassy of Japan
5	April 2013	European Union
6	April 2013	Danish International Development Agency
7	April 2013	Ministry of Finance and Economic Planning
8	April 2013	Ministry of Finance and Economic Planning
9	April 2013	United Nations Development Programme
10	April 2013	Kreditanstalt für Wiederaufbau (KfW)
11	April 2013	UK Department for International Development
12	April 2013	National Development Planning Commission
13	April 2013	Ministry of Finance and Economic Planning
14	April 2013	IMANI Centre for Policy and Education
15	April 2013	Ministry of Finance and Economic Planning
16	April 2013	Centre for Democracy and Development
17	April 2013	Korea International Cooperation Agency
18	April 2013	Institute for Democratic Governance
19	May 2013	Canadian International Development Agency
20	May 2013	Embassy of Switzerland
UGANDA	**DATE**	**ORGANIZATION**
1	Sept. 2013	U.S. Agency for International Development
2	Sept. 2013	Centre for Performance Management and Evaluative Research
3	Sept. 2013	European Union
4	Sept. 2013	UK Department for International Development

(Continued)

UGANDA	DATE	ORGANIZATION
5	Sept. 2013	United Nations Development Programme
6	Sept. 2013	Danish International Development Agency
7	Sept. 2013	Japan International Cooperation Agency
8	Sept. 2013	Independent consultant
9	Sept. 2013	Kreditanstalt für Wiederaufbau (KfW)
10	Sept. 2013	Irish Aid
11	Sept. 2013	Office of the Prime Minister
12	Sept. 2013	Office of the Prime Minister
13	Sept. 2013	Civil Society Budget Advocacy Group
14	Sept. 2013	Ministry of Finance, Planning, and Economic Development
15	Oct. 2013	European Union
16	Oct. 2013	Economic Policy Research Centre
17	Oct. 2013	Makarare University, Department of Political Science
18	Oct. 2013	Reeve Consulting
19	Oct. 2013	Italian Development Cooperation
20	Oct. 2013	Ministry of Finance, Planning, and Economic Development
21	Oct. 2013	African Development Bank
22	Oct. 2013	Korea International Cooperation Agency
23	Oct. 2013	Danish International Development Agency
24	Oct. 2013	Action Aid
25	Oct. 2013	World Bank
26	Oct. 2013	World Bank
27	Oct. 2013	Embassy of Austria
28	Oct. 2013	Embassy of Sweden
29	Oct. 2013	National Planning Authority
30	Oct. 2013	Embassy of the Kingdom of Belgium

RWANDA	DATE	ORGANIZATION
1	Oct. 2009	Kreditanstalt für Wiederaufbau (KfW)
2	Oct. 2009	U.S. Agency for International Development
3	Oct. 2009	Swedish International Development Cooperation Agency
4	Oct. 2009	Rwanda Governance Advisory Council
5	Oct. 2009	United Nations Development Programme
6	Oct. 2009	Swedish International Development Cooperation Agency
7	Nov. 2009	Norwegian People's Aid
8	Nov. 2009	Search for Common Ground
9	Nov. 2009	Rwandan Governance Advisory Council
10	Nov. 2009	European Commission
11	Nov. 2009	Department of International Development
12	Nov. 2009	United Nations Development Programme / Rwanda National Parliament
13	Nov. 2009	United Nations Development Programme
14	Nov. 2009	Rwanda Governance Advisory Council
15	Nov. 2009	Swedish International Development Cooperation Agency
16	Nov. 2009	Ministry for Local Government
17	Nov. 2009	European Commission
18	Nov. 2009	U.S. Agency for International Development
19	Nov. 2009	African Development Bank
20	Nov. 2009	Canadian International Development Agency
21	Nov. 2009	World Bank
22	Nov. 2009	Ministry of Finance and Economic Planning
23	June 2010	Ministry of Finance and Economic Planning
24	June 2010	Ministry of Finance and Economic Planning
25	June 2010	Rwanda Civil Society Platform

RWANDA	DATE	ORGANIZATION
26	June 2010	Institute for Research and Dialogue for Peace
27	June 2010	Ministry of Finance and Economic Planning
28	June 2010	Rwanda Governance Advisory Council
29	June 2010	Rwanda Governance Advisory Council
30	June 2010	U.S. Agency for International Development
31	June 2010	World Bank
32	June 2010	UK Department for International Development
33	June 2010	United Nations Development Programme
34	June 2010	Netherlands Embassy in Kigali
35	June 2010	Embassy of Belgium in Rwanda
36	June 2010	Action Aid
37	June 2010	Independent consultant
38	June 2010	Kreditanstalt für Wiederaufbau (KfW)
39	June 2010	Japan International Cooperation Agency
40	June 2010	Japan International Cooperation Agency
41	June 2010	Norwegian People's Aid
42	June 2010	United Nations Development Programme
43	July 2010	Ministry of Finance and Economic Planning
44	July 2010	Trocaire
45	July 2010	Kreditanstalt für Wiederaufbau (KfW)
46	Oct. 2013	European Commission
47	Oct. 2013	Kreditanstalt für Wiederaufbau (KfW)
48	Oct. 2013	Ministry of Finance and Economic Planning
49	Oct. 2013	Netherlands Embassy in Kigali

TANZANIA	DATE	ORGANIZATION
1	May 2012	Development Partners Group
2	May 2012	Netherlands Embassy in Dar es Salaam
3	May 2012	Embassy of Denmark, Tanzania
4	May 2012	Foundation for Civil Society
5	May 2012	Kreditanstalt für Wiederaufbau (KfW)
6	May 2012	Gesellschaft für Internationale Zusammenarbeit (GiZ)
7	May 2012	European Commission
8	June 2012	GBS Secretariat
9	June 2012	Netherlands Embassy in Dar es Salaam
10	June 2012	Irish Aid
11	June 2012	Planning Commission, President's Office
12	June 2012	Swedish International Development Cooperation Agency
13	June 2012	U.S. Agency for International Development
14	June 2012	Gesellschaft für Internationale Zusammenarbeit (GiZ)
15	June 2012	World Bank
16	June 2012	GBS Secretariat
17	June 2012	Norwegian Agency for Development Cooperation
18	June 2012	African Development Bank
19	June 2012	Economic and Social Research Foundation
20	June 2012	World Bank
21	June 2012	Policy Forum
22	June 2012	Independent consultant / Economic and Social Research Foundation
23	June 2012	Research on Poverty Alleviation
24	June 2012	Ministry of Finance, External Finance Unit and MKUKUTA Department

(Continued)

TANZANIA	DATE	ORGANIZATION
25	July 2012	Japanese Embassy
26	July 2012	Canadian International Development Agency
27	July 2012	UK Department for International Development
28	Oct. 2013	Planning Commission, President's Office
29	Oct. 2013	Ministry of Finance, External Finance Unit
30	Oct. 2013	UK Department for International Development
31	Oct. 2013	Tanzania Association of NGOs
32	Oct. 2013	Embassy of the Republic of Germany
33	Oct. 2013	Bank of Tanzania
34	Oct. 2013	European Commission
35	March 2015	Ministry of Finance, External Finance Unit
36	March 2015	Development Partners Group
37	March 2015	African Development Bank

DESCRIPTION OF SURVEY SAMPLE

TABLE A.1 Countries included in the survey and response rates

	COUNTRY	ODA AS A PERCENT OF GNI (2000–2011)	SAMPLE SIZE	PARTICIPATED	RESPONSE RATE (%)
1st wave	Ghana	9.20	15	10	67
	Mozambique	25.00	21	10	48
	Uganda	13.28	15	8	53
	Rwanda	19.98	14	11	79
	Tanzania	12.76	21	11	52
2nd wave	Burundi	28.31	10	6	60
	Ethiopia	13.86	16	7	44
	Guinea	7.09	7	5	71
	Mauritania	13.53	8	4	50
	Zambia	15.04	15	7	47
3rd wave	Sierra Leone	30.37	6	3	50
	Niger	13.57	12	5	42
	Comoros	9.10	4	2	50
	Liberia	73.38	6	5	83
	Malawi	20.62	8	6	75
4th wave	Togo	7.20	5	2	40
	Chad	8.59	6	2	33
	Congo	6.92	5	3	60
	Ivory Coast	3.76	7	2	29
	Kenya	4.53	14	5	36
Total/average			**215**	**114**	**53**

TABLE A.2 Donor agencies represented in the survey

DONOR NAME	FREQUENCY
Australia	2
Austria	3
Belgium	3
Canada	1
Denmark	5
Finland	2
France	10
Germany	7
Ireland	6
Japan	7
Netherlands	4
Norway	3
South Korea	3
Spain	2
Sweden	4
Switzerland	4
United Kingdom	3
United States	4
Total bilateral	**73**
African Development Bank	10
European Commission	12
United Nations Development Programme	9
World Bank	6
Total multilateral	**37**
Total all	*114*

SURVEY PROTOCOL

Aid Effectiveness and Donor–Government Relations in Sub-Saharan Africa

Haley J. Swedlund, Principal Investigator
Radboud University Nijmegen

Dear [insert name],

Thank you very much for your willingness to participate in this survey on donor–government relations and aid coordination. This survey is part of a multi-country research project and will provide us with valuable data on how development cooperation operates not only in [Country] but globally.

All data collected through this survey will be kept anonymous by the research team. Your answers will not be associated with either your name or your agency. You are free to discontinue the survey at any time.

The survey should take you approximately 15 minutes to complete. You will be given space to provide feedback on the survey at its conclusion.

If you have questions about the survey or would like more information about the project, please feel free to contact the Principal Investigator:

Haley Swedlund, PhD
Assistant Professor
Radboud University Nijmegen (the Netherlands)
E: h.swedlund@fm.ru.nl
T: 0031 (0) 24361 5687

Thank you very much for your assistance!

Question 1

We would like to know more about your agency's country-level priorities. Please rank the following sectors in order of importance **for your agency in [Country].**

To rank, drag and drop the sectors in order of importance (1 = most important / 9 = least important).

Health
Public Financial Management and Public Sector Capacity
Private Sector Development and Extractive Industries
Education
Social Protection
Transport, Energy and Infrastructure
Water and Sanitation
Agriculture
Democratization, Human Rights and Civil Society Promotion

Question 2

Are there any other sectors that are similarly important for your agency in [Country] and not listed above?
[OPTIONS: Yes, No]
IF YES:
Please indicate what these specific sectors are: [WRITE-IN TEXT BOX]

Question 3

In your opinion, are the following sectors over-emphasized, just right or under-emphasized in your agency's development portfolio for [Insert] (as represented by funding, staff-time and attention paid to the topic)?

Please drag to the appropriate box.

Note: If a sector is not currently part of your agency's development portfolio, you may still rank it as "just right" if you think it is appropriately excluded or "under-emphasized" if you think more attention is needed.

[OPTIONS: Over-emphasized, Just Right, Under-emphasized]
Health
Public Financial Management and Public Sector Capacity
Private Sector Development and Extractive Industries
Education
Social Protection
Transport, Energy and Infrastructure
Water and Sanitation

Agriculture
Democratization, Human Rights and Civil Society Promotion

Question 4

In your opinion, are the following sectors over-emphasized, just right or under-emphasized in the policy dialogue between donors and the Government of [Country]? Please drag to the appropriate box.

Note: If a sector is not currently part of the policy dialogue, you may still rank it as "just right" if you think it is appropriately excluded or "under-emphasized" if you think more attention is needed.

[OPTIONS: Over-emphasized, Just Right, Under-emphasized]
Health
Public Financial Management and Public Sector Capacity
Private Sector Development and Extractive Industries
Education
Social Protection
Transport, Energy and Infrastructure
Water and Sanitation
Agriculture
Democratization, Human Rights and Civil Society Promotion

Question 5

How are your agency's country-level sector priorities formed? Please rank the following stakeholders in order of how much influence they have over your agency's country-level strategy in [Country].

To rank, drag and drop the stakeholders in order of influence (1 = most influential / 11 or 12 = least influential).

Note: Please use the "other" option to indicate if there are stakeholders other than those listed that are influential over your agency's country-level strategy.

Your home ministry and/or agency's headquarters
Domestic business interests in your home country or in your agency's member countries
International Civil Society
Civil Society in [Country]
Bilateral Donors in [Country]
Government of [Country]
Your agency's mission or country office
Multilateral Donors (including the European Commission) in [Country]

Domestic public opinion in your home country or in your agency's member
  countries
Parliament of [Country]
Local Government in [Country]
Other: [WRITE-IN TEXT BOX]

(Question was randomized.)

Question 6

Has your agency ever provided budget support (either sector or general) to
[Country]?

My agency currently provides budget support to [Country].

My agency provided budget support to [Country] in the past but no longer
  does so.

My agency has never provided budget support to [Country].

Question 7

*(Only if "My agency provides budget support" or "My agency has provided budget
support in the past" was selected in q6)*

In what calendar year did your agency first begin providing budget support
to [Country]?

[WRITE-IN TEXT BOX]

Question 8

*(Only if "My agency provides budget support" or "My agency has provided budget
support in the past" was selected in q6)*

Which of the following was a motivating factor in your agency's decision to
begin budget support in [Country]?

[Options: Motivating Factor—Not a Motivating Factor]

desire to increase your agency's policy influence over the Government of
  [Country]

desire to decrease recipient country transaction costs

desire to increase recipient country ownership

desire to increase donor harmonization

strategic shift by your agency's headquarters

pressure from the Government of [Country] to participate in budget support

pressure from other donors to participate in budget support

(Question was randomized.)

Question 9

(Only if "My agency provides budget support" was selected in q6)
Were there any other motivating factors in your country's decision to begin budget support in [Country]?
[OPTIONS: Yes—No]
If yes: What were these motivating factors?
[WRITE-IN TEXT BOX]

Question 10

(Only if "My agency provided budget support in the past" was selected in q6)
Why did your agency decide to end budget support to [Country]?
[WRITE-IN TEXT BOX]

Question 11

(Only if "My agency provided budget support in the past" was selected in q6)
Does your agency have any tentative plans to reintroduce budget support in the future?
[OPTIONS: Yes—No—Not Sure]

Question 12

(Only if "My agency has never provided budget support" was selected in q6)
Does your agency have any tentative plans to introduce budget support in the future?
[OPTIONS: Yes—No—Not Sure]

Question 13

In your personal opinion, is it a good idea for your agency to provide budget support to [Country]?
[OPTIONS: Yes—No—Not Sure]
Why or why not?
[WRITE-IN TEXT BOX]

Question 14

In your opinion, do donors that provide budget support have more influence with the Government of [Country]?
[OPTIONS: Yes—No]

Question 15

Which of the following best describes your agency?

Last year, my agency's actual disbursements were lower than agreed amounts in [Country].

Last year, my agency's actual disbursements were roughly equal to agreed amounts in [Country].

Last year, my agency's actual disbursements were higher than agreed amounts in [Country].

(Respondents selected one option.)

Question 16

How long in advance can your agency accurately predict disbursements in [Country]?

Three Months
Six Months
One Year
Two Years
Three Years
Other: [WRITE-IN TEXT BOX]

Question 17

In [Country], is it difficult for your agency to:

disburse promised aid on time?
give accurate predictions of disbursements one year in advance?
give accurate predictions of disbursements three years in advance?

[OPTIONS: Very difficult—Moderately difficult—Not difficult]

Question 18

How often do the following scenarios influence your agency's ability to disburse agreed amounts?

[OPTIONS: Often—Sometimes—Rarely—Never influence my agency's ability to disburse agreed amounts]

limited authority at the mission level
disbursement delays at headquarters
recipient country failing to meet required performance indicators
changing public opinion in your home country or member countries
recipient country failing to meet technical requirements for disbursement

political turnover in your home country or member countries

development partner(s) failing to meet required performance indicators

(Question was randomized.)

Question 19

Are there other factors that could negatively influence your agency's ability to make agreed disbursements?

[OPTIONS: Yes—No]

If yes, what other factors could negatively influence your agency's ability to disburse agreed amounts?

[WRITE-IN TEXT BOX]

Question 20

What are the most politically contentious issues regularly discussed by your agency and the Government of [Country]?

[WRITE-IN TEXT BOX]

Question 21

Are there issues that are important to your agency but regularly avoided in discussions with the Government of [Country] due to their political sensitivity?

[OPTIONS: Yes—No]

IF YES: What are these issues (in order of political sensitivity)?

[WRITE-IN TEXT BOX]

Question 22

When faced with contentious issues in [Country], which of the following strategies does your agency use to advocate for reform?

[OPTIONS: Often used to advocate for reform—Sometimes used to advocate for reform—Never used to advocate for reform]

local government in [Country]

civil society in [Country]

bilateral negotiations in [Country]

aid conditionalities

the policy dialogue structure

parliament of [Country]

media in [Country]

(Question was randomized.)

Question 23

Are there any other important strategies your agency uses to advocate for reform?
    [OPTIONS: Yes—No]
    IF YES: What are these strategies?
    [WRITE-IN TEXT BOX]

Question 24

Has participating in general budget support changed how your agency addresses contentious issues in [Country]?
    [OPTIONS: Yes—No]
    Please explain:
    [WRITE-IN TEXT BOX]

Question 25

For each of the following events, how likely is it that your agency would suspend aid to [Country], if the event occurred at some point in the future?
    [OPTIONS: Very Likely—Moderately Likely—Unlikely]
    corruption scandal in a project your agency is supporting
    deterioration in the investment climate
    moderately fraudulent elections
    changes in headquarters priorities
    corruption scandal in the government at large
    deterioration in respect for civil liberties
    highly fraudulent elections

    (Question was randomized.)

Question 26

In [Country], how much does your agency consider China during the following scenarios?
    (0 = not a consideration—10 = major consideration)
    aid negotiations
    drafting of your country strategy
    decisions about future aid allocations
    decisions about development cooperation in the extractive/natural resource
        sector

    (Question was randomized.)

Question 27

Does the possibility of Chinese assistance or investment promises currently reduce your agency's bargaining power with the Government of [Country]?
[OPTIONS: Yes—No—Not sure]
Please explain:
[WRITE-IN TEXT BOX]

Question 28

Please rate the chances of success for each of the following donors, if they attempt to negotiate an administrative reform program in the transportation sector with the Government of [Country].
[OPTIONS: Very likely to be successful—Moderately likely to be successful—Unlikely to be successful]

Control Group

A multilateral organization with access to 4 million USD in trust fund resources for administrative reform.
Your own agency.
A major bilateral European donor (does not provide budget support in [Country]) who is able to allocate an additional 5 million USD to support administrative reform.

Treatment Group

A multilateral organization with access to 4 million USD in trust fund resources for administrative reform.
Your own agency.
A major bilateral European donor (provides budget support in [Country]) who is able to allocate an additional 5 million USD to support administrative reform.

(Question was randomized.)

Question 29

Please read the following statements and indicate how many are true.

Control Group

I believe my development agency should focus more on HIV/AIDS reduction globally.

I think all development agencies should establish priority countries.

I believe that OECD countries should take a backseat to south-south cooperation.

I believe that too much development aid is currently spent in Africa.

Treatment Group

I believe my development agency should focus more on HIV/AIDS reduction globally.

I think all development agencies should establish priority countries.

I believe that OECD countries should take a backseat to south-south cooperation.

I believe that too much development aid is currently spent in Africa.

As long as [Country]'s government remains cooperative on our agency's main priorities, political repression (including suspected assassinations of opposition leaders) would not lead to the suspension of aid.

Question 30

Please read the following statements and indicate how many are true.

Control Group

I believe my development agency should allocate more aid toward wildlife support.

I think that countries with a port should receive more development aid per capita.

Lack of clean and safe water is a big problem in Africa.

Staff turnover is a large problem for my agency.

Treatment Group

I believe my development agency should allocate more aid toward wildlife support.

I think that countries with a port should receive more development aid per capita.

Within the past two years, my agency has threatened to withhold funding or promised additional funding to get the Government of [Country] to support a business interest from my home country.

Lack of clean and safe water is a big problem in Africa.

Staff turnover is a large problem for my agency.

(Question was randomized.)

Thank you very much for completing the anonymous survey. Your answers will be stored in an anonymized format and not associated with your name or your agency's name.

To complete the questionnaire, we would also like to ask you a few background questions. These questions will not be anonymized but will be treated strictly confidentially. This information will help us in our research process and help us to identify other potential respondents. Your assistance is greatly appreciated.

What is your current title?
[WRITE-IN TEXT BOX]
For how long have you held your current position?
[SLIDING SCALE: number of months (0–48)]
In what country were you previously posted?
[WRITE-IN TEXT BOX]
What was your previous position?
[WRITE-IN TEXT BOX]

Would you like to be kept informed about the results of the survey and/or the larger results of the study?

Please keep me informed about the results of the survey.
Please keep me informed about the result of the survey and the larger results of the study.
I am not interested in receiving the findings from either the survey or the larger study.
(Respondents selected one option)

We would also find it very valuable to speak with your predecessor. If possible, please enter the name and e-mail address of your predecessor.

Name of predecessor:
[WRITE-IN TEXT BOX]
Predecessor's e-mail address:
[WRITE-IN TEXT BOX]

We would be very happy to have your feedback on the survey. Please use the space below to provide us with any comments about the survey you may have. Thank you again for your time.

[LARGE WRITE-IN TEXT BOX]

Notes

1. THE DEVELOPMENT DANCE

1. In fiscal year (FY) 2015, USAID distributed $297.5 million in aid to Uganda.

2. A basket fund is a "type of joint financial mechanism whereby parties contribute funds to a common pooled account; subsidiary accounts may then be set up to fund specific clusters of activities. Pooled funds usually involves the use of a holding account reserved for particular purposes identified by agreement between a government and donors participating in the pool" (United Nations 2015).

3. To classify as ODA, aid flows must be "official financing administered with the promotion of the economic development and welfare of developing countries as the main objective, and which are concessional in character with a grant element of at least 25 percent (using a fixed 10 percent rate of discount)" (IMF 2003, 263). Historically, financial assistance given through the military was excluded from being classified as ODA. Recent changes, however, allow some military assistance to be classified as ODA (see OECD 2016).

4. Development aid is distinguishable from humanitarian aid in that it focuses on long-term poverty alleviation rather than a short-term response to an acute crisis or natural disaster. While this distinction is not always clear in practice, my focus is on aid delivered in the context of long-term development programs, rather than short-term or crises-related aid.

5. Largely because the data simply was not there, most of the seminal studies on development aid do not distinguish between different aid delivery mechanisms in their analysis. This is a significant limitation in the literature on foreign aid. Recent scholarship that does distinguish between different types of aid finds differences in allocation patterns (Dietrich 2013; Reinsberg 2015; Winters and Martinez 2015).

6. Prior to World War II, aid was largely distributed in an ad hoc manner, with donor countries providing assistance to specific countries that they choose to prioritize for historical, political, or economic reasons. Early antecedents include relief aid given by the United States and Europe to the Soviet Union following World War I, development aid to the colonies during the interwar years, and technical assistance provided by the United States to Latin America at the beginning of World War II (Lancaster 2007, 25–27).

7. In 1960, Canada created an External Aid Office, which became the Canadian International Development Agency (CIDA) in 1968. In 1961, France established a Ministry for Co-operation, and the United States enacted the Foreign Assistance Act, which created the Agency for International Development (USAID). Also in 1961, Japan established a cooperation fund, and Sweden established an Agency for International Assistance, which became the Swedish International Development Agency (SIDA) in 1965 (Führer 1996).

8. Throughout the 1950s, developing countries expressed a great deal of frustration at being unable to access funding from the IBRD. In September 1960, with strong support from the United States, the World Bank launched IDA with an initial funding of $912.7 million and fifteen signatory countries. Within eight months, IDA had fifty-one members (IDA 2016).

9. The original members of the DAG were Belgium, Canada, France, Germany, Italy, Portugal, the United Kingdom, the United States, and the Commission of the European Economic Community. Japan and the Netherlands joined shortly thereafter (IDA 2016).

10. Instead of functioning as competitors, NGOs and other development contractors largely work alongside bilateral and multilateral donors in recipient countries.

11. Source: Aiddata.org (Tierney et al. 2011). Accurate data on budget support is difficult to come by. For a long time, official ODA numbers did not differentiate between different types of aid. As a result, these figures should be used with care. However, the fact that budget support grew in popularity in the late 1990s and early 2000s is undisputed.

12. Source: Aiddata.org (Tierney et al. 2011).

13. For more details see Whitfield and Jones 2009, 190–91.

14. Quoted in Pomerantz 2004, 21.

15. Bilateral donor official, September 24, 2013, Uganda.

16. This is in fact exactly what happened. In 2005, DAC donors committed to disbursing $1,258 million in ODA to Tanzania. Only $977 million was actually disbursed (source: OECD Creditor Reporting System).

17. There is a great deal of contestation about the meaning of the term "ownership" (Buiter 2007; de Renzio, Whitfield, and Bergamaschi 2008; Faust 2010; Zimmermann 2007). As Whitfield and Fraser explain, some define ownership as "commitment," while others define ownership as "control" (see 2009a, 3–6, for a discussion). Taking their lead, I opt for the latter definition.

2. IT TAKES TWO TO TANGO

1. Alesina and Dollar (2000) first posed the question in this way. However, a number of scholars have weighed in on this debate (e.g., Alesina and Weder 2002; Claessens, Cassimon, and Van Campenhout 2009; Clist 2011; Collier and Dollar 2002; Reinsberg 2015; Wright and Winters 2010). This body of literature is also closely linked with debates on whether donors reward governments with better governance (e.g., Berthélemy and Tichit 2004; Burnside and Dollar 2000; Dollar and Levin 2006).

2. Radelet (2006a) divides views on the relationship between foreign aid and growth into three categories: (1) On average, aid has a positive relationship with growth (e.g., Hansen and Tarp 2000, 2001; Lensink and White 2001; Sachs 2005; Sachs et al. 2004). (2) Aid has no effect on growth and may actually undermine development and growth (e.g., Boone 1996; Mosley 1980; Mosley, Hudson, and Horrell 1987; Rajan and Subramanian 2008). (3) Aid has a conditional relationship with growth (e.g., Burnside and Dollar 2000; Svensson 1999). For an excellent summary of cross-country studies on aid effectiveness see table A.1 in Sumner and Mallett (2013, 63–73).

3. A notable exception is the literature on multilateral versus bilateral aid (e.g., McLean 2012, 2015; Milner and Tingley 2012).

4. Official diplomatic ties were restored in 2009.

5. A standby agreement in 1986 not only unlocked funds from the IMF, but also made available funds from the World Bank and several bilateral agencies that had conditioned their aid on an agreement with the IMF (Edwards 2014a).

6. How the specific preferences of individual donor agencies are determined is a different question and will likely be influenced by the accountability structures of the donor agency, as well as certain normative preferences (e.g., Dietrich 2016; Faust and Koch 2014). For our purposes, it is not important what the specific preferences of individual donor agencies are. Instead, what is important is that donor agencies have a preference for having more technical control over aid, so that they can monitor how their aid is spent.

7. In response to the purchase, the UK cut aid by approximately £3 million (Banda 2010).

8. As two scholars eloquently put it, "While most economists assume that aid is fungible, most aid donors behave as if it is not" (D. van de Walle and Mu 2007, 667).

9. The literature on structural adjustment is extensive. For a flavor of the debates see Babb (2005), Crisp and Kelly (1999), Easterly (2003b), Loxley (1990), Sahn, Dorosh, and Younger (1997), and Schatz (1994). For a history of structural adjustment loans see chapter 2 in Mosley, Harrigan, and Toye (1995).

10. A moral-hazard problem exists when one party has a tendency to take on risk because it knows that the potential costs or burdens of taking such a risk will be borne in whole or in part by others.

11. Applying these insights to regime survival, several scholars have pointed out that the influx of aid may actually encourage the recipient government to *put off* reforms by removing pressures from domestic constituents (e.g., Bräutigam 2000; Bräutigam and Knack 2004; Bueno de Mesquita and Smith 2010; Knack 2004; Morrison 2007; Svensson 2000a, 2000b; N. van de Walle 2001).

12. White House spokesman Jay Carney cited in Plumer (2013).

13. In contrast, North defines organizations as groups of individuals bound by a certain purpose.

14. In game theoretical terms, the utility function of the players.

15. Government official, September 30, 2013, Uganda.

3. STUDYING THE DANCE

1. The bulk of the fieldwork was conducted from 2012 to 2014. In 2009 and 2010, I conducted fieldwork in Rwanda for the dissertation project that served as the inspiration for this book. Between 2012 and 2014, I traveled to Tanzania, Uganda, and Ghana, and back to Rwanda. In 2015, I made shorter visits to Ghana and Tanzania to conduct workshops with participants on the findings.

2. Other benefits of the approach include the ability to identify paths to an outcome, point out variables that were left out in the initial comparison of cases, check for spuriousness, and to permit causal inference on the basis of a few cases or even a single case (Bennett and George 2001).

3. One limitation of the data collection process was that political and contextual realities sometimes prevented me from audio recording my interviews, especially with government officials, and particularly in Rwanda. As a result, for some interview records I am forced to rely on detailed notes rather than a full transcription. For more on collecting data in Rwanda see Swedlund (2011).

4. Official names for HoCs vary by donor agency. For example, at UNDP the equivalent would be the resident representative, while at the World Bank it would be the country director. Most bilateral agencies, however, have a head of cooperation or head of development cooperation.

5. Cross-national figures on budget support are notoriously poor. I use data from the Paris Surveys of Aid Effectiveness, because it is the most comprehensive and comparable during the time period of concern. The accuracy of the data is, however, subject to a number of critiques, the most important being that it is self-reported.

6. The NDC and NPP are largely seen as having avoided ethnic polarization by having a strong support base across the country's different regions and membership based on cross-cutting social cleavages (Whitfield 2009b).

7. Government official, March 23, 2013, Accra. In 1995, the Rawlings government presented a long-term economic plan titled *Ghana: Vision 2020* to parliament with the core aim of making Ghana a middle-income country in twenty-five years. The idea was to produce a medium-term economic plan every five years in order to reach the goals set out in the long-term vision. These plans were forced to change when the country opted into HIPC.

8. Ghana Poverty Reduction Strategy, 2003–2005, an Agenda for Prosperity and Growth (Republic of Ghana 2003).

9. The Growth and Prosperity Reduction Strategy (GPRS) II, 2006–2009 (Republic of Ghana 2006), and the Ghana Shared Growth and Development Agenda (GSGDA), 2010–2013 (Republic of Ghana 2010c).

10. Additional observers include the UN, the IMF, Norway, and the United States.

11. The government of Ghana officially announced the discovery of commercial quantities of oil in 2007, and oil production began in December 2010. Exploration activities are concentrated in two major oil fields: the Jubilee fields and the Tweneboa-Enyenra-Ntomme (TEN) fields. Production has begun only in the Jubilee fields. Tullow Oil PLC, which owns 49.95 percent of the Jubilee fields, estimates that between 600 million and 1.8 billion barrels of oil lie in the Jubilee fields (Gary 2009).

12. For a critical view on GDP calculations see Jerven (2013).

13. Nyerere remained chairman of the CCM until 1990 and handpicked his successor.

14. For an excellent analysis of the political and economic history of Tanzania, particularly under Nyerere, see Coulson (2013).

15. Efforts to manage aid contributions got under way in Tanzania as early as 1973, when an External Finance Unit was created at the Ministry for Finance and the first External Finance Manual was published. However, economic crises in the seventies and eighties led to a hiatus in efforts to more efficiently manage foreign aid contributions.

16. Following the first report of the Independent Monitoring Group led by Helleiner, the IMG has published reports in 1997, 1999, 2000, 2002, 2005, and 2010.

17. MKUKUTA stands for "Mkakati wa Kukuza Uchumi na Kupunguza Umaskini," or the National Strategy for Growth and Reduction of Poverty (United Republic of Tanzania 2005, 2010). Because of its semiautonomous status, Zanzibar has its own PRSP, the Zanzibar Strategy for Growth and Reduction of Poverty, known in Swahili as the MKUZA. The first PRSP simply went by the name "Poverty Reduction Strategy Paper" (United Republic of Tanzania 2000).

18. The JAST was preceded by the Tanzania Assistant Strategy (TAS), which was published in 2002 and provided a framework for donor–government relations and a three-year strategy for development assistance. Preparations for the TAS began in 1998–1999. Its publication was delayed, however, because donors prioritized the ongoing PRSP process (Wohlgemuth 2006).

19. At one time, the Netherlands and Switzerland also provided budget support to Tanzania.

20. For more on Uganda's political trajectory since independence see Mutibwa (1992), Mwakikagile (2012), and Kasozi, Musisi, and Sejjengo (1994).

21. Interview with Margaret Kakande by David Hulme, reported in Hulme (2010, 4).

22. For a timeline of oil exploration and discoveries in Uganda see http://www.oilinuganda.org/categories/oil-timeline.

23. The first signatories to the Uganda Joint Assistance Strategy were the AfDB, Germany, the Netherlands, Norway, Sweden, DfID, and the World Bank Group. Later, Austria, Belgium, and Ireland also signed (Ugandan Development Partners 2005).

24. Bilateral donor official, October 11, 2013.

25. For a more detailed historical look at Rwanda, including the genocide period and its antecedents, see Des Forges (1999), Prunier (1995), Straus (2006), and Uvin (1998). Particularly relevant to this study is Uvin's work, which explicitly addresses the role of development aid in the genocide. According to Uvin, development aid contributed to increasing structural violence in Rwanda in the years preceding the genocide, making donor agencies at least partially culpable for the violence.

26. Kagame is widely thought to have ruled from behind the scenes during the postwar transition period (Kinzer 2008). For a critical perspective on the transition years and the RPF see Reyntjens (2004).

27. The EDPRS focused on implementation of the first PRSP (Republic of Rwanda 2007), while the EDPRS II, which runs from 2013 to 2018, tries to address more explicitly the need to raise GDP per capita by increasing the country's growth rate (Republic of Rwanda 2013d). To reach the target GNP per capita laid out in its long-term development plan, *Vision 2020*, Rwanda needs to grow at a rate of at least 11.5 percent per year over the duration of the EDPRS II (Republic of Rwanda 2013b).

28. To be a member of the BSHG, donors needed to provide at least $10 million or more in budget support annually, with the major budget support donors to Rwanda being the UK, the EU, the World Bank, and the AfDB. Germany, Belgium, and the Netherlands provided smaller levels of largely sector budget support.

4. MAY I HAVE THIS DANCE?

1. Multilateral donor official, September 30, 2013, Tanzania.

2. As a respondent in Uganda explained, "The dialogue is for us to hear from government what they are doing, what they're planning to do, but also to say, okay, maybe more could be done here" (bilateral donor official, October 10, 2013, Uganda).

3. Bilateral donor official, July 4, 2012, Tanzania.

4. In the mid-2000s, former U.S. president George W. Bush established the President's Emergency Plan for AIDS Relief (PEPFAR), channeling billions of dollars into anti-HIV/AIDS programs on the continent. PEPFAR continues to be a cornerstone of U.S. development aid in Africa.

5. As one respondent in Ghana put it, the annual policy dialogue is "more ceremonial than it is important content to us" (multilateral donor official, April 10, 2013, Ghana).

6. It is also within these spaces that the content for the high-level meetings is decided.

7. Multilateral donor official, March 25, 2015, Tanzania.

8. Bilateral donor official, October 7, 2013, Uganda.

9. In Uganda this unit is called the Aid Liaison Department.

10. All four countries have in recent years implemented a database to help better monitor foreign aid commitments and disbursements. Because such databases rely on donor input, they have had mixed success in practice.

11. Government official, June 23, 2012, Ghana. A copy of Ghana's constitution is available at https://www.constituteproject.org/constitution/Ghana_1996.pdf. The National Development Planning Commission is covered in paragraphs 86 and 87.

12. For more on the PRSP process, including in the countries of the study, see Alonso, Judge, and Klugman (2006), Ansoms (2007), Craig and Porter (2003), Danida (2001), Fraser (2005), Gould (2005), Killick and Abugre (2001), Selbervik (2006), Wangwe (2002), and Whitfield (2005).

13. In Tanzania, the six priority areas are energy and natural gas, agriculture, water, education, transport, and mobilization of resources.

14. Bilateral donor official, October 29, 2013, Tanzania.

15. Bilateral donor official, October 28, 2013, Tanzania; emphasis added.

16. Multilateral donor official, June 21, 2012, Tanzania.

17. Government official, September 30, 2013, Uganda. It is for precisely this reason that I do not refer to donor agencies and recipient governments as development partners, despite the fact that this term is common at the recipient-country level.

18. Multilateral donor official, May 22, 2012, Tanzania.

19. Multilateral donor official, June 21, 2012, Tanzania.

20. The targets and policy objectives relate to three pillars: (1) promoting growth, income, and employment; (2) human development productivity and employment; and (3) transparency and accountable governance (Republic of Ghana 2010a).

21. Bilateral donor official, April 23, 2013, Ghana.

22. Government official, April 12, 2012, Ghana.

23. Government official, April 25, 2013, Ghana.

24. Multilateral donor official, October 13, 2013, Rwanda.

25. She went on to explain that while such work is not captured in any assessment framework, it is a necessary part of their job and occupies a significant portion of their time. In fact, her donor agency has even gone so far as to develop tip sheets to help its staff effectively communicate with the recipient government (bilateral donor official, April 2, 2013, Ghana).

26. Bilateral donor official, September 23, 2013, Uganda.

27. Forty-one percent of respondents reported that the government was the number one stakeholder, with an additional 21 percent ranking the government as the second and third most important stakeholder. In contrast, 32 percent reported that the agency's headquarters was the most important stakeholder.

28. Bilateral donor official, July 4, 2012, Tanzania.

29. As one respondent noted, "One thing is what is technically possible to move and remove and reform and change, and the other is what is politically possible" (bilateral donor official, June 20, 2012, Tanzania).

30. Multilateral donor official, October 2, 2013, Uganda. As another donor official, this time from Tanzania, put it, "Politicians want to get reelected, right? And they want to look good, so they usually tend to set very high targets and ambitious policies. . . . Then you come to the technical level, and you sit down and you realize there's no money for it. There is not the capacity to do it" (bilateral donor official, May 24, 2012, Tanzania).

31. Bilateral donor official, October 10, 2013, Uganda.

32. Of course, it can also sometimes be difficult for locals to make sense of the political environment. As one donor official put it, "I think the first challenge is for the government to know what it wants. It's not always clear" (multilateral donor official, June 20, 2012).

33. Bilateral donor official, July 4, 2012, Tanzania.

34. Civil society representative, September 27, 2013, Uganda.

35. Economist and consultant, June 17, 2012, Tanzania.

36. Government official, April 12, 2013, Ghana.

37. Bilateral donor official, October 10, 2013, Uganda.

5. A HALFHEARTED SHUFFLE

1. Civil society representative, September 27, 2013, Uganda; emphasis added.

2. Bilateral donor representative, May 2, 2013, Ghana.

3. Multilateral donor official, October 30, 2013, Uganda.

4. Multilateral donor official, June 25, 2012, Tanzania.

5. Bilateral donor official, April 22, 2013, Ghana.

6. Government official, June 6, 2012, Tanzania.

7. Bilateral donor official, July 4, 2012, Tanzania. Similarly, a donor official in Ghana noted that government is "quite polite," frequently agreeing to do things but then just not doing them (bilateral donor official, April 23, 2013, Ghana).

8. Bilateral donor official, May 23, 2012, Tanzania.

9. A clear example of this is when a respondent told me, "If you want to influence and to improve national systems, that's when you have to work with the government. Nevertheless . . . I think, sometimes we take more care of [Ugandans] than the [Ugandan] government [does]" (bilateral donor official, October 18, 2014, Uganda).

10. It is not uncommon for donor officials, for example, to use the metaphor of giving an allowance to a child while talking about aid.

11. As one donor official crudely put it, donors are attracted to people who speak their language "like flies on a piece of poop" (multilateral donor official, June 21, 2012, Tanzania).

12. Similarly, a respondent in Ghana told me that "those who actually execute things as planned get trusted, but there are some donors who commit once but actually don't do it. And then, obviously, I don't think they will get such trust from the government" (bilateral donor official, April 10, 2013, Ghana).

13. Bilateral donor official, May 23, 2012, Tanzania.

14. Multilateral donor official, October 2, 2013, Uganda.

15. Bilateral donor official, May 24, 2012, Tanzania.

16. Government official, April 25, 2012, Ghana.

17. Government official, April 25, 2012, Ghana; emphasis added.

18. Donor officials clearly recognize that aid unpredictability can be a big problem for recipient governments. As a donor official in Tanzania remarked, "If you plan a budget, and a large part of your budget is supposed to be funded by donor money, if then only some of it comes in, you have a major problem, of course. . . . I think it must be a huge frustration for the minister of finance and for the government, I mean, to be in that situation" (bilateral donor official, June 20, 2012, Tanzania).

19. While the two are often conflated, aid volatility is not equivalent to aid predictability; it is entirely possible that volatile aid is predictable. Predictability is the ex ante description of the difference between expected disbursements and actual disbursements. Alternatively, volatility is the ex post description of how much aid fluctuates over time (Celasun and Walliser 2008).

20. Multilateral donor official, April 9, 2013, Ghana.

21. Government official, September 30, 2013, Uganda.

22. Respondents were asked, "How long in advance can your agency accurately predict disbursements in [country]?" and then given the following options: three months, six months, one year, two years, three years, other [write-in text box].

23. An additional nineteen respondents selected "other" and wrote in an answer. Only one respondent indicated a higher level of predictability than was made available in the questionnaire (four years). Instead, the vast majority indicated a difficulty in making predictions *at all*, with respondents writing remarks such as "it varies," "it depends on the project," and "we basically can't predict."

24. For more on the political implications of district creation in Uganda see Grossman and Lewis (2014).

25. Multilateral donor official, September 23, 2013, Uganda.

26. According to another respondent, "The president a few months ago said he has put a moratorium on the creation of districts, something we have been demanding for the last six years. But now it suits his purpose, so maybe he has discovered another frontier for patronage which may not be as expensive" (civil society representative, October 11, 2013, Uganda).

27. Multilateral donor official, April 8, 2013, Ghana.

28. In previous years, they were 7.2 percent and 4 percent, respectively (Joint Budget Support Development Partners 2012).

29. To quote directly from the document, the joint statement made the point, "For the budget support partners—as for Ugandan citizens—it is crucially important to know how public funds are being used. . . . The published budget is the means by which we do this but last year, unfortunately, we could not. So we hope you can reassure us today that . . . we will not be seeing further supplementary requests for *foreseeable* expenditures, and that we can expect to be consulted" (Joint Budget Support Development Partners 2012, 3).

30. Bilateral donor official, October 14, 2013, Rwanda.

31. Bilateral donor official, October 10, 2013, Uganda.

32. Bilateral donor official, June 5, 2012, Tanzania.

33. Civil society representative, June 26, 2012, Tanzania.

34. Multilateral donor official, September 23, 2013, Uganda.

35. Bilateral donor official, October 30, 2013, Tanzania; emphasis added.

36. For many years after the genocide, Rwanda was still considered a "hardship" country by many donor agencies. Therefore, appointments were shorter. Many donor officials were posted to the country for two years or less.

37. Standard error 1.5 months.

38. Government official, October 24, 2013, Tanzania.

39. It is donor agencies that typically fund aid management systems, at least initially. This suggests that donor agencies understand that it is also in their interest for aid funds to be properly accounted for.

40. A popular tool is Development Gateway's "Aid Management Program." See http://www.developmentgateway.org/expertise/amp/.

41. Government official, April 24, 2013, Ghana.

42. Bilateral donor official, June 5, 2012, Tanzania.

43. Bilateral donor official, April 11, 2013, Ghana.

44. Bilateral donor official, October 7, 2013, Uganda.

6. TRACKING A CRAZE

1. All figures in this paragraph come from AidData.org (Tierney et al. 2011).

2. Multilateral donor official, April 8, 2013, Ghana.

3. Multilateral donor official, October 2, 2013, Uganda.

4. Question 8 in the survey protocol (see appendix 3).

5. Forty-five out of fifty-seven respondents selected that increased influence was a motivating factor in their agency's decision to provide budget support. This question was asked only if the HoCs had previously indicated that (a) their agency currently provides budget support to the recipient government or (b) their agency previously provided budget support. Other motivating factors included a desire to reduce recipient-country transaction costs (85 percent); desire to increase recipient-country ownership (92 percent); desire to increase donor harmonization (83 percent); and a strategic shift by the agency headquarters (76 percent) (Swedlund 2015).

6. Bilateral donor official, October 18, 2013, Uganda.

7. Bilateral donor official, September 24, 2013, Uganda.

8. Multilateral donor official, June 21, 2012, Tanzania. Discussing the DPG, another respondent told me, "[The] DPG, come on. That's like a social forum for everyone to come together, drink coffee, beer, [complain] about the government and their home" (technical assistant to the government, June 6, 2012, Tanzania).

9. The same respondent also claimed that whatever budget support donors want happens. While this is likely a simplification, it is further evidence of the envy that many non–budget support donors feel (bilateral donor official, September 24, 2013, Uganda).

10. Multilateral donor official, April 9, 2013, Ghana.

11. One respondent told me that while donors such as the United States do not need to provide budget support to get influence, he has heard of some donors just throwing in a bit of money into the budget support pool to get a seat at the table (bilateral donor official, June 5, 2012, Tanzania).

12. Bilateral donor official, June 2, 2013, Ghana.

13. Bilateral donor official, July 4, 2012, Tanzania. Similarly, another respondent said that despite being the smallest partner, "We're an accepted partner at the table" (bilateral donor official, October 28, 2013, Tanzania).

14. Bilateral donor official, October 10, 2013, Uganda.

15. Multilateral donor official, June 21, 2012, Tanzania.

16. Bilateral donor official, October 10, 2013, Uganda.

17. A policy report on changing aid delivery mechanisms in Tanzania noted that the prominence of new aid modalities, such as budget support, has made it more important for donors to participate in the Public Expenditure Review. Access to the review means that donors have substantial information on the effectiveness of public funds in PRSP priority sectors (Wohlgemuth 2006).

18. Bilateral donor official, April 10, 2013, Ghana.

19. Government official, October 30, 2013, Tanzania.

20. Multilateral donor official, April 9, 2013, Ghana.

21. Bilateral donor official, June 5, 2012, Tanzania.

22. Independent development consultant, June 27, 2012, Tanzania.

23. Multilateral donor official, September 19, 2013, Uganda.

24. Bilateral donor official, April 10, 2013, Uganda.

25. Civil society official, October 11, 2013, Uganda.

26. Bilateral donor official, October 28, 2013, Tanzania.

27. For this reason it is not surprising that while ministries of finance prefer budget support, many line ministries are opposed to it. As one donor official put it, "The line ministries hate general budget support" (bilateral donor official, October 10, 2013, Uganda).

28. Multilateral donor official, April 9, 2013, Ghana.

29. Bilateral donor official, October 10, 2013, Uganda; author's emphasis.

30. In all four countries of the study, the government expressed an explicit preference for budget support in its aid policy or similar document.

31. Multilateral donor official, September 19, 2013, Uganda.

32. Government official, June 5, 2010, Rwanda.

33. Officials of the External Finance Unit in Tanzania told me, for example, that with project aid you have many different priorities and that having to manage multiple competing demands is extremely difficult for the government.

34. Government official, June 6, 2012, Tanzania.

35. Bilateral donor official, June 5, 2012, Tanzania.

36. Bilateral donor official, June 7, 2012, Tanzania.

37. Bilateral donor official, June 8, 2012, Tanzania.

38. Bilateral donor official, May 24, 2012, Tanzania.

39. Bilateral donor official, June 20, 2012, Tanzania. Similarly, an official of the GBS Secretariat in Tanzania noted that the advantage of GBS for the government is that "they get the views of all donors in one" (GBS Secretariat, June 20, 2012, Tanzania).

40. Multilateral donor official, April 10, 2013, Ghana.

41. Bilateral donor official, April 11, 2013, Ghana.

42. Sometimes a donor will break up its disbursement into two or three "tranches," but the underlying logic is that the aid funds are disbursed in large chunks at prespecified intervals.

43. Multilateral donor official, June 20, 2012, Tanzania.

44. This was not the first time the Rwandan government had been accused of supporting instability in the DRC. In 2010, the UN released a mapping report of human rights violations committed in the DRC between 1993 and 2003. The document was quite critical of the government of Rwanda's role in the conflict (OHCHR 2010). A previous version of the report, which was leaked early, went as far as to accuse the government of possible genocide, as well as war crimes. The final version was significantly watered down following heavy protests and threats by the Rwandan government to withdraw peacekeepers active in UN peacekeeping missions abroad (Republic of Rwanda 2010c).

45. While general budget support constituted 23 percent of aid flows in FY 2010/11, in FY 2012/13 it was only 6 percent of ODA (source: World Development Indicators).

46. It was also later revealed that the country had hundreds of "ghost workers" on the payroll, which further frustrated donors (Bigg 2014).

47. In November 2014, Tanzania's public accounts committee revealed fraudulent payments made under the guise of energy contracts to offshore banking accounts amounting to roughly $180 million. Investigations into the scandal revealed that the state-owned energy provider Tanesco had formed a joint escrow (holding) account in 2006, transferring funds to private businesspeople and government officials. Several top-level Tanzanian officials were implicated in the scandal (Kabendera and Anderson 2014a, 2014b; Kabendera 2015).

48. Question 12 in the survey protocol (see appendix 3).

49. Bilateral donor official, July 4, 2012, Tanzania.

50. Bilateral donor official, June 7, 2012, Tanzania.

51. As one donor official put it, "The dialogue structure has become very complicated here, and it's very much formalized, so in that sense, it's rusting, and the rust causes new transaction costs" (bilateral donor official, May 23, 2012, Tanzania).

52. According to a 2013 evaluation, there was "virtual unanimous agreement that the transaction costs per unit of aid remained lower for Budget Support than for other modalities but that during the evaluation period the transaction costs for Budget Support had increased, as a result of the expansion of the PAF and the increasingly protracted discussions" (European Commission et al. 2013, 25).

53. A good example of this is the European Commission, which passed a communication in 2011 that obliges the EC to use budget support to promote democracy and human rights (European Commission 2011). Under the new communication, GBS is now referred to as "Good Governance and Development Contracts". For more on the changes see Faust et al. (2012).

54. A colleague noted here that donors are now calling aid GBS even when it is actually earmarked 30 percent to education. He also explained that while performance tranches once composed only one-third of funding, they now make up 50 percent of budget support funding (government officials, October 24, 2013, Tanzania).

55. Grant project aid provided as financial support was 75 percent predictable, while grant project (i.e., aid provided as in-kind) was 95 percent predictable. Alternatively, GBS provided as either a grant or a loan was predictable over 90 percent of the time, and SBS was 98 percent and 75 percent predictable when provided as either a grant or loan respectively (Republic of Rwanda 2013b).

56. Independent development consultant, June 27, 2012, Tanzania.

57. In FY 2011/12, of the $113 million in GBS promised to the Rwandan government, only approximately $55 million was disbursed by the time of the annual ODA report.

58. Furtado and Smith similarly note that after donors withdrew budget support to Ethiopia (following postelection violence), "the level of trust between donors and the government deteriorated quickly," with the government arguing that "donors had failed to fulfil their commitment to provide predictable support based on an objective assessment of the government's performance to date" (2009, 137).

59. According to the respondent, the auditor general's report is an example of the reforms actually working, and hence the suspension represents a punishment for doing something right: "The reforms helped us to know where the problems are, and we were penalized for that" (government official, September 30, 2013, Uganda).

60. Bilateral donor official, July 4, 2012, Tanzania.

61. Molenaers (2012), for example, notes that although donor agencies have policies that "sanctions" cannot be applied in-year, if a breach is deemed serious and extreme a donor agency will not hesitate to cut off aid immediately.

62. According to a donor official, the financial crises increased the perception by citizens that "money is worth something." This, combined with a perception that little has been accomplished in terms of poverty reduction, has placed a good deal of pressure on donor agencies (multilateral donor official, May 29, 2012, Tanzania).

63. The 2012 scandal was certainly not the first—nor the largest—corruption scandal in recent memory in Uganda (*New Vision* 2012). However, it was the one with the biggest fallout.

64. Bilateral donor official, September 26, 2013, Tanzania.

65. Bilateral donor official, March 23, 2012, Tanzania.

66. More specifically, the respondent is referring to the high-level forums in Accra, Ghana, in 2008 and Busan, South Korea, in 2011 (multilateral donor official, May 29, 2012, Tanzania).

67. The respondent went on to explain that as soon as they know about this, they "start to dialogue with our partners here, so we don't overnight suddenly dump something new." However, he admitted that such events still endanger the time horizon of their commitments (bilateral donor official, June 20, 2012, Tanzania).

68. Multilateral donor official, October 11, 2013, Uganda.

69. Bilateral donor official, June 20, 2012, Tanzania.

70. Government official, October 24, 2013, Tanzania.

71. Multilateral donor official, October 11, 2013, Uganda.

72. Bilateral donor official, June 20, 2012, Tanzania.

73. Bilateral donor official, May 2, 2013, Ghana.

74. Multilateral donor official, September 11, 2013, Uganda.

75. Multilateral donor official, October 30, 2013, Tanzania.

7. THE FUTURE OF THE DEVELOPMENT DANCE AND WHY WE SHOULD CARE

1. Bilateral donor official, October 10, 2013, Uganda.

2. One challenge with this approach is that some goals and objectives are easier to measure than others. Accordingly, there is concern among practitioners and scholars alike that the need to have measurable indicators will lead to the prioritization of certain reforms merely because they are easily measured and quantified.

3. RBA is also referred to as cash on delivery, output-based aid, or payment by results.

4. The actual dollar amount per student ranges from £30 to £100. See http://www.odi.org/sites/odi.org.uk/files/odi-assets/events-presentations/1374.pdf.

5. One important limitation of RBA is that it can be used only in areas where it is possible to identify a clear indicator. For more on the pros and cons of RBA see Binnedijk (2000); Klingebiel (2011, 2012); Pearson, Johnson, and Ellison (2010); de Renzio and Woods (2010); and Rogerson (2011).

6. The emergence of China on the African continent is not actually new. The People's Republic of China has provided development assistance to African countries for over sixty years, first giving aid to Egypt in 1956 and then gradually expanding across the continent as states won their independence (Bräutigam 2009). Nonetheless, it is clear that China has expanded its activities in Africa more recently.

7. China refuses to publicly release data on aid and investments, arguing that transparency standards regarding financial assistance should be different for South–South cooperation (Tran 2011). As a result, estimates regarding the value of Chinese assistance vary widely. For example, while Bräutigam (2011) estimates that China spent approximately $1.4 billion continent-wide in 2007, Lum et al. (2009) put the figure at closer to $18 billion.

8. Government consultant, April 10, 2013, Ghana.

9. Government official, September 30, 2013, Uganda.

10. The interviewee was presumably referring to a 542-kilometer natural gas pipeline between Mtwara and Dar es Salaam built by the Chinese. The pipeline was financed by a $1.2 billion loan from the Export-Import Bank of China and included the construction of a gas processing plant. Construction started in July 2013, and the pipeline was commissioned in October 2015 (Senelwa 2015).

11. Multilateral donor official, June 20, 2012, Tanzania.

12. Bilateral donor official, April 23, 2013, Ghana.

13. As one civil society representative put it, "since the discovery of oil, the donor has been a little bit on the quiet side because I think they've gotten to realize that Ghana is no longer a low-income country; once the oil funds start flowing they might not listen to us" (CSO representative, April 25, 2013, Ghana). Similarly, a donor official told me that "the donor's leverage will become less and less, as Ghana has alternative sources of income from oil, from commercial loans, private sector, more domestic resources" (multilateral donor official, April 10, 2013, Ghana). This view is not necessarily uniform across all donor agencies. According the one respondent, for example, the need for technical assistance will likely still be there. As he put it, just because a government finds out it has oil "doesn't mean that government will be better at buildings, courts, or roads or health centers, and planning for them. Those technical needs will be pretty much the same in five years' time [as] what they are today" (multilateral donor official, September 23, 2013, Uganda).

14. Bilateral donor official, June 20, 2012, Tanzania.

15. Bilateral donor official, July 4, 2012, Tanzania.

16. Individual development consultant, September 25, 2013, Uganda.

17. Civil society representative, October 27, 2013, Uganda.

18. See "IMF Approves US$918 Million ECF Arrangement to Help Ghana Boost Growth, Jobs and Stability," IMF press release, April 3, 2015, https://www.imf.org/exter nal/np/sec/pr/2015/pr15159.htm.

Works Cited

Abbey, Richard Annerquaye. 2015. "AfDB to Provide US $100m Budget Support." *B&FT Online*, October 23. http://thebftonline.com/business/banking-finance/15685/AfDB-to-provide-US$100m-budget-support.html.

ActionAid Uganda. 2012. "How Much Oil (and Gas) Does Uganda Have, and Where Is It?" Oil in Uganda, March 5. http://www.oilinuganda.org/facts-faqs/uganda-oil-facts-faqs/how-much-oil-and-gas-does-uganda-have-and-where-is-it.html.

Akello, Joan, and Ivan Rugambwa. 2013. "Is the Government Broke?" *Independent*, August 2. http://www.independent.co.ug/cover-story/8066-is-the-government-broke.

Akwetey, Emmanuel. 2007. "Effect of Implementation on Civil Society Funding and Policy Space in Ghana." Alliance2015 Report, December. http://www.alliance2015.org/fileadmin/user_upload/Alliance2015_Ghana_Governance___Education_Aid_Effectiveness_Study_2007.pdf.

Alden, Chris. 2005. "Leveraging the Dragon: Toward 'An Africa That Can Say No.'" *YaleGlobal Online Magazine*, March 1. http://yaleglobal.yale.edu/content/leveraging-dragon-toward-africa-can-say-no.

———. 2007. *China in Africa: Partner, Competitor or Hegemon?* London: Zed Books.

Alesina, Alberto, and David Dollar. 2000. "Who Gives Foreign Aid to Whom and Why?" *Journal of Economic Growth* 5, no. 1: 33–63. doi:10.1023/a:1009874203400.

Alesina, Alberto, and Beatrice Weder. 2002. "Do Corrupt Governments Receive Less Foreign Aid?" *American Economic Review* 92, no. 4: 1126–37. http://www.jstor.org/stable/3083301.

Alonso, Rosa, Lindsey Judge, and Jeni Klugman. 2006. "PRSPS and Budgets: A Synthesis of Five Case Studies." In Koeberle, Stavreski, and Walliser, 155–92.

Anderson, Mark. 2014. "UK and International Donors Suspend Tanzania Aid after Corruption Claims." *Guardian*, October 13. http://www.theguardian.com/global-development/2014/oct/13/uk-and-international-donors-suspend-tanzania-aid-after-corruption-claims.

Ansoms, An. 2007. "How Successful Is the Rwandan PRSP? Growth, Poverty and Inequality." *Review of African Political Economy* 34, no. 112: 371–79. doi:10.1080/03056240701449752.

Arakawa, Hiroto. 2006. "Budget Support and Aid Effectiveness: Experience from East Asia." In Koeberle, Stavreski, and Walliser 2006, 431–45.

Arellano, Cristina, Aleš Bulíř, Timothy Lane, and Leslie Lipschitz. 2009. "The Dynamic Implications of Foreign Aid and Its Variability." *Journal of Development Economics* 88, no. 1: 87–102. doi:10.1016/j.jdeveco.2008.01.005.

Armon, Jeremy. 2007. "Aid, Politics and Development: A Donor Perspective." *Development Policy Review* 25, no. 5: 653–56. doi:10.1111/j.1467-7679.2007.00390.x.

Armstrong, Robert P. 1996. *Ghana Country Assistance Review: A Study in Development Effectiveness*. Washington, DC: World Bank.

Arndt, Channing. 2000. "Technical Co-Operation." In *Foreign Aid and Development: Lessons Learnt and Directions for the Future*, edited by Finn Tarp and Peter Hjertholm, 154–77. London: Routledge.

Arndt, Channing, Sam Jones, and Finn Tarp. 2014. "Problems, Promises, and Paradoxes of Aid: Africa's Experience." In *Problems, Promises, and Paradoxes of Aid: Africa's Experience*, edited by Muna Ndulo and Nicolas van de Walle, 16–37. Cambridge: Cambridge Scholars.

Aryeetey, Ernest, and Finn Tarp. 2000. "Structural Adjustment and After: Which Way Forward?" In *Economic Reforms in Ghana: The Miracle and the Mirage*, edited by Ernest Aryeetey, Jane Harrigan, and M. Nissanke, 344–65. Oxford: James Currey.

Axelrod, Robert. 2004. "Theoretical Foundations of Partnership." In *Evaluation and Development: The Partnership Dimension*, World Bank Series on Evaluation and Development, vol. 6, edited by Andres Liebenthal, Osvaldo N. Feinstein, and Gregory K. Ingram, 9–20. New Brunswick, NJ: Transaction.

Azam, Jean-Paul, and Jean-Jacques Laffont. 2003. "Contracting for Aid." *Journal of Development Economics* 70, no. 1: 25–58. doi:10.1016/S0304-3878(02)00085-8.

Babb, Sarah. 2005. "The Social Consequences of Structural Adjustment: Recent Evidence and Current Debates." *Annual Review of Sociology* 31, no. 1: 199–222. doi:10.1146/annurev.soc.31.041304.122258.

Baffoe, John K. 2000. "Structural Adjustment and Agriculture in Uganda." Sectoral Activities Programme Working Paper, WP.149. Geneva: International Labor Organization. http://www.ilo.org/public/libdoc/ilo/2000/100B09_70_engl.pdf.

Banda, Mabvuto. 2010. "Britain Reduces Aid to Malawi over Presidential Jet." Thomson Reuters, March 10. http://af.reuters.com/article/malawiNews/idAFLDE6292 1I20100310?pageNumber=1&virtualBrandChannel=0.

Barder, Owen. 2005. "Reforming Development Assistance Lessons from the UK Experience." Working Paper 70. Washington, DC: Center for Global Development.

BBC. 2009. "Rwanda and France Restore Ties." *BBC News*, November 30. http://news.bbc.co.uk/2/hi/africa/8385887.stm.

Bearce, David H., and Daniel C. Tirone. 2010. "Foreign Aid Effectiveness and the Strategic Goals of Donor Governments." *Journal of Politics* 72, no. 3: 837–51. doi:10.1017/S0022381610000204.

Bennett, Andrew. 2010. "Process Tracing and Causal Inference." In *Rethinking Social Inquiry: Diverse Tools, Shared Standards*, 2nd ed., edited by Henry E. Brady and David Collier, 207–10. Lanham, MD: Rowman & Littlefield.

Bennett, Andrew, and Jeffrey T. Checkel, eds. 2014. *Process Tracing: From Metaphor to Analytic Tool*. Cambridge: Cambridge University Press.

Bennett, Andrew, and Colin Elman. 2006. "Qualitative Research: Recent Developments in Case Study Methods." *Annual Review of Political Science* 9, no. 1: 455–76. doi:10.1146/annurev.polisci.8.082103.104918.

Bennett, Andrew, and Alexander L. George. 2001. "Case Studies and Process Tracing in History and Political Science: Similar Strokes for Different Foci." In *Bridges and Boundaries: Historians, Political Scientists, and the Study of International Relations*, edited by Colin Elman and Miriam Fendius Elman, 137–66. Cambridge, MA: MIT Press.

Berthélemy, Jean-Claude, and Ariane Tichit. 2004. "Bilateral Donors' Aid Allocation Decisions: A Three-Dimensional Panel Analysis." *International Review of Economics & Finance* 13, no. 3: 253–74. doi:10.1016/j.iref.2003.11.004.

Bhavnani, Rikhil, Nancy Birdsall, and Isaac Shapiro. 2004. "Whither Development Assistance? An Analysis of the President's 2005 Budget Request." Washington, DC: Center for Global Development & Center on Budget and Policy Priorites. http://www.cgdev.org/files/14140_file_Birdsall_WhitherAssistance_04.pdf.

Bigg, Matthew Mpoke. 2014. "Ghana Must Cut 'Ghost Workers' from Payroll before Aid Resumes—EU." Reuters, December 16, http://www.reuters.com/article/ghana-eu-idUSL6N0U04JZ20141216.

Binnedijk, Annette. 2000. "Results Based Management in the Development Co-Operation Agencies: A Review of Experience (Background Report)." Paris: DAC Working Party on Aid Evaluation. http://www.oecd.org/development/evaluation/1886527.pdf.

Birdsall, Nancy. 2005. "Seven Deadly Sins: Reflections on Donor Failings." Working Paper 50. Washington, DC: Center for Global Development. http://www.cgdev.org/sites/default/files/2737_file_WP50_rev12_05_2.pdf.

Birdsall, Nancy, and Rita Perakis. 2012. "Cash on Delivery Aid: Implementation of a Pilot in Ethiopia." Washington, DC: Center for Global Development. https://www.oecd.org/dac/peer-reviews/Ethiopia_RBA_pilot_report.pdf.

Boone, Peter. 1996. "Politics and the Effectiveness of Foreign Aid." *European Economic Review* 40, no. 2: 289–329. doi:10.1016/0014-2921(95)00127-1.

Bourguignon, François, and Jean-Philippe Platteau. 2015. "The Hard Challenge of Aid Coordination." *World Development* 69: 86–97. doi:10.1016/j.worlddev.2013.12.011.

Bräutigam, Deborah. 1992. "Governance, Economy, and Foreign Aid." *Studies in Comparative International Development* 27, no. 3: 3–25. doi:10.1007/BF02687132.

———. 2000. *Aid Dependence and Governance*. Stockhom: Almqvist & Wiksell International.

———. 2008. "China's Foreign Aid in Africa." In *China into Africa—Trade, Aid and Influence*, edited by Robert I. Rotberg, 197-216. Washington, DC: Brookings Institution.

———. 2009. *The Dragon's Gift: The Real Story of China in Africa*. Oxford: Oxford University Press.

———. 2011. "Aid 'with Chinese Characteristics': Chinese Foreign Aid and Development Finance Meet the OECD-DAC Aid Regime." *Journal of International Development* 23:752–64. doi:10.1002/jid.1798.

Bräutigam, Deborah, and Stephen Knack. 2004. "Foreign Aid, Institutions, and Governance in Sub-Saharan Africa." *Economic Development and Cultural Change* 52, no. 2: 255–85. doi:10.1086/380592.

Brown, Stephen. 2005. "Foreign Aid and Democracy Promotion: Lessons from Africa." *European Journal of Development Research* 17, no. 2: 179–98. doi:10.1080/09578810500130799.

———. 2011. "Well, What Can You Expect? Donor Officials' Apologetics for Hybrid Regimes in Africa." *Democratization* 18, no. 2: 512–34. doi:10.1080/13510347.2011.553368.

Brown, William. 2013. "Sovereignty Matters: Africa, Donors, and the Aid Relationship." *African Affairs* 112, no. 447: 62–82. doi:10.1093/afraf/adt001.

Bueno de Mesquita, Bruce, and Alastair Smith. 2010. "Leader Survival, Revolutions, and the Nature of Government Finance." *American Journal of Political Science* 54, no. 4: 936–50. doi:10.1111/j.1540-5907.2010.00463.x.

Buiter, Willem H. 2007. "'Country Ownership': A Term Whose Time Has Gone." *Development in Practice* 17, nos. 4–5: 647–52. doi:10.1080/09614520701469856.

Bulíř, Aleš, and A. Javier Hamann. 2001. "How Volatile and Predictable Are Aid Flows, and What Are the Policy Implications?" IMF Working Paper No. 01/167. Washington, DC: International Monetary Fund.

———. 2006. "Volatility of Development Aid: From the Frying Pan into the Fire?" IMF Working Paper WP/06/65. Washington, DC: International Monetary Fund.

Burgess, James. 2016. "$8 Billion Natural Gas Find Re-Af Rms Tanzania's Status As Gas Giant." *Oilprice.com*. March 28. http://oilprice.com/Energy/Energy-General/8-Billion-Natural-Gas-Find-Re-Affirms-Tanzanias-Status-As-Gas-Giant.html.

Burnside, Craig, and David Dollar. 2000. "Aid, Policies, and Growth." *American Economic Review* 90, no. 4: 847–68. http://www.jstor.org/stable/117311.

Carlin, Alan. 1966. "Project versus Program Aid: From the Donor's Viewpoint." Santa Monica, CA: RAND Cooperation. https://www.rand.org/content/dam/rand/pubs/papers/2008/P3283.pdf.

Celasun, Oya, and Jan Walliser. 2006. "Predictability of Budget Aid: Recent Experiences." In Koeberle, Stavreski, and Walliser, 215–28.

———. 2008. "Predictability of Aid: Do Fickle Donors Undermine Aid Effectiveness?" *Economic Policy* 23, no. 55: 545–94. doi:10.1111/j.1468-0327.2008.00206.x.

Checkel, Jeffery T. 2008. "Process-Tracing." In *Qualitative Methods in International Relations: A Pluralist Guide*, edited by Audie Klotz and Deepa Prakash, 114–30. Basingstoke, UK: Palgrave Macmillan.

Claessens, S., D. Cassimon, and B. Van Campenhout. 2009. "Evidence on Changes in Aid Allocation Criteria." *World Bank Economic Review* 23, no. 2: 185–208. doi:10.1093/wber/lhp003.

Clist, Paul. 2011. "25 Years of Aid Allocation Practice: Whither Selectivity?" *World Development* 39, no. 10: 1724–34. doi:10.1016/j.worlddev.2011.04.031.

Collier, Paul. 1997. "The Failure of Conditionality." In *Perspectives on Aid and Development*, edited by Catherine Gwin and Joan M. Nelson, 51–78. Washington, DC: Overseas Development Council; distributed by Johns Hopkins University Press.

———. 2007. *The Bottom Billion: Why the Poorest Countries Are Failing and What Can Be Done about It.* Oxford: Oxford University Press.

Collier, Paul, and David Dollar. 2002. "Aid Allocation and Poverty Reduction." *European Economic Review* 46, no. 8: 1475–1500. doi.org/10.1016/S0014-2921(01)00187-8.

Commonwealth of Nations. 2015. "Tanzania General Elections: Report of the Commonweath Observer Group." Dar es Salaam, Tanzania: Commonweath Observer Group. http://thecommonwealth.org/sites/default/files/inline/2015 Tanzania COG FINAL REPORT_PRINT.PDF.

Coulson, Andrew. 2013. *Tanzania: A Political Economy.* 2nd ed. Oxford: Oxford University Press.

Council on Foreign Relations. 2006. "More Than Humanitarianism: A Strategic U.S. Approach toward Africa; Report of an Independent Task Force." Independent Task Force Report No. 56. New York: Council on Foreign Relations. http://www.cfr.org/africa-sub-saharan/more-than-humanitarianism/p9302.

Craig, David, and Doug Porter. 2003. "Poverty Reduction Strategy Papers: A New Convergence." *World Development* 31, no. 1: 53–69. doi:10.1016/S0305-750X(02)00147-X.

Crisp, Brian F., and Michael J. Kelly. 1999. "The Socioeconomic Impacts of Structural Adjustment." *International Studies Quarterly* 43, no. 3: 533–52. http://www.jstor.org/stable/2600942.

Daima and ODI. 2005. "Joint Evaluation of General Budget Support Tanzania, 1995–2004." Dar es Salaam, Tanzania: Daima Associates Limited and Overseas Development Institute. https://www.odi.org/sites/odi.org.uk/files/odi-assets/publications-opinion-files/3234.pdf.

Danida—Danish Ministry of Foreign Affairs. 2001. "Review of the PRS Processes in Tanzania: A Contribution to the International Review of the PRSP Process." Danish Ministry of Foreign Affairs. http://siteresources.worldbank.org/INTPRS1/Resources/Comprehensive-Review/danish4.pdf.

de Renzio, Paolo, and Sarah Mulley. 2006. "Promoting Mutual Accountability in Aid Relationships." Briefing paper, April. London: Overseas Development Institute.

http://www.odi.org/sites/odi.org.uk/files/odi-assets/publications-opinion-files/2017.pdf.

de Renzio, Paolo, Lindsay Whitfield, and Isaline Bergamaschi. 2008. "Reforming Foreign Aid Practices: What Country Ownership Is and What Donors Can Do to Support It." Briefing paper, June. Oxford: Global Economic Governance Programme. http://www.globaleconomicgovernance.org/sites/geg/files/Reforming%20Foreign%20Aid%20PB%202008.pdf.

de Renzio, Paolo, and Ngaire Woods. 2010. "The Trouble with Cash on Delivery Aid: A Note on Its Potential Effect on Recipient Country Institutions." Note prepared for CGD initiative on "Cash on Delivery Aid." Washington, DC: Center for Global Development. http://cgdev.org.488elwb02.blackmesh.com/doc/Cash on Delivery AID/Derenzio Woods.pdf.

Des Forges, Alison. 1999. *Leave None to Tell the Story: Genocide in Rwanda.* New York: Human Rights Watch.

Deverajan, Shantayanan, and Vinya Swaroop. 2006. "The Implications of Foreign Aid Fungibility for Development Assistance." In *The World Bank: Structure and Policies*, edited by Christopher L. Gilbert and David Vines, 196–209. Cambridge: Cambridge University Press.

Dietrich, Simone. 2013. "Bypass or Engage? Explaining Donor Delivery Tactics in Foreign Aid Allocation." *International Studies Quarterly* 57, no. 4: 698–712. doi:10.1111/isqu.12041.

———. 2016. "Donor Political Economies and the Pursuit of Aid Effectiveness." *International Organization* 70, no. 1: 65–102. doi:http://dx.doi.org/10.1017/S0020818315000302.

Dollar, David, and Victoria Levin. 2006. "The Increasing Selectivity of Foreign Aid, 1984–2003." *World Development* 34, no. 12: 2034–46. doi:10.1016/j.worlddev.2006.06.002.

Dollar, David, and Jakob Svensson. 2000. "What Explains the Success or Failure of Structural Adjustment Programmes?" *Economic Journal* 110, no. 466: 894–917. http://www.jstor.org/stable/2667857.

Dreher, Axel, Andreas Fuchs, Roland Hodler, Bradley C. Parks, Paul A. Raschky, and Michael J. Tierney. 2014. "Aid on Demand: African Leaders and the Geography of China's Foreign Assistance. (AidData Working Paper #3)." Williamsburg, VA: AidData.

Dunning, Thad. 2004. "Conditioning the Effects of Aid: Cold War Politics, Donor Credibility, and Democracy in Africa." *International Organization* 58, no. 2: 409–23. doi:10.1017/S0020818304582073.

Easterly, William. 2003a. "Can Foreign Aid Buy Growth?" *Journal of Economic Perspective* 17, no. 3: 23–48.

———. 2003b. "IMF and World Bank Structural Adjustment Programs and Poverty." In *Managing Currency Crises in Emerging Markets*, edited by Michael P. Dooley and Jeffrey A. Frankel, 361–92. Chicago: University of Chicago Press.

———. 2007. "Are Aid Agencies Improving?" *Economic Policy* 22, no. 52: 633–78. doi:10.1111/j.1468-0327.2007.00187.x.

———. 2010. "Reader Exercise: Please Explain 'Aid Fungibility' to Our Secretary of State." *Aid Watch Blog*, October 21. http://aidwatchers.com/2010/10/reader-exercise-please-explain-aid-fungibility-to-our-secretary-of-state/.

Economist. 2013. "The Pain of Suspension." January 12. http://www.economist.com/news/middle-east-and-africa/21569438-will-rwandas-widely-praised-development-plans-now-be-stymied-pain.

ECOSOC. 2008. "Background Study for the Development Cooperation Forum: Trends in South–South and Triangular Development Cooperation." United

Nations Economic and Social Council. http://www.un.org/en/ecosoc/docs/pdfs/south-south_cooperation.pdf.

Edwards, Sebastian. 2014a. "Economic Development and the Effectiveness of Foreign Aid: A Historical Perspective." Working Paper 20685. Cambridge, MA: National Bureau of Economic Research.

———. 2014b. *Toxic Aid: Economic Collapse and Recovery in Tanzania*. Oxford: Oxford University Press.

Ernst, Jessica. 2011. "Aid Collaboration in Uganda." *International Affairs Review* 20, no. 1: 1–17.

European Commission. 2011. "The Future Approach to EU Budget Support to Third Countries." 3/10/11 COM(2011) 638. http://eur-lex.europa.eu/LexUriServ/LexUriServ.do?uri=COM:2011:0638:FIN:EN:PDF.

European Commission et al. 2013. "Joint Evaluation of Budget Support to Tanzania: Lessons Learned and Recommendations for the Future." Final Report: Vol. 1. https://ec.europa.eu/europeaid/sites/devco/files/evaluation-budget-support-tanzania-1321-main-report-2013_en.pdf.

Falleti, Tulia G. 2006. "Theory-Guided Process-Tracing in Comparative Politics: Something Old, Something New." *APSA-CP, Newsletter of the Organized Section in Comparative Politics of the American Political Science Association* 17, no. 1: 9–14.

Faust, Jörg. 2010. "Policy Experiments, Democratic Ownership and Development Assistance." *Development Policy Review* 28, no. 5: 515–34. doi:10.1111/j.1467-7679.2010.00496.x.

Faust, Jörg, and Svea Koch. 2014. "Foreign Aid and the Domestic Politics of European Budget Support." Discussion paper. Bonn: German Development Institute. https://www.die-gdi.de/uploads/media/DP_21.2014.pdf.

Faust, Jörg, et al. 2012. "The Future of EU Budget Support: Political Conditions, Differentiation and Coordination." European Think-Tanks Group in collaboration with the Institute of Development Policy and Management, University of Antwerp, May. http://www.oecd.org/dac/evaluation/dcdndep/50363784.pdf.

Fisher, Jonathan. 2013. "The Limits—and Limiters—of External Influence: Donors, the Ugandan Electoral Commission and the 2011 Elections." *Journal of Eastern African Studies* 7, no. 3: 471–91. doi:10.1080/17531055.2013.809206.

Fraser, Alastair. 2005. "Poverty Reduction Strategy Papers: Now Who Calls the Shots?" *Review of African Political Economy* 32, no. 104–5: 317–40. doi:10.1080/03056240500329346.

———. 2009. "Aid-Recipient Sovereignty in Historical Context." In Whitfield 2009a, 45–73.

Fraser, Alastair, and Lindsay Whitfield. 2009. "Understanding Contemporary Aid Relationships." In Whitfield 2009a, 74–107.

Führer, Helmut. 1996. "The Story of Official Development Assistance: A History of the Development Assistance Committee and the Development Co-operation Directorate in Dates, Names and Figures." Paris: Organisation for Economic Co-operation and Development. http://www.oecd.org/dac/1896816.pdf.

Furia, Annalisa. 2015. *The Foreign Aid Regime: Gift-Giving, States and Global Dis/Order*. London: Palgrave Macmillan.

Furtado, Xavier, and W. James Smith. 2009. "Ethiopia: Retaining Sovereignty in Aid Relations." In Whitfield 2009a, 131–55.

Gary, Ian. 2009. "Ghana's Big Test: Oil's Challenge to Democratic Development." Oxfam America and Integrated Social Development Centre (ISODEC). https://www.oxfamamerica.org/static/media/files/ghanas-big-test.pdf.

George, Alexander L., and Andrew Bennett. 2005. *Case Studies and Theory Development in the Social Science*. Cambridge, MA: MIT Press.

Gibson, Clark C., Krister Andersson, Elinor Ostrom, and Sujai Shivakumar. 2005. *The Samaritan's Dilemma: The Political Economy of Development Aid*. Oxford: Oxford University Press.

Gould, Jeremy. 2005. *The New Conditionality: The Politics of Poverty Reduction Strategies*. London: Zed Books.

Grossman, Guy, and Janet I. Lewis. 2014. "Administrative Unit Proliferation." *American Political Science Review* 108, no. 1: 196–217. doi:10.1017/S0003055413000567.

Hanna, William. 2015. "EU Resumes Budgetary Assistance to Ghana." Press statement, December 6. http://eeas.europa.eu/delegations/ghana/press_corner/all_news/news/2015/20150612_pressstatementbudgetsupport_en_01.htm.

Hansen, Henrik, and Finn Tarp. 2000. "Aid Effectiveness Disputed." In *Foreign Aid and Development: Lessons Learnt and Directions for the Future*, edited by Finn Tarp, 103–28. London: Routledge.

———. 2001. "Aid and Growth Regressions." *Journal of Development Economics* 64, no. 2: 547–70. doi:10.1016/S0304-3878(00)00150-4.

Harrison, Graham. 2001. "Post-conditionality Politics and Administrative Reform: Reflections on the Cases of Uganda and Tanzania." *Development and Change* 32, no. 4: 657–79. doi:10.1111/1467-7660.00221.

Harrison, Graham, Sarah Mulley, and Duncan Hotom. 2009. "Tanzania: A Genuine Case of Recipient Leadership in the Aid System?" In Whitfield 2009a, 271–98.

Hawkins, Darren G., et al., eds. 2006. *Delegation and Agency in International Organizations*. Cambridge: Cambridge University Press.

Hayman, Rachel. 2009a. "Rwanda: Milking the Cow; Creating Policy Space in Spite of Aid Dependence." In Whitfield 2009a, 156–84.

———. 2009b. "From Rome to Accra via Kigali: 'Aid Effectiveness' in Rwanda." *Development Policy Review* 27, no. 5: 581–99. doi:10.1111/j.1467-7679.2009.00460.x.

Hjertholm, Peter, and Howard White. 2000. "Foreign Aid in Historical Perspective: Background and Trends." In *Foreign Aid and Development: Lessons Learnt and Directions for the Future*, edited by Finn Tarp, 59–77. London: Routledge.

Hudson, John. 2015. "Consequences of Aid Volatility for Macroeconomic Management and Aid Effectiveness." *World Development* 69:62–74. doi:10.1016/j.worlddev.2013.12.010.

Hudson, John, and Paul Mosley. 2001. "Aid Policies and Growth: In Search of the Holy Grail." *Journal of International Development* 13, no. 7: 1023–38. doi:10.1002/jid.819.

Hulme, David. 2010. *Global Poverty: How Global Governance is Failing the Poor*. London: Routledge.

Hyden, Gordan. 2008. "After the Paris Declaration: Taking on the Issue of Power." *Development Policy Review* 26, no. 3: 259–74. doi:10.1111/j.1467-7679.2008.00410.x.

IDA (International Development Association). 2007. "Aid Architecture: An Overview of the Main Trends in Official Development Assistance Flows." Background paper. http://www.worldbank.org/ida/papers/IDA15_Replenishment/Aidarchitecture.pdf.

———. 2016. "History." Washington, DC: World Bank Group. https://ida.worldbank.org/about/history.

IDD and Associates. 2006. "Evaluation of General Budget Support: Synthesis Report." In *Joint Evaluation of General Budget Support, 1994–2004*. Birmingham, UK: International Development Department (IDD), School of Public Policy, University of Birmingham. http://www.oecd.org/development/evaluation/dcdndep/37426676.pdf.

IMF. 2003. "Official Development Assistance." In *External Debt Statistics: Guide for Compilers and Users*. Appendix 3, glossary. Washington, DC: International Monetary Fund. http://www.imf.org/external/pubs/ft/eds/Eng/Guide/index.htm.

Janus, Heiner, and Niels Keijzer. 2015. "Big Results Now? Emerging Lessons from Results-Based Aid in Tanzania." Discussion paper 4/2015. Bonn: German Development Institute. https://www.die-gdi.de/en/discussion-paper/article/big-results-now-emerging-lessons-from-results-based-aid-in-tanzania/.

Jeanne, Dear, and John Njoroge. 2012. "Donors Cut All Direct Aid to Government until 2013." *Daily Monitor*, April 16. http://www.monitor.co.ug/News/National/Donors--cut--all-direct-aid--government--until-2015/-/688334/1635792/-/tc4u1pz/-/index.html.

Jeanne, Olivier, Jonathan D. Ostry, and Jeromin Zettelmeyer. 2008. "A Theory of International Crisis Lending and IMF Conditionality." IMF working paper, WP/08/236. Washington, DC: International Monetary Fund. doi:10.5089/9781451870947.001.

Jerven, Morten. 2013. *Poor Numbers: How We Are Misled by African Development Statistics and What to Do about It*. Ithaca, NY: Cornell University Press.

Jerven, Morten, and Magnus Ebo Duncan. 2012. "Revising GDP Estimates in Sub-Saharan Africa: Lessons from Ghana." *African Statistical Journal* 15:13–22.

Joint Budget Support Development Partners. 2012. "JBSF Co-chair Speaking Points for the PCC Meeting on 24 January." Unpublished document. Kampala, Uganda.

Kabendera, Erick. 2015. "Tanzania Cabinet Reshuffled as Energy Scandal Claims Fourth Politician." *Guardian*, January 28. http://www.theguardian.com/global-development/2015/jan/28/tanzania-cabinet-reshuffle-energy-scandal-jakaya-kikwete.

Kabendera, Erick, and Mark Anderson. 2014a. "Tanzanian PM under Pressure to Resign over Alleged Fraudulent Payments." *Guardian*, November 28. https://www.theguardian.com/global-development/2014/nov/28/tanzania-prime-minister-mizengo-pinda-alleged-fraudulent-payments-energy-contracts.

———. 2014b. "Tanzania Energy Scandal Ousts Senior Politicians." *Guardian*, December 24. http://www.theguardian.com/global-development/2014/dec/24/tanzania-energy-scandal-ousts-senior-politicians.

Kasozi, A., Nakanyike Musisi, and James Mukooza Sejjengo. 1994. *Social Origins of Violence in Uganda, 1964–1985*. Montreal: McGill–Queen's University Press.

Kharas, Homi J. 2008. "Measuring the Cost of Aid Volatility." Wolfensohn Center for Development Working Paper 3. July. Washington, DC: Brookings Institution. https://www.brookings.edu/wp-content/uploads/2016/06/07_aid_volatility_kharas.pdf.

Killick, Tony. 1998. *Aid and the Political Economy of Policy Change*. London: Overseas Development Institute.

———. 2004. "Politics, Evidence and the New Aid Agenda." *Development Policy Review* 22, no. 1: 5–29. doi:10.1111/j.1467-8659.2004.00235.x.

Killick, Tony, and Charles Abugre. 2001. "Institutionalising the PRSP Approach in Ghana." In *PRSP Institutionalisation Study: Final Report*. Accra, Ghana: Overseas Development Institution. http://www.odi.org/sites/odi.org.uk/files/odi-assets/publications-opinion-files/2191.pdf.

Kinzer, Stephen. 2008. *A Thousand Hills: Rwanda's Rebirth and the Man Who Dreamed It*. Hoboken, NJ: John Wiley & Sons.

Klingebiel, Stephan. 2011. "Results Based Financing—the Potential for a Greater Results Focus." Discussion paper for an event with members of the German Parliament (Bundestag). September 28. Berlin. https://www.die-gdi.de/uploads/media/DP_RBA_bn.pdf.

———. 2012. "Results-Based Aid (RBA): New Aid Approaches, Limitations and the Application to Promote Good Governance." Discussion paper 14/2012. Bonn:

German Development Institute. https://www.die-gdi.de/uploads/media/ DP_14.2012.pdf.

Klingebiel, Stephan, and Heiner Janus. 2014 "Results-Based Aid: Potential Limits of an Innovative Modality in Development Cooperation." *International Development Policy* 5, no. 2: doi:10.4000/poldev.1746.

Knack, Stephen. 2004. "Does Foreign Aid Promote Democracy?" *International Studies Quarterly* 48, no. 1: 251–66. doi:10.1111/j.0020-8833.2004.00299.x.

———. 2013. "Building or Bypassing Recipient Country Systems: Are Donors Defying the Paris Declaration?" World Bank Policy Research Working Paper 6423. Washington, DC: World Bank.

Knoll, Martin. 2008. "Budget Support: A Reformed Approach or Old Wine in New Skins?" UNCTAD Discussion Papers. Geneva: United Nations Conference on Trade and Development. http://unctad.org/en/docs/osgdp20085_en.pdf.

Koeberle, Stefan, Zoran Stavreski, and Jan Walliser. 2006. *Budget Support as More Effective Aid? Recent Experiences and Emerging Lessons.* Washington, DC: World Bank.

Kragelund, Peter. 2008. "The Return of Non-DAC Donors to Africa: New Prospects for African Development?" *Development Policy Review* 26, no. 5: 555–84. doi:10.1111/j.1467-7679.2008.00423.x.

———. 2010. "The Potential Role of Non-traditional Donors' Aid in Africa." ICTSH Issue Paper No. 11. Geneva: International Centre for Trade and Sustainable Development. http://www.ictsd.org/downloads/2011/03/the-potential-role-of-non-traditional-donorse28099-aid-in-africa.pdf.

———. 2011. "Back to BASICs? The Rejuvenation of Non-traditional Donors' Development Cooperation with Africa." *Development and Change* 42 no. 2: 585–607. doi:10.1111/j.1467-7660.2011.01695.x.

Kroslak, Daniela. 2007. *The Role of France in the Rwandan Genocide.* London: Hurst.

Kuteesa, Florence N., and Rosetti Nabbumba. 2004. "HIPC Debt Relief and Poverty Reduction Strategies: Uganda's Experience." In *HIPC Debt Relief: Myths and Reality,* edited by Jan Joost Teunissen and Age Akkerman, 48–56. The Hague: Forum on Debt and Development.

Lancaster, Carol. 2007. *Foreign Aid: Diplomacy, Development, Domestic Politics.* Chicago: University of Chicago Press.

Lensink, Robert, and Howard White. 2001. "Are There Negative Returns to Aid?" *Journal of Development Studies* 37, no. 6: 42–65. doi:10.1080/713601082.

Loxley, John. 1990. "Structural Adjustment in Africa: Reflections on Ghana and Zambia." *Review of African Political Economy* 17, no. 47: 8–27. doi:10.1080/03056249008703845.

Lu, Chunling, Matthew T. Schneider, Paul Gubbins, Katherine Leach-Kemon, Dean Jamison, and Christopher J. L. Murray. 2010. "Public Financing of Health in Developing Countries: A Cross-National Systematic Analysis." *Lancet* 375, no. 9723: 1375–87. doi:10.1016/S0140-6736(10)60233-4.

Lum, Thomas, Hannah Fischer, Julissa Gomez-Granger, and Anne Leland. 2009. "China's Foreign Aid Activities in Africa, Latin America, and Southeast Asia." Washington, DC: Congressional Research Service Report for Congress. https://www.fas.org/sgp/crs/row/R40361.pdf.

Lundsgaarde, Erik. 2012. *The Domestic Politics of Foreign Aid.* Abingdon, Oxon, UK: Routledge.

Mande, Mike. 2011. "Tanzania: Netherlands Slashes Budget Support to Dar es Salaam." *East African,* May 29. http://allafrica.com/stories/201105302217.html.

Martens, Bertin. 2002. *The Institutional Economics of Foreign Aid.* New York: Cambridge University Press.

———. 2005. "Why Do Aid Agencies Exist?" *Development Policy Review* 23, no. 6: 643–63. doi:10.1111/j.1467-7679.2005.00306.x.

McLean, Elena V. 2012. "Donors' Preferences and Agent Choice: Delegation of European Development Aid." *International Studies Quarterly* 56, no. 2: 381–95. doi:10.1111/j.1468-2478.2012.00727.x.

———. 2015. "Multilateral Aid and Domestic Economic Interests." *International Organization* 69, no. 1: 97–130. doi:10.1017/S0020818314000289.

Milner, Helen V., and Dustin Tingley. 2012. "The Choice for Multilateralism: Foreign Aid and American Foreign Policy." *Review of International Organizations* 8, no. 3: 313–41. doi:10.1007/s11558-012-9153-x.

———, eds. 2013. *The Geopolitics of Foreign Aid*. Cheltenham, UK: Edward Elgar.

Mohan, Giles, and Marcus Power. 2008. "New African Choices? The Politics of Chinese Engagement in Africa and the Changing Architecture of International Development." *Review of African Political Economy* 35, no. 1: 23–42. doi: 10.1080/03056240802011394.

Molenaers, Nadia. 2012. "The Great Divide? Donor Perceptions of Budget Support, Eligibility and Policy Dialogue." *Third World Quarterly* 33, no. 5: 37–41. doi:10.1080/01436597.2012.677311.

Morrison, Kevin. 2007. "Natural Resources, Aid, and Democratization: A Best-Case Scenario." *Public Choice* 131:365–86. doi:10.1007/s11127-006-9121-1.

Mosley, Paul. 1980. "Aid, Savings, and Growth Revisited." *Oxford Bulletin of Economics and Statistics* 42, no. 2: 79–95. doi:10.1111/j.1468-0084.1980.mp42002002.x.

Mosley, Paul, Blessing Chiripanhua, Jean Grugel, and Ben Thirkell-White. 2012. *The Politics of Poverty Reduction*. Oxford: Oxford University Press.

Mosley, Paul, and Marion J. Eeckhout. 2000. "From Project Aid to Programme Assistance." In *Foreign Aid and Development: Lessons Learnt and Directions for the Future*, edited by Finn Tarp and Peter Hjertholm, 131–53. London: Routledge.

Mosley, Paul, Jane Harrigan, and John Toye. 1995. *Aid and Power: The World Bank and Policy-Based Lending*. Vol. 1. London: Routledge.

Mosley, Paul, John Hudson, and Sara Horrell. 1987. "Aid, the Public Sector and the Market in Less Developed Countries." *Economic Journal* 97, no. 387: 616–41. http://www.jstor.org/stable/2232927.

Moss, Todd. 2010. "Ghana Says: Hey, Guess What? We're Not Poor Anymore!" *Blog of Global Development: Views from the Center*, November 5. http://www.cgdev.org/blog/ghana-says-hey-guess-what-we%E2%80%99re-not-poor-anymore.

Moss, Todd, and Sarah Rose. 2006. "China Exim Bank and Africa: New Lending, New Challenges." Washington, DC: Center for Global Development. November. http://www.cgdev.org/sites/default/files/11116_file_China_and_Africa.pdf.

Moyo, Dambisa. 2009. *Dead Aid: Why Aid Is Not Working and How There Is a Better Way for Africa*. New York: Farrar, Straus and Giroux.

Museveni, Yoweri. 1997. *Sowing the Mustard Seed: The Struggle for Freedom and Democracy in Uganda*. London: Macmillian.

———. 2013. "Statement by H. E. Yoweri Kaguta Museveni, President of the Republic of Uganda, at the 68th United Nations General Assembly." New York: September 24.

Musoni, Protais. 2003. "Challenges and Opportunities of Foreign Aid in a Post-conflict Situation: The Case of Rwanda." Paper presented at the Expert Group Meeting on Aid Delivery and Aid Management, Mexico City, November 2–3.

Mutibwa, Phares Mukasa. 1992. *Uganda since Independence: A Story of Unfulfilled Hopes*. Trenton, NJ: Africa World Press.

Mwakikagile, Godfrey. 2012. *Obote to Museveni: Political Transformation in Uganda since Independence*. Dar es Salaam, Tanzania: New Africa Press.

Neureiter, Katharina. 2012. "Tanzania: Reserving Judgment on Tanzania's Natural Gas Discoveries." Think Africa Press, September 4. http://thinkafricapress.com/ tanzania/nascent-gas-industry-potential-or-potentially-dangerous-430billion.

New Vision. 2012. "Nine Corruption Scandals to Look Back At." November 11. http:// www.newvision.co.ug/new_vision/news/1309873/corruption-scandals-look.

Ng'wanakilala, Fumbuka. 2015. "Donors Agree to Release $44 Million of Aid to Tanzania." Reuters, March 12. http://af.reuters.com/article/topNews/idAFK BN0M81U520150312.

NISR. 2014. "Rwanda Poverty Profline Report 2013/14: Results of Integrated Household Living Conditions Survey [EICV]." Kigali, Rwanda: National Institute of Statistics of Rwanda. http://www.statistics.gov.rw/publication/rwanda-poverty-profile-report-results-eicv-4.

North, Douglass C. 1990. *Institutions, Institutional Change and Economic Performance.* Cambridge: Cambridge University Press.

North, Douglass C., and Barry R. Weingast. 1989. "Constitutions and Commitment: The Evolution of Institutional Governing Public Choice in Seventeenth-Century England." *Journal of Economic History* 49, no. 4: 803–32.

OECD. 2005. "The Paris Declaration on Aid Effectiveness." Approved at the Paris High Level Forum on Aid Effectiveness, March 2. Paris: Organisation for Economic Co-operation and Development.

———. 2011. "Survey on Monitoring the Paris Declaration (Database)." OECD.stat. http://stats.oecd.org/Index.aspx?lang=en&DataSetCode=SURVEYDATA.

———. 2016. "DAC High Level Meeting: Communique." February 19. Paris: Organisation for Economic Co-operation and Development. http://www.oecd.org/dac/ DAC-HLM-Communique-2016.pdf.

OHCHR. 2010. "Democratic Republic of the Congo, 1993–2003, UN Mapping Report." Office of the UN High Commissioner for Human Rights. http://www. ohchr.org/EN/Countries/AfricaRegion/Pages/RDCProjetMapping.aspx.

Ostrom, Elinor, Clark Gibson, Sujai Shivakumar, and Krister Andersson. 2002. "Aid, Incentives, and Sustainability: An Institutional Analysis of Development Cooperation." Sida Studies in Evaluation 02/01. Stockholm: Swedish International Development Cooperation Agency.

Pearson, Lester B. 1969. *Partners in Development: Report of the Commission on International Development.* Edited by the Commission on International Development. New York: Praeger.

Pearson, Mark, Martin Johnson, and Robin Ellison. 2010. "Review of Major Results Based Aid (RBA) and Results Based Financing Schemes-Final Report." London: DFID Human Development Resource Centre. http://www.oecd.org/dac/ peer-reviews/Review-of-Major-RBA-and-RBF-Schemes.pdf.

Pedersen, Karl R. 1996. "Aid, Investment and Incentives." *Scandinavian Journal of Economics* 98, no. 3: 423–37. http://www.jstor.org/stable/3440735.

Plumer, Brad. 2013. "The U.S. Gives Egypt $1.5 Billion a Year in Aid. Here's What It Does." *Washington Post's Wonkblog,* July 9. https://www.washingtonpost.com/news/wonk/ wp/2013/07/09/the-u-s-gives-egypt-1-5-billion-a-year-in-aid-heres-what-it-does/.

Pomerantz, Phyllis R. 2004. *Aid Effectiveness in Africa: Developing Trust between Donors and Governments.* Lanham, MD: Lexington Books.

Prunier, Gérard. 1995. *The Rwanda Crisis: History of a Genocide.* New York: Columbia University Press.

Quadir, Fahimul. 2013. "Rising Donors and the New Narrative of 'South–South' Cooperation: What Prospects for Changing the Landscape of Development Assistance Programmes?" *Third World Quarterly* 34, no. 2: 321–38. doi: 10.1080/01436597.2013.775788.

Rabe, Stephen G. 1988. *Eisenhower and Latin America: The Foriegn Policy of Anti-communism.* Chapel Hill: University of North Carolina Press.

Radelet, Steven. 2006a. "A Primer on Foreign Aid." Working Paper 92. Washington, DC: Center for Global Development. http://www.cgdev.org/publication/primer-foreign-aid-working-paper-92.

———. 2006b. "Bush and Foreign Aid." *Foreign Affairs* 82, no. 5: 104–17. www.jstor.org/stable/20033686.

Radelet, Steven, and Ruth Levine. 2008. "Can We Build a Better Mousetrap? Three New Institutions Designed to Improve Aid Effectiveness." In *Reinventing Foreign Aid*, edited by William Easterly, 431–60. Cambridge, MA: MIT Press.

Rajan, Raghuram G., and Arvind Subramanian. 2008. "Aid and Growth: What Does the Cross-Country Evidence Really Show?" *Review of Economics and Statistics* 90, no. 4: 643–65. doi:10.1162/rest.90.4.643.

Reinsberg, Bernhard. 2015. "Foreign Aid Responses to Political Liberalization." *World Development* 75:46–61. doi:10.1016/j.worlddev.2014.11.006.

Reisen, Helmut, and Jean-Philippe Stijns. 2011. "Emerging Partners Create Policy Space for Africa." *VoxEU.org*, July 12. http://www.voxeu.org/article/how-emerging-donors-are-creating-policy-space-africa.

Republic of Ghana. 2003. "Ghana Poverty Reduction Strategy, 2003–2005: An Agenda for Growth and Prosperity." Accra, Ghana: National Development Planning Commission.

———. 2005. "Partnering for Growth and Poverty Reduction." *Multi-donor Budget Support Newsletter* 1, no. 1. Accra, Ghana: MDBS Secretariat.

———. 2006. "Growth and Poverty Reduction Strategy (GPRS) II, 2006–2009." Accra, Ghana: National Development Planning Commission.

———. 2008. "Partnering for Growth and Poverty Reduction." *Multi-donor Budget Support Newsletter* 4, no. 5. Accra, Ghana: MDBS Secretariat.

———. 2010a. "Performance Assessment Framework 2010 (Summary)." Accra, Ghana: Multi-donor Budget Support (MDBS) and Ministry of Finance and Economic Planning.

———. 2010b. "Ghana Aid Policy and Strategy, 2011–2015." Accra, Ghana: Ministry of Finance and Economic Planning.

———. 2010c. "Medium-Term National Development Policy Framework: Ghana Shared Growth and Development Agenda (GSGDA), 2010–2013." Accra, Ghana: National Development Planning Commission.

———. 2012. "Leveraging Partnership for Shared Growth and Development: Government of Ghana—Development Partners Compact, 2012–2022." Accra, Ghana: Ministry of Finance and Economic Planning.

Republic of Rwanda. 2006. "Rwanda Aid Policy." Kigali, Rwanda. Endorsed by the cabinet July 26.

———. 2007. "Economic Development and Poverty Reduction Strategy (2008–2012)." Kigali, Rwanda: Ministry of Finance and Economic Planning.

———. 2010a. "Donor Division of Labour in Rwanda." Kigali, Rwanda: Ministry of Finance and Economic Planning.

———. 2010b. "Donor Performance Assessment Framework (DPAF), FY 2009–2010." Kigali, Rwanda: Ministry of Finance and Economic Planning.

———. 2010c. "Official Government of Rwanda Comments on the Draft UN Mapping Report on the DRC." Kigali, Rwanda: Office of the UN High Commissioner for Human Rights.

———. 2011a. "Rwanda Aid Policy Manual of Procedures." Kigali, Rwanda: Ministry of Finance and Economic Planning.

———. 2011b. "Donor Performance Assessment Framework (DPAF), FY 2010–2011." Kigali, Rwanda: Ministry of Finance and Economic Planning.

———. 2013a. "Donor Performance Assessment Framework (DPAF), FY 2011–12." Kigali, Rwanda: Ministry of Finance and Economic Planning.

———. 2013b. "Official Development Assistance Report, FY2011–2012: Aid for Development." Kigali, Rwanda: Ministry of Finance and Economic Planning.

———. 2013c. "Rwanda's Official Development Assistance Report, FY 2012–2013." Kigali, Rwanda: Ministry of Finance and Economic Planning.

———. 2013d. "Economic Development and Poverty Reduction Strategy, 2013–2018." Kigali, Rwanda: Ministry of Finance and Economic Planning.

Republic of Uganda. 2000. "Uganda's Poverty Eradication Plan (PEAP), 1997–2007." Kampala, Uganda: Ministry of Finance, Planning and Economic Development.

———. 2005. "Poverty Eradication Action Plan (2004/5–2007/8)." Kampala, Uganda: Ministry of Finance, Planning and Economic Development.

———. 2010. "National Development Plan (2010/11–2014/15)." Kampala, Uganda: Ministry of Finance, Planning and Economic Development.

———. 2012. "Uganda: Letter of Intent, Memorandum of Economic and Financial Policies, and Technical Memorandum of Understanding (December 21, 2012)." Kampala, Uganda: Ministry of Finance, Planning and Economic Development.

———. 2013. "Report on Loans, Grants and Guarantees for Financial Year 2012/2013." Kampala, Uganda: Ministry of Finance, Planning and Economic Development.

Reuters. 2016. "Tanzania Makes Big Onshore Natural Gas Discovery—Local Newspapers." February 25. http://www.reuters.com/article/tanzania-gas-idUSL8N16427G.

Reyntjens, Filip. 2004. "Rwanda, Ten Years On: From Genocide to Dictatorship." *African Affairs* 103, no. 411: 177–210. doi:10.1093/afraf/adh045.

Riddell, Roger C. 1999. "The End of Foreign Aid to Africa? Concerns about Donor Policies." *African Affairs* 98, no. 392: 309–35. doi:10.1093/oxfordjournals.afraf.a008042.

Rogerson, Andres. 2011. "What If Development Aid Really Rewarded Results? Revisiting the Cash-on-Delivery (CoD) Aid Model." OECD Development Brief no. 1. Paris: OECD Development Co-operation Directorate. http://www.oecd.org/dac/47041528.pdf.

Rotberg, Robert I., ed. 2008. *China into Africa—Trade, Aid and Influence.* Washington, DC: Brookings Institution.

Rwanda Civil Society Platform, and Network of International NGOs. 2010. "Rwanda Civil Society Joint Statement on Making Aid Effective to Leverage Private Investments and Meet the Millennium Development Goals." Presentation at Ninth Government of Rwanda and Development Partners Meeting, November 4–5, Kigali, Rwanda.

Sachs, Jeffrey D. 2005. *The End of Poverty: Economic Possibilities for Our Time.* London: Penguin.

Sachs, Jeffrey D., et al. 2004. "Ending Africa's Poverty Trap." *Brookings Papers on Economic Activity* 1:117–216. http://www.jstor.org/stable/3217964.

Sahn, David E., Paul A. Dorosh, and Stephen D. Younger. 1997. *Structural Adjustment Reconsidered: Economic Policy and Poverty in Africa.* Cambridge: Cambridge University Press.

Sathyamurthy, T. V. 1986. *The Political Development of Uganda: 1900–1986.* London: Gower.

Schain, Martin, ed. 2001. *The Marshall Plan: Fifty Years After.* New York: Palgrave.

Schatz, Sayre P. 1994. "Structural Adjustment in Africa: A Failing Grade So Far." *Journal of Modern African Studies* 32, no. 4: 679–92. doi:10.1017/S0022278X00015901.

Schneider, Christina J., and Jennifer L. Tobin. 2013. "Interest Coalitions and Multilateral Aid Allocation in the European Union." *International Studies Quarterly* 57, no. 1: 103–14. doi:10.1111/isqu.12062.

Seabright, Paul. 2002. "Conflicts of Objectives and Task Allocation in Aid Agencies." In Martens 2002, 34–68.

Selbervik, Hilde. 2006. "PRSP in Tanzania: Do Mkukuta and the CCM Election Manifesto Pull in the Same Direction?" CIM Report, R 2006: 9. Bergen, Norway: Chr. Michelsen Institue. http://hdl.handle.net/10202/79.

Senelwa, Kennedy. 2015. "Tanzania to Start Tests on 542km Long New Mtwara-Dar Gas Pipeline." *East African*, July 25. http://www.theeastafrican.co.ke/business/Tanzania-tests-on-542km-long-new-Mtwara-Dar-gas-pipeline/2560-2808568-item-0-bl4a2fz/index.html.

Spitz, Gabi, Roeland Muskens, and Edith Van Ewijk. 2013. "The Dutch and Development Cooperation: Ahead of the Crowd or Trailing Behind." Amsterdam: NCDO. http://www.ncdo.nl/sites/default/files/Report Analysis The Dutch and Development Cooperation FINAL 2013 03 04.pdf.

Straus, Scott. 2006. *The Order of Genocide: Race, Power, and War in Rwanda*. Ithaca, NY: Cornell University Press.

Straus, Scott, and Lars Waldorf. 2011. *Remaking Rwanda: State Building and Human Rights after Mass Violence*. Madison: University of Wisconsin Press.

Sumner, Andy, and Richard Mallett. 2013. *The Future of Foreign Aid: Development Cooperation and the New Geography of Global Poverty*. London: Palgrave Macmillan.

Sundaram, Anjan. 2014. "Rwanda : The Darling Tyrant." *Politico*, March/April. ttp://www.politico.com/magazine/story/2014/02/rwanda-paul-kagame-americas-darling-tyrant-103963.

Svensson, Jakob. 1999. "Aid, Growth and Democracy." *Economics & Politics* 11, no. 3: 275–97. doi:10.1111/1468-0343.00062.

———. 2000a. "When Is Foreign Aid Policy Credible? Aid Dependence and Conditionality." *Journal of Development Economics* 61, no. 1: 61–84. doi:10.1016/S0304-3878(99)00061-9.

———. 2000b. "Foreign Aid and Rent-Seeking." *Journal of International Economics* 51, no. 2: 437–61. doi:10.1016/S0022-1996(99)00014-8.

———. 2003. "Why Conditional Aid Does Not Work and What Can Be Done about It?" *Journal of Development Economics* 70, no. 2: 381–402. doi:10.1016/S0304-3878(02)00102-5.

———. 2006. "The Institutional Economics of Foreign Aid." *Swedish Economic Policy Review* 13, no. 115–37. doi:10.1017/CBO9780511492563.

Swedlund, Haley J. 2011. "From Donorship to Ownership? Evolving Donor-Government Relationships in Rwanda. " PhD diss., Syracuse University.

———. 2013a. "From Donorship to Ownership? Budget Support and Influence in Rwanda and Tanzania." *Public Administration and Development* 33, no. 5: 357–70. doi:10.1002/pad.1665.

———. 2013b. "The Domestication of Governance Assessments: Evidence from the Rwandan Joint Governance Assessment." *Conflict, Aid and Development* 13, no. 4: 449–70. doi:10.1080/14678802.2013.834117.

———. 2014. "Assessing the Promises of Budget Support: Case Study Evidence from Rwanda." In *Problems, Promises, and Paradoxes of Aid: Africa's Experience*, edited by Muna Ndulo and Nicolas van de Walle, 238–65. Cambridge: Cambridge Scholars.

———. 2015. "Data Report: Survey on Aid Effectiveness and Donor-Government Relations." POL15-01. Nijmegen, Netherlands. http://haleyswedlund.com/files/SurveyDataReport.pdf.

——. 2017a. "Can Foreign Aid Donors Credibly Threaten to Suspend Aid? Evidence from a Cross-National Survey of Donor Officials." *Review of International Political Economy* online (March 29): 1–43. doi: 10.1080/09692290.2017.1302490.

——. 2017b. "Is China Eroding the Bargaining Power of Traditional Donors in Africa?" *International Affairs* 93, no. 2: 389–408. doi:10.1093/ia/iiw059.

Taylor, Ian. 2006. "China's Oil Diplomacy in Africa." *International Affairs* 82, no. 5: 937–59. doi:10.1111/j.1468-2346.2006.00579.x.

Tierney, Michael J., et al. 2011. "More Dollars Than Sense: Refining Our Knowledge of Development Finance Using AidData." *World Development* 39, no. 11: 1891–1906. doi:10.1016/j.worlddev.2011.07.029.

Tran, Mark. 2011. "Transparency Could Be the Sticking Point for China at Busan." *Guardian's Poverty Matters Blog*, November 14. http://www.theguardian.com/global-development/poverty-matters/2011/nov/14/busan-aid-china-rejects-transparency.

Tsekpo, Anthony K. 2008. "A Game Theoretic Rationalisation of Development Management: From Public Investments Programme to Budget Support." Policy Research Series No. 4. Accra, Ghana: Institute for Democratic Governance.

Tsikata, Yvonne M. 2001. "Ghana." In *Aid and Reform in Africa*, 45–100. Washington, DC: World Bank.

Tuffour, Joe Amoaka. 2005. "Multi-donor Direct Budget Support in Ghana: The Implications for Aid Delivery and Aid Effectiveness." Ghana: Selected Economic Issues. No. 11. Accra, Ghana: Centre for Policy Analysis. http://www.cepa.org.gh/archives/Multi_donor_Direct_budget_No_11-200525.pdf.

Tull, Denis M. 2006. "China's Engagement in Africa: Scope, Significance and Consequences." *Journal of Modern African Studies* 44, no. 3: 459. doi:10.1017/S0022278X06001856.

Ugandan Development Partners. 2005. "Joint Assistance Strategy for the Republic of Uganda (2005–2009)." Kampala, Uganda.

United Nations. 2015. "Basket Fund." UNTERM. https://unterm.un.org.

United Republic of Tanzania. 2000. "Poverty Reduction Strategy Paper." Dar es Salaam, Tanzania.

——. 2005. "National Strategy for Growth and Reduction of Poverty." Dar es Salaam, Tanzania: Vice President's Office.

——. 2006a. "Joint Assistance Strategy for Tanzania (JAST)." Dar es Salaam, Tanzania.

——. 2006b. "Memorandum of Understanding on the Joint Assistance Strategy for Tanzania (JAST) between the Government of the United Republic of Tanzania and Development Partners." Dar es Salaam, Tanzania.

——. 2010. "National Strategy for Growth and Reduction of Poverty II." Dar es Salaam, Tanzania: Ministry of Finance and Economic Affairs.

——. 2012. "The Tanzania Five Year Development Plan (2011/12–2015/16)." Dar es Salaam, Tanzania: President's Office Planning Commission.

——. 2014. "Aid Management Platform: Analysis of ODA Report for FY 2012/13." Dar es Salaam, Tanzania: Ministry of Finance and Economic Affairs.

Uvin, Peter. 1998. *Aiding Violence: The Development Enterprise in Rwanda*. West Hartford, CT: Kumarian.

Uwiringiyimana, Clement. 2015. "Rwanda's President Thanks Nation after Referendum Allowing Him to Stay On." Reuters, December 21. http://www.reuters.com/article/us-rwanda-politics-idUSKBN0U41A420151221.

van de Walle, Dominique, and Ren Mu. 2007. "Fungibility and the Flypaper Effect of Project Aid: Micro-evidence for Vietnam." *Journal of Development Economics* 84, no. 2: 667–85. doi:10.1016/j.jdeveco.2006.12.005.

van de Walle, Nicolas. 2001. *African Economies and the Politics of Permanent Crisis, 1979–1999*. Cambridge: Cambridge University Press.

Wangwe, Samuel. 2002. "The PRSP Process in Rwanda." Second Meeting of the African Learning Group on the Poverty Reduction Strategy Papers, November 18–21. Brussels: Economic Commission for Africa.

Wenar, Leif. 2011. "Accountability in International Development Aid." *Ethics & International Affairs* 20, no. 1: 1–23. doi:10.1111/j.1747-7093.2006.00001.x.

Whitfield, Lindsay. 2005. "Trustees of Development from Conditionality to Governance: Poverty Reduction Strategy Papers in Ghana." *Journal of Modern African Studies* 43, no. 4: 641–64. doi:10.1017/S0022278X05001254.

———, ed. 2009a. *The Politics of Aid: African Strategies for Dealing with Donors*. Oxford: Oxford University Press.

———. 2009b. "'Change for a Better Ghana': Party Competition, Institutionalization and Alternation in Ghana's 2008 Elections." *African Affairs* 108, no. 433: 621–41. doi:10.1093/afraf/adp056.

Whitfield, Lindsay, and Alastair Fraser. 2009a. "Introduction: Aid and Sovereignty." In Whitfield 2009a, 1–26.

———. 2009b. "Negotiating Aid." In Whitfield 2009a, 27–44.

———. 2010. "Negotiating Aid: The Structural Conditions Shaping the Negotiating Strategies of African Governments." *International Negotiation* 15, no. 3: 341–66. doi:10.1163/157180610X529582.

Whitfield, Lindsay, and Emily Jones. 2009. "Ghana: Breaking Out of Aid Dependence? Economic and Political Barriers to Ownership." In Whitfield 2009a, 185–216.

WHO. 2000. *The World Health Report 2000, Health Systems: Improving Performance*. Geneva: World Health Organization. http://www.who.int/whr/2000/en/.

Williams, David Gareth. 1997. "The Emergence and Implementation of the World Bank's Good Governance Agenda." PhD diss., University of London, School of Oriental and African Studies.

Williamson, Oliver. 1985. *Economic Institutions of Capitalism*. New York: Free Press.

Winters, Matthew S., and Gina Martinez. 2015. "The Role of Governance in Determining Foreign Aid Flow Composition." *World Development* 66:516–31. doi:10.1016/j.worlddev.2014.09.020.

Wohlgemuth, Lennart. 2006. "Changing Aid Modalities in Tanzania." *Policy Management Brief* No. 17. Maastricht: European Centre for Development Policy Management.

Woods, Ngaire. 2010. "Whose Aid? Whose Influence? China, Emerging Donors and the Silent Revolution in Development Assistance." *International Affairs* 84, no. 6: 1205–21. doi:10.1111/j.1468-2346.2008.00765.x.

World Bank. 1999. *Tanzania: Social Sector Review (A World Bank Country Study)*. Washington, DC: World Bank.

———. 2009. *Doing Business 2010: Reforming through Difficult Times*. Washington, DC: World Bank, IFC, and Palgrave Macmillan. doi:10.1596/978-0-8213-7961-5.

———. 2010. "Poverty Reduction Support Credits—an Evaluation of World Bank Support." Washington, DC: World Bank Group. http://ieg.worldbank.org/Data/reports/prsc_eval_0.pdf.

———. 2014. "World Development Indicators." Washington, DC: World Bank Group. http://data.worldbank.org/data-catalog/world-development-indicators.

World Bank and IMF. 2013. "Heavily Indebted Poor Countries (HIPC) Initiative and Multilateral Debt Relief Initiative (MDRI)—Statistical Update." Washington, DC: International Monetary Fund.

World Bank et al. 2011. "Joint Budget Support Framework: Assessment of JAF3." December 22. Kampala, Uganda: World Bank, Delegation of the European

Union, and Governments of Austria, Belgium, Denmark, Germany, Ireland, Netherlands, Norway, Sweden, and the United Kingdom.

Wright, Joseph, and Matthew Winters. 2010. "The Politics of Effective Foreign Aid." *Annual Review of Political Science* 13, no. 1: 61–80. doi:10.1146/annurev. polisci.032708.143524.

Zimmermann, Felix. 2007. "Ownership in Practice: The Key to Smart Development." Informal Experts' Workshop, September 27–28, Sèvres, France: OECD Development Centre. http://www.oxfamamerica.org/static/oa3/files/ownership-in-practice.pdf.

Index

Page numbers followed by letters *f* and *t* refer to figures and tables, respectively.

development aid: vs. humanitarian aid, 151n4.
 See also foreign aid
Development Assistance Committee (DAC), 7
Development Assistance Group (DAG), 7,
 152n9
development dance, 2, 60*f*, 122
Development Partner Performance Assessment
 Framework (DP-PAF), Ghana, 94
Development Partners Coordination Group
 (DPCG), Rwanda, 54, 63
Development Partners Group (DPG),
 Tanzania, 49, 63, 102, 158n8
DFID. *See* Department for International
 Development
disbursement of aid: assessment frameworks
 and, 124; budget support and criteria for,
 108–9, 111; vs. commitments, deviations
 from, 84–85, 85*t*; donor agencies' budget
 cycle and, 85–86; pressures for, 96; in
 project aid vs. budget support, 110–11;
 reforms as precondition for, 10, 13
discounting of aid, by recipient governments,
 33, 86
discretionary funds: recipient governments'
 preference for, 26. *See also* budget support
donor agencies: and aid policy bargaining,
 preferences in, 25–26, 25*t*; assessment of
 performance of, 94, 115; attractiveness
 of aid provided by, need to increase, 130;
 budget cycles of, and aid disbursement,
 85–86; budget support and benefits for, 15,
 99–107, 120; commitment problems of, 2,
 13–14, 30–31, 81–88, 90–91; country-level
 strategies of, government as key stakeholder
 in formation of, 72–73; credibility of
 commitments by, ensuring, 17; declining
 bargaining power of, 127–30, 162n13;
 donor countries distinguished from,
 20–21; efficiency of, factors undermining,
 88–93; enforcement mechanisms used
 by, 30, 95–96; formal vs. real schedules
 used by, 33; goals of, 59–60; influence
 in recipient countries, limits to, 73–74;
 information disadvantage of, 74–75; as
 mediators between donors and recipients,
 21; need to negotiate with recipient
 governments, 23–24; political preferences
 of donor countries and, 24; and poverty
 reduction strategy papers (PRSPs), drafting
 of, 66; pressure to spend aid funds, 30;
 proliferation of, 7; reform delays and,
 80–81; reforms sought by, 3, 11, 24, 31; role
 in policy dialogue, 70–73; shifting priorities
 and agendas ("moving goalposts") of,
 82–83; staff turnover in country offices,

31, 59, 92–93; unpredictability of aid
 disbursements by, 13–14, 83–88, 85*t*–87*t*,
 91. *See also* aid architecture; coordination
 among donor agencies; donor-government
 relations; donor officials; policy influence
donor countries: vs. donor agencies, 20–21;
 political shifts in, impact on budget
 support, 117, 118–19; shifting priorities
 in, 24, 30–31
donor-government relations, 59–60, 60*f*;
 discovery of oil and, 129–30; during
 election years, 89–90; end of Cold War and
 shift in, 9; exogenous shocks and, 5; highs
 and lows in, 3–4, 121; joint workshops,
 36; mutual dependence in, 13, 68, 75–76,
 120–21; political interests in maintaining,
 30. *See also* bargaining; policy dialogue
donor officials: corruption scandals and, 79–80;
 frustrations over recipient commitment
 problems, 78–79, 80, 81; lessons for, 124–25,
 130; opportunity to influence spending and
 allocation patterns, 18; positions on budget
 support, 113, 114*f*; pressure to show results,
 80; relationships with recipient-government
 officials, importance of, 71; responsibilities
 of, 1; rotations of, 31, 59, 92–93; survey of,
 16, 37, 39–40
Donor Performance Assessment Framework
 (DPAF), Rwanda, 94
DPCG. *See* Development Partners
 Coordination Group
DPG. *See* Development Partners Group
DP-PAF. *See* Development Partner
 Performance Assessment Framework

economic growth: foreign aid and, 152n2; in
 Ghana, 46, 55*t*–56*t*; in Rwanda, 52–53,
 55*t*–56*t*; in Tanzania, 48, 55*t*–56*t*; in
 Uganda, 51, 55*t*–56*t*
economic institutionalism. *See* institutional
 economics
efficiency of foreign aid institutions, factors
 undermining, 88–93; bureaucratic hurdles
 and, 91–93; donor country politics and,
 90–91; recipient country politics and, 89–90
efficiency of institutions, factors determining,
 32, 34–35, 88
Egypt, U.S. aid to, 30
elections, donor-government relations during,
 89–90
electronic aid management systems, 93–94
enforcement, lack of: budget support and, 120,
 121; and commitment problems, 93–96,
 124–25; results-based aid and, 126;
 structural adjustment lending and, 29

Short, Clare, 21
"short leash" lending, 10
SIDA. *See* Swedish International Development Cooperation Agency
Sierra Leone, World Bank road projects in, 5
social sectors, Millennium Development Goals (MDGs) and, 9, 82–83
structural adjustment lending, 5, 8; enforcement difficulties associated with, 29; origins of, 8–9; recipient commitment problems emphasized in, 125; variety of designs for, 20
sub-Saharan Africa: importance of foreign aid in, 41–42. *See also specific countries*
survey, of heads of cooperation (HOCs), 16, 37, 39–40, 137–49
suspension of aid: budget support, 112, 117; donor agencies' inability to make credible threats of, 30; as enforcement mechanism, 95–96; Ugandan corruption scandal and, 112
Swedish International Development Cooperation Agency (SIDA), 151n7; disbursements in final months of budget cycle, 86; education project in Tanzania, 23–24; work in Burkina Faso, 6

Tanzania: aid architecture in, 48–49, 63, 102, 154n18; "Big Results Now" (BRN) program in, 67; budget support group in, 102; budget support in, 42t, 49, 117; Chinese aid to, 129; commitment problems in, 78–79; corruption in, efforts to combat, 47; corruption scandal in, 160n47; donor-government relations in, 68, 69; Dutch aid to, 5, 91, 118; economic growth in, 48, 55t–56t; External Finance Department of, 64–65; Five-Year Development Plans of, 66–67; foreign direct investment (FDI) in, 48, 56t; German aid to, 103; Heavily Indebted Poor Countries (HIPC) program in, 48, 66, 66t, 67; IMF expelled from, 23; national development planning process in, 65–66; natural gas discoveries in, 48, 129; negotiations with donors, 69; official development assistance (ODA) to, 48, 57t–58t; policy dialogue in, time invested in, 68; political and economic history of, 46–47; poverty reduction strategy paper (PRSP) process in, 48, 66, 154n17; reduction in budget support to, 112, 118; SIDA education project in, 23–24; unpredictability of aid disbursement in, 14, 85t, 152n16; war with Uganda, 47, 50

technical control, donor vs. recipient preferences regarding, 25t, 26
transactional costs: budget support and reduction in, 109, 114, 116, 160n52; factors increasing, 88; and institutional change, 12; project aid and, 159n33
triggers: last-minute completion of, 78; in performance assessment frameworks (PAFs), 69

Uganda: aid architecture in, 51–52; aid unpredictability in, 85t; budget support in, 42t, 52; Chinese aid to, 128; corruption scandal in, 52, 79–80, 112, 117, 118, 161n63; discounting of aid commitments in, 33, 86; discovery of oil in, 51, 129–30; economic growth in, 51, 55t–56t; faith-based groups in, role in health sector, 64; foreign direct investment (FDI) in, 56t; Heavily Indebted Poor Countries (HIPC) program in, 50, 51, 66t; off-budget spending in (2010–2011), 90; official development assistance (ODA) to, 51, 57t–58t; political and economic history of, 49–50; politics of decentralization in, 89; Poverty Eradication Action Plan (PEAP) in, 10, 50–51; suspension of budget support in, 112, 117, 118, 119; war with Tanzania, 47, 50
Uganda Joint Assistance Strategy, 51–52, 154n23
Ugandan National Development Plan, on importance of aid predictability, 84
UNDP. *See* United Nations Development Programme
United Kingdom. *See* Department for International Development (DFID)
United Nations Development Programme (UNDP): and aid architecture in Rwanda, 65; and aid architecture in Tanzania, 49; resident representatives in, 153n4
United Nations General Assembly, Declaration on the Establishment of the New International Economic Order, 8
United States: aid to Bolivia, 7; Cold War politics and foreign aid by, 27; Foreign Assistance Act in, 30; and Marshall Plan, 6–7; President's Emergency Plan for AIDS Relief (PEPFAR), 31, 155n4
United States Agency for International Development (USAID): country directors in, responsibilities of, 1; origins of, 151n7; priorities in African countries, 62; reductions in spending on long-term programs, 31; U.S. government distinguished from, 20–21

Vision 2020: in Ghana, 153n7; in Rwanda, 53, 155n27

Wangwe, Sam, 48
Wolfensohn, James, 15
working groups, budget support and, 64, 101
workshops, donor-government, 36
World Bank: and agricultural policy reform in Kenya, 29; Berg Report of, 9; and budget support, 10; Chinese assistance compared to, 128; coordination efforts of, 7; country directors of, 153n4; focus on poverty alleviation, 8; Heavily Indebted Poor Countries (HIPC) initiative of, 10; and International

Development Association (IDA), 7, 151n8; negotiations with Ghana on structural adjustment, 12–13, 23, 26; and poverty reduction strategy paper (PRSP) process, 10; reforms sought by, 13; road projects in Sierra Leone, 5; on Rwanda's economic development, 53; structural adjustment lending by, 9; work in Ghana, 44, 45; work in Tanzania, 47, 48, 78; work in Uganda, 50–51, 52
World War II: foreign aid prior to, 151n6; Marshall Plan after, 6–7

Zanzibar, poverty reduction strategy paper (PRSP) process in, 154n17